**THE EXPERIMENTS
THE PROJECTS
THE WEAPONS**

V-1, V-2, V-3 *and* V-4
Japanese Balloon Bombs
American Bat Bombs
Norden Bombsight
Aphrodite and Anvil
Gorgon
Tallboy and Grand Slam
Project Bumblebee
Anzio Annie and Her Sisters
Channel Guns
Grizzly Bear and Mavs
Kamikaze Torpedoes
Zeppelin Rammers
Lippisch Flying Wings
Foo Fighters
and many more

*Secret Weapons of
World War II*

**William Yenne** is the author of more than two
dozen books on aviation and space-related topics.

# Secret Weapons of World War II

*William Yenne*

BERKLEY BOOKS, NEW YORK

SECRET WEAPONS OF WORLD WAR II

A Berkley Book / published by arrangement with
the author

PRINTING HISTORY
Berkley edition / August 2003

Copyright © 2003 by William Yenne
Cover design by Steven Ferlauto
Book design by Julie Rogers

ISBN: 0-425-18992-9

BERKLEY®
Berkley Books are published by The Berkley Publishing Group,
a division of Penguin Group (USA) Inc.,
375 Hudson Street, New York, NY 10014.
BERKLEY and the "B" design
are trademarks belonging to Penguin Group (USA) Inc.

PRINTED IN THE UNITED STATES OF AMERICA

10  9  8  7  6  5  4  3  2  1

# Contents

# Introduction

What are the characteristics of a "secret weapon" or a "wonder weapon"?

Clearly, they are not merely weapons that are kept secret from an enemy. They are, literally, both secret *and* they elicit a sense of wonder. They are weapons that add a new dimension to the technology of war. They are weapons that theoretically provide the potency to tip the balance of power on the battlefield in favor of the armies that possess them.

Secret wonder weapons have existed throughout history. At the Battle of Agincourt in 1415, the English longbow represented a ratcheting up of technology that stunned the French and resulted in a victory for the vastly outnumbered English. In the Civil War, the use of telegraph for communications and of railroads to transport troops quickly and efficiently altered the face of warfare. In World War I, the use of automatic weapons resulted in casualties beyond the wildest imaginations of the politicians who launched the war. Had the capricious princelings who initiated that horrible conflict known this, they might have been less hasty.

Of course, the development of a new level of technology by one side often leads to a new level of technology to counter it. In World War I again, the use of barbed wire and machine guns made trenches secure and invincible, but this led to a stalemate. Other weapons, such as tanks and poison gas, were introduced to break the stalemate.

In no war in history has the leap in the evolution of weapons technology been greater than in World War II. From nuclear weapons to jet propulsion, World War II marked the most important turning point in military technology in history.

For example, most of the world's air forces began the war with a sizable proportion of their fleets composed of open-cockpit biplanes. Six years later, Germany, Britain, and the United States had jet aircraft in squadron service. At sea, the war started with aircraft carriers merely a novelty and ended with carrier warfare having defined the future of naval power for the rest of the century. On the ground, one has only to compare the Panzer II tanks used in the Blitzkrieg of 1939 to the tanks in service in Europe in 1945.

Radar was a major technological breakthrough virtually unknown when the war began. By 1940, land-based radar was playing a pivotal role in winning the Battle of Britain. By 1944, radar was equipping night-flying aircraft and allowing them to fight in complete darkness. The night-fighting aircraft of 1945 have more in common with the all-weather aircraft of today than they do with the warplanes of 1939.

There were bizarre secret projects such as spaceplanes and sound cannons. As strange as they seem, both of these weapons were actually being built when the war ended.

In Germany, where a long scientific and technical tradition was hijacked by a sociopathic cult, secret weapons became an obsession in World War II. Germany entered the war with perhaps the most up-to-date military in the world. After 1941, when the Nazis imagined themselves on the verge of victory, there was a brief hiatus in their interest in continuing to invest in advanced technology. By 1944, however, with their fortunes in reversal, the tune changed. From Adolf Hitler on down, the cry went out for "secret weapons" to stun the Allies and win the war. Had this call been made in 1942, it would have been technologically possible for Germany to have achieved in 1944—especially in aviation—what took the rest of the world another decade. The weapons created against the backdrop of this call to action could not have been made available in time to save the Nazis, but they provide us with fascinating stories.

The Allied side also developed weapons of staggering proportions. The United States created the world's first nuclear weapons. In Britain, the efforts to break Germany's Enigma code led to Colossus, a harbinger of the computer age. Both of these technologies influenced the history of the world throughout the remainder of the century.

Also of interest as we read of the secret weapons of World War II is the length of time they remained secret. This book would not have been possible in 1965. Even two decades after World War II, much of the material in this book was unknown or unavailable to the general public. Certainly that would be true of nuclear and intercontinental missile technology. However, the Ultra program that developed Colossus—and indeed the existence of this computer itself—was not revealed until 1974. The work of the Navajo Code Talkers—one of the most low-tech secrets of the war—was not declassified until 1968, a quarter century after they went into action. Germany's super-submarines were developed under a tight cloak of secrecy that kept the details from being known until the war was long over. Technology developed during the war, especially in aviation and missiles, was still being explored—and kept secret—decades later.

Many of the secret weapons of World War II would stay secret for a generation. Perhaps there are others that are *still* secret.

This book is a look at more than 175 secret and wonder weapons from air to land to sea—and beyond. Included are weapons developed by all the major warring powers.

It is also an acknowledgment of the scientists and innovators, both sung and unsung, who created the technology that changed the history of warfare during World War II and in the years that followed.

# The Nuclear Genie

Nuclear weapons were certainly the ultimate weapons of World War II. They were the most amazing weapons used during the war. They were the weapons that ended the war, and they were the weapons that cast the longest and darkest shadow across the next half-century.

They did not determine *who* won the war, but they might have. They almost certainly determined *when* the war was won. Without the two American weapons that were used, the war would have ended with the same victor and the same vanquished, but almost certainly not for another six to nine months or more, and not without hundreds of thousands more casualties. However, if they had been developed and used by either Germany or Japan, the outcome might have been quite different.

The theory of nuclear energy was first advanced by the renowned physicist Albert Einstein in his theory of relativity (1905), in which he stated that energy was equal to mass at the speed of light ($E=mc^2$). In other words, mass could be converted into energy if it was propelled at the speed of light. Einstein's hypothesis remained in the realm of the theoretical until 1938 when three German scientists—Otto Hahn, Lise Meitner, and Fritz Strassman—discovered that uranium, when bombarded by neutrons, broke down into barium and krypton, and released tremendous quantities of heat in a process known as nuclear fission.

Meanwhile, Danish physicist Niels Henrik David Bohr learned of these experiments and realized the potential of using the process to create a military explosive, or atomic bomb. In 1939, he emigrated to the United States, determined to urge the Americans to undertake the development of such a weapon before the Germans did.

The race was on.

## The Manhattan Project

The American "atom bomb" was the war's conclusive weapon and arguably its most important secret. Except for a few insiders who sold secrets to the Soviets—then American allies—the secrecy was practically absolute. There were virtually no credible rumors of its existence, and almost no one within the U.S. government was briefed about it. Indeed, President Truman wasn't even fully aware of it until after he became president. When the bomb was finally used, the most common reaction of people everywhere was disbelief.

The project, which broke new ground scientifically, was also the most expensive and challenging engineering project in the history of the world. From Albert Einstein's famous letter to FDR to Hiroshima and Nagasaki, the U.S. government devoted more money and manpower to the Manhattan Project—the program to develop the bomb—than to any other weapon.

Curiously, the "chain reaction" of events that got the American nuclear weapons program rolling involved four

European émigrés—a Dane, a Hungarian, a German, and an Italian—who would not have relocated to the United States had it not been for the bellicosity of Germany under Hitler.

In 1939, Niels Bohr, who was newly arrived in the United States, told expatriate Hungarian physicist Leo Szilard about the work being done in Germany. Szilard approached Albert Einstein, the German physicist whose theory had opened the door to nuclear fission, and asked him to write a letter to President Franklin D. Roosevelt. Einstein, who was one of the most respected scientists in the world, did indeed write the letter. Dated August 2, 1939, it outlined the danger of Germany having such a terrible weapon and the danger of American inaction. Though he would later claim to regret this, Einstein also recommended to Roosevelt that the United States be the first to undertake the development of an atomic bomb.

Recognizing the weapon's potential, and imagining what would happen if he did nothing, Roosevelt made the decision to build the bomb. The project was instantly draped in secrecy and was assigned to the Manhattan district of the U.S. Army Corps of Engineers under the command of Major General Leslie R. Groves.

Many widely available volumes have been written about the Manhattan Project and the dropping of the bomb, so we will restrict our comments to a brief sketch of the program.

The construction of a nuclear reactor, a device built to contain a self-sustaining nuclear chain reaction, was a first step toward the development of a full-scale nuclear weapon. The world's first nuclear reactor was constructed under the direction of the Manhattan district on a squash court beneath the bleachers at Stagg Field at the University of Chicago, under the direction of the Italian physicist Enrico Fermi.

Fermi, who had won the 1938 Nobel Prize for his work in neutron physics, had theorized that a nuclear chain reaction was possible. The Chicago reactor contained 50 tons of uranium, cadmium control rods, and 500 tons of graphite. The latter was to slow down the world's first controlled nuclear chain reaction, which was finally achieved on December 2, 1942.

At the same time, J. Robert Oppenheimer and a team of scientists at the University of California at Berkeley were also working on the problem of nuclear fission. Using a cyclotron (a subatomic particle accelerator), they had discovered that plutonium 239, like uranium 235, was also potentially fissionable.

Achieving the elusive nuclear chain reaction proved, at least theoretically, that an atomic bomb was possible. Armed with this information, General Groves established three Manhattan Project centers to conduct various elements of the program—as quickly and as quietly as possible. The requirement for the location of the first two would be abundant electrical power. There would be a secret uranium-235 factory at Oak Ridge, Tennessee, which would take advantage of the electricity output of the series of hydroelectric dams of the recently completed Tennessee Valley Authority. There would also be a plutonium-239 plant at Hanford, Washington, which would take advantage of the electricity output of the series of hydroelectric dams built on the Columbia River by the federally owned Bonneville Power Administration.

The third site was a secret government laboratory located in a remote site near Los Alamos, New Mexico. It would be here that the actual atomic bombs would be built. Szilard and Fermi were joined by J. Robert Oppenheimer, as well as by Arthur H. Compton of the University of Chicago and a team of many other chemists, physicists, and engineers.

The first nuclear weapon, a uranium-235 bomb, was successfully detonated on July 16, 1945, at a site in the New Mexico desert north of Alamogordo that was code-named Trinity.

Meanwhile, the USAAF (U.S. Army Air Corps, the U.S. Air Force after 1947) had created the 509th Composite Group, which would train to drop a special bomb of unusual shape from modified Boeing B-29 Superfortress bombers. At Wendover AAF in Utah, crews trained with dummy bombs without knowing that their "secret" weapons would be atomic bombs. By July 1945, the crews and aircraft of the 509th Composite Group had been assigned to the XXI Bomber Command of the 20th Air Force, which was flying long-range conventional attacks against the Japanese homeland from bases in the Marianas Islands of Guam, Tinian, and Saipan.

By this time, the political and military situation had changed considerably from just a few months earlier. President Roosevelt had died on April 12 and on May 7 Germany had formally accepted Allied terms for unconditional surrender. World War II had finally ended in Europe. With the defeat of Germany, the Allies turned their attention to conquering the Japanese Empire.

Many of the scientists working on the Manhattan Project had favored developing the atomic bomb out of a sense of moral revulsion toward Hitler and Nazism, but they were ambivalent toward Imperial Japan, despite its equally brutal disregard for the Geneva Convention and its initiation of the Pacific phase of World War II with attacks on American territory. Of course, by this time, it was not their choice to make.

As the American and Allied forces moved closer to Japan during the first half of 1945, the Japanese had become more and more tenacious. During this period, the Iwo Jima and Okinawa campaigns had proven to be the

bloodiest major battles of the war for the Americans. With
this in mind, the Allies estimated that it would cost them a
million casualties—most of these American—to invade
and defeat the Japanese home islands. The only answer
was a secret weapon.

President Harry S. Truman, who had became president
upon the death of Franklin Roosevelt on April 12, decided
that the prospect of a million American casualties was un-
acceptable. He had a secret weapon, and he decided to use
it. Along with his cabinet and top military advisers, he decided to drop two of the new bombs on Japan with the hope
that such a maneuver would cause the Japanese to surrender unconditionally and immediately.

The first nuclear weapon used in wartime was a 9,700-
pound uranium bomb nicknamed "Little Boy," dropped on
Hiroshima by the B-29 *Enola Gay* on August 6, 1945. The
second was a 10,000-pound plutonium bomb nicknamed
"Fat Man," dropped on Nagasaki three days later by the B-
29 *Bock's Car*. Coincidentally, it was in Hiroshima Prefecture that the Japanese manufactured the chemical weapons
that they had used extensively in China for nearly a decade.

Implicit in the two nuclear attacks three days apart was
the menage that the United States had the capability to
drop many more in rapid succession, but this was not actually the case. However, the bombs, which each had the explosive power of 50,000 tons of TNT, had the desired
effect.

Japan's Emperor Hirohito and most members of the
military government ruling the country could see that the
misadventure that began at Pearl Harbor was now hope-
less, and on August 15, they sent word that Japan would
accept Allied conditions for an unconditional surrender.

The weapon that had been a carefully guarded secret
became one of the most important topics of discussion in
the years just after World War II, and a subject of interna-

tional dread when the United States lost its monopoly on these terrible bombs a few years later. Working in large part with data stolen from the U.S. Manhattan Project, the Soviet Union became the world's second nuclear power in 1949. Thus began an arms race of unprecedented scale.

## Heisenberg, Germany's Bomb, and the V-4 Project

During the 1920s and 1930s, the theoretical work that would lead to the development of atomic energy was more advanced in Germany than in America. It is entirely probable that scientists there would have been the first to achieve a self-sustaining nuclear chain reaction had they not been disrupted by a very unlikely person. The man who would have later benefited most from Germany being the first to have nuclear weapons was the same man who sabotaged their development.

Many of the important German nuclear physicists happened to be Jewish. Indeed, Albert Einstein himself was a Jew. Einstein was born in Germany in 1879, and although he lived abroad from 1894 to 1914, he had reestablished himself in Germany for nearly two decades when Adolf Hitler came to power in 1933. When Hitler came in, Jewish scientists began heading out—most of them to the United States. In 1933, few people outside the scientific community paid any attention to nuclear energy. It was merely theoretical physics and it seemed to have little practical value. Within a few years, this would all change.

As noted, the awesome potential power of nuclear weapons was first theorized about in 1938—in Germany— in the work of Otto Hahn, Lise Meitner, and Fritz Strassman. By this time, Einstein was in the United States, and in August 1939, less than a month before the start of World

War II, he would write his letter to President Roosevelt. The American leader took the bomb more seriously than Hitler did, and Germany squandered an early lead in what the Nazis did not perceive as a race to the ultimate weapon.

Nevertheless, Germany did begin a nuclear weapons program, although it was denied the funding levels enjoyed by the Manhattan Project.

The leading figure in Germany's nuclear project was physicist Werner Karl Heisenberg, who is best known for the Heisenberg uncertainty principle, which he discovered in 1927. Two years earlier, he had invented matrix mechanics, the first version of quantum mechanics. Heisenberg published *The Physical Principles of Quantum Theory* in 1928, and in 1932 he was awarded the Nobel Prize in Physics for this work.

In 1932, Heisenberg wrote a three-part paper that described the modern picture of the nucleus of an atom. He treated the structure of the various nuclear components, discussing their binding energies and their stability. This series of papers opened the way for other scientists to apply quantum theory to the atomic nucleus.

In December 1938, while working at the Kaiser Wilhelm Institute for Chemistry in Berlin, Otto Hahn demonstrated nuclear fission using uranium 235. This was a major scientific breakthrough that took the world closer to the dawn of a nuclear era—and Germany closer to a nuclear weapons capability. Paul Hartek and Wilhelm Groth, both chemistry professors at Hamburg University, contacted the Oberkommando Wehrmacht (German High Command) to remind them that Hahn's discovery paved the way for explosives of immense power.

On April 29, 1939, just five days after Hartek and Groth penned their memo, Adolf Hitler spoke to the Reichstag. William Shirer, author of *The Rise and Fall of the Third Reich,* lists this as Hitler's definitive address to the nation on

Germany's destiny and its ambitions to dominate Europe. Reading between the lines, one might infer that the words spoken at the podium that day were the opening salvo of World War II.

German industry had mobilized for war well before April 1939, but within days of Hitler's Reichstag speech, the industrial component of the German nuclear weapons program was mobilized. The Reich Ordnance Office, which coordinated and funded the weapons work of such armaments giants as Krupp and Rheinmetall-Borsig, got into the act.

The technical reports of the physicists went to Erich Schuman, head of research for the Reich Ordnance Office, who was now playing the role of coordinator of the nuclear weapons program. Kurt Diebner, who was doing uranium research at the Army test center at Kummersdorf was also on the team. Also at Kummersdorf at the time—and sharing the parking lot with Diebner—was Walter Dornberger, who would, along with Wernher von Braun, soon develop Germany's Intermediate Range Ballistic Missile (IRBM) capability.

The group of physicists working on the program as the war began included Paul Hartek and Otto Hahn as well as Werner Heisenberg, now on the faculty of the University of Leipzig. Heisenberg soon became the de facto head of the scientific side of the German nuclear weapons program.

As an international team in the United States was working toward the same objective, the Germans set about building a nuclear reactor. For this, they needed fissionable material and a liquid moderator. Graphite could be used for the latter, but it is subject to deterioration.

For use as fissionable material, the German nuclear weapons program needed uranium. A leading source of uranium in the world at the time was the mines of the Belgian Congo. By May 1940, Germany had defeated Belgium and and its forces had occupied the country, including the big uranium refinery and warehouse complex at Oolen.

In order to use water for the liquid moderator, the reactor team needed enriched uranium that was at least 3 percent uranium 235, the "critical mass." Natural uranium is mostly uranium 238, and less than 1 percent uranium 235. This can be utilized, but only by using deuterium oxide (so-called heavy water) instead of water. Heavy water required an enormous amount of electricity in its manufacture, and in 1940, the largest European heavy-water producer was Norsk-Hydro at Rjukan in Norway, where there was abundant hydroelectric power. Coincidentally, by June 1940, Norway had been defeated and occupied by German forces.

The pieces were falling into place. Tons of uranium and a steady flow of heavy water were now available. By the summer of 1940, the Germans were arguably ahead of the team in the United States in developing a nuclear weapons program.

However, it was like the "tortoise and the hare" story. What the scientists in the United States had spurring them on was that they *knew* there was a German program, and they were sure that the Germans could and would build the first reactor and the first bomb. They assumed they were behind and that they were playing catch-up.

In Germany, however, the nuclear weapons program had taken a curious turn. While their competition across the Atlantic looked on theirs as a crash program, the Germans approached the task as a leisurely academic exercise. They bickered and debated about such things as the size and nature of the reactor. To them, it was like a school project not a nuclear weapons program.

There was a disagreement between Heisenberg and Hartek over the nature of the reactor that would, in retrospect, cause serious delays. Despite a great deal of fussing, there was simply no sense of urgency that things *should* be sorted out.

There was even a parallel nuclear project being conducted by Professor Fritz Houtermans of the German Postal Service Research Institute that allegedly had nothing to do with *weapons*. Hartek, a proponent of the low-temperature reactor, became peripherally involved in this effort, as did Walther Gerlach, late of the physics department of the University of Munich, who became head of the Reich Research Council in 1943. By now, there were many cooks, but no real sense of how to make the soup.

If Heisenberg had explained the potential to Hitler with the same fervor Einstein had used to explain it to Roosevelt, things would have gone differently.

Reich Armaments Minister Albert Speer reportedly knew enough about the nature of the nuclear weapons program to be aware of its great potential, and he also had the power to get things rolling. At one point in June 1942, Heisenberg had a meeting with Speer in which he might have made the case for a crash program, but instead, he expressed the feeling that at the present pace of development, the atomic bomb was a weapon of the future, not of World War II. Six months later, the world's first controlled nuclear reaction was achieved in Chicago. Heisenberg, Speer, and Hitler had no idea.

Nevertheless, the Oberkommando Wehrmacht seems to have been preparing the way for an operational nuclear weapon. As early as 1943, Hitler and others referred to a Vergeltungswaffe (Vengeance Weapon), designated V-4, which was capable of destroying all life within an area having a diameter of about four miles. Such a description would be consistent with what the Führer and his cronies would have been told about nuclear weapons by the physicists. This was probably the secret weapon about which

Hitler raved with such confidence even until the end of the Third Reich and the day that he went to his dusty grave in the Reichstag garden.

During 1943 and early 1944, engineering work that was being done at the Watten V-2 site in northern France—as well as at the secret underground factory at Nordhausen in Germany—indicated preparations for a larger weapon of some sort. Though details are apparently *still* secret, these preparations also indicate that a radiation hazard was being anticipated.

Heisenberg and the others continued their work as the Reich began to implode. They were now confidently predicting that a reactor would be built in 1943 or 1944. It was not. In February 1943, saboteurs hit the Norsk-Hydro plant, and within a year, Allied air raids assured that it would no longer be a source of heavy water.

By the end of 1944, two teams were coming very close to building Germany's first nuclear reactor. Walther Gerlach and Paul Hartek were at work in a basement near Erfurt, while Heisenberg was building a reactor in a cave near Hechingen. It would be Heisenberg who would come the closest. On the first of March in 1945, with the Allies already spilling into Germany from all sides, he powered up his reactor—but he failed to achieve a chain reaction. He did not have a critical mass of fissionable uranium.

Meanwhile, the United States and the other Allies were convinced that the German program was much further advanced than it was. General Leslie Groves, commander of the Manhattan Project, had created a parallel secret project code-named "Alsos" (the Greek word for "groves") to investigate what the Germans had done.

Just as the U.S. Army's Operation Paperclip scampered into the defeated Reich to snatch up rocket scientists, Project Alsos entered Germany on the heels of combat troops to snatch up the nuclear scientists.

The Americans were very surprised to learn how little the Germans had accomplished. Several months later, after word of the Hiroshima attack became headline news, it was the turn of the German physicists to be surprised. They had no idea that the Americans had come so far.

After the war, Heisenberg was interned in Britain with other leading German scientists. When he returned to Germany in 1946, he was appointed director of the Max Planck Institute for Physics and Astrophysics at Göttingen. He and Hartek would continue to squabble in the ensuing decades, each insisting that the other didn't know what he was doing when it came to nuclear chain reactions.

## Not Just a Target: Japan's Bomb

While most details of the German nuclear program have been revealed in recent years, history traditionally treats Japan as the Axis partner who was a nuclear victim not a potential nuclear perpetrator. Indeed, Japan has created a cottage industry out of its role as a hapless victim, conveniently ignoring the fact that the chemical weapons manufactured in Hiroshima Prefecture were widely used against civilians in China.

While Japan was the target of the only two nuclear attacks conducted in wartime during the twentieth century, it is also true that its imperial government has a good many skeletons in its own closet. These include such Japanese-initiated atrocities as the Rape of Nanking, the use of Allied prisoners as slave laborers, and the unspeakable horrors of Japanese chemical and biological weapons programs. Undisclosed for decades, Japan also had a nuclear weapons program.

As a backdrop to the study of the Japanese nuclear program, it should be pointed out that there was considerable rivalry between the Imperial Japanese Navy and Imperial Japanese Army throughout the war. While such rivalry is present in the armed forces of many nations, it reached its most extreme levels with Imperial Japan. The competition between the two services existed even when it led to needless duplication that hurt the common goal of winning the war. The Imperial Japanese Navy and Imperial Japanese Army kept secrets from each other and often maintained independent and parallel command and supply structures in the field when a coordinated system would have ultimately saved time and effort.

By 1940, each of the services had independent nuclear weapons projects under way. The Army's program was under the direction of General Takeo Yasuda, director of the service's Aviation Technology Research Center. Among the scientists involved were Yoshio Nishina, Ryokichi Sagane, and Lieutenant Colonel Tatsusaburo Susuki. Nishina had studied at the California Institute of Technology and had consulted with Ernest O. Lawrence at the University of California. Lawrence had earned 1939 Nobel Prize in Physics for his invention of the cyclotron.

Suzuki, meanwhile, had also conducted a study of American and European nuclear projects. He outlined for Yasuda all the potential sources of uranium in the Far East, especially in Korea and in Burma. Both were occupied by the Imperial Japanese Army.

The Imperial Japanese Army's nuclear project was terminated in 1944, but the Navy project, centered at the University of Kyoto and the Riken laboratory complex in Tokyo, continued. However, this effort was hampered by a lack of the fissionable uranium necessary for a nuclear chain reaction.

While Japan did not have the fissionable material that it needed, Germany did. In one of the war's more interesting tales, the German submarine U-234 was sent from Norway on April 16, 1945, to take uranium to Japan. The submarine also carried a Messerschmitt Me.262 jet fighter and other secret documents and equipment. When Germany capitulated three weeks later, the U-boat sailed into Portsmouth, New Hampshire, and surrendered to U.S. forces. All the contents were captured, although 1,200 pounds of uranium oxide later disappeared.

Little is known about the Japanese nuclear weapons program. Some sources report the rumor that the Imperial Japanese Navy had completed one nuclear bomb by August 1945 and were prepared to use it against the U.S. Fleet at the time that Hiroshima was attacked. The tight lid of security on information about the Japanese chemical and biological weapons also remained in place—until the 1990s. Details are discussed in Chapters 24 and 25.

Other sources speculate that there may have been a plan in the works to use radioactive material—such as that being transported by the U-234—in a "dirty bomb" attack against cities on the U.S. West Coast. These attacks would have been made using aircraft launched from I-400–class submersible aircraft carriers. In fact, when the war ended, two such vessels were en route to the United States. These remarkable ships and their activities are discussed in Chapter 15.

## Conventional Bombs

Though overshadowed by nuclear weapons, conventional bombs obviously played a much wider role in World War II. Technological advances in conventional bombs during World War II were many, and a great many resources were brought to bear on these projects. Most of these weapons were created in a highly classified environment, and clearly the weapons listed below were secret weapons. Among these projects were the British large bombs, American and German guided bombs, and an innovative means of delivery developed by the Japanese.

The guided bombs included in this chapter are what we now refer to popularly as "smart" bombs. Both the Germans and the Americans were working on such secret weapons simultaneously, and both sides created examples that were amazingly successful. More accurately called "glide bombs," the American weapons were the first generation of weapons that evolved into the GBU-8 Pave Strike bomb used during the Vietnam War, and the GBU-15, and GBU-27 that have been an integral part of the U.S. arsenal in both Gulf Wars and Afghanistan.

The British led the way in the creation of really large high-explosive bombs. Indeed, the largest nonnuclear bombs used in World War II—and indeed the largest in the history of warfare—were all of British design. As a point of reference, bombs in the 500-pound class were then, and are today, considered standard. Bombs weighing one or two tons were less common but hardly unusual. The British went beyond this, first deploying a 4,000-pound bomb in April 1941 against Emden, and using an 8,000-pound bomb in September 1942. By way of comparison, the modern American GBU-28 "Bunker Buster" weighs 4,700 pounds.

Yet these British bombs, called "Blockbusters" and "Cookies," were not the true super-bombs of World War II.

## Barnes Neville Wallis

Any discussion of British World War II super-bombs must begin with the aeronautical genius who invented them. After an apprenticeship in an engineering company and a short stint as a shipyard worker, Barnes Wallis joined the Vickers aircraft company in 1913 at the age of 26. Among his earliest projects were the R80 and R100 airships, for which he utilized a revolutionary geodetic structural design. He would eventually apply this to aircraft design, culminating in the remarkable Vickers Wellington bomber, which was designed in 1936. The geodetic structure permitted twice the payload capacity than what had been expected when the project was envisioned. The Wellington was to be widely used in World War II, and remained in production until 1945. Over 11,000 Wellingtons were built, more than any other British bomber.

When World War II began, Wallis turned his attention to designing ordnance, where his understanding of aircraft design would help him push the limits of what was possible. His Tallboy and Grand Slam were the largest bombs ever used operationally.

After World War II, he continued to pioneer new designs in military aircraft, but this unfortunately coincided with a constriction in the funding available in Britain. He became Sir Barnes in 1968, and passed away in 1979.

## Upkeep

In prioritizing strategic industrial targets, Allied planners noted that most, such as factories, could be dispersed and relocated. Those that could not included coal mines, oil fields, and hydroelectric dams. This conclusion led to the first major ordnance problem that Barnes Wallis was asked to solve during World War II.

Wallis decided that coal mines were too easily repaired. The oil fields on which the German war machine depended were in Romania, and in 1942, these were at or beyond the limit of the range of Royal Air Force and USAAF bombers. For this reason, Barnes Wallis chose to focus on creating a special weapon to be used against the hydroelectric dams in the Ruhr Valley, Germany's industrial heartland.

Wallis realized that the electricity provided by the dams was essential to the German steel industry and that steel was essential to the manufacture of tanks, guns, U-boats, and nearly every weapon being produced by German industry. Furthermore, destroying the dams would greatly degrade the usefulness of the waterways throughout northern Germany.

The problem was that the dams were invulnerable to conventional bombing. Destroying their incredibly thick reinforced concrete would require a weapon of immense explosive capability, but that was only part of the trouble.

The bombs would have to impact the dams below the waterline of their reservoirs, and the dams were protected by torpedo nets to prevent this. In what was known as Project Upkeep, Barnes Wallis was handed the daunting challenge of solving this problem.

To do so, Wallis created a secret weapon that would essentially do the impossible. His Upkeep bomb would be among the heaviest ever built, yet it would be delivered by *bouncing it* for 400 yards across the surface of the water!

The Upkeep bomb was a barrel-shaped weapon that weighed 9,250 pounds. This included 5,720 pounds of a high explosive called torpex, which was a mix of TNT (trinitrotoluene), cyclotrimethylene trinitranmine, and aluminum. It was intended to bounce across the surface of the water and sink when it hit the back of the dam. It would then be exploded by a hydrostatic fuse set to detonate at a depth of 30 feet.

Tests done in December 1942 with a Wellington bomber proved that a bomb could be made to bounce across the surface of a body of water. Since the Wellington would be too small for what was required of it, the Avro Lancaster, Britain's largest World War II bomber, was chosen for the actual missions. Twenty Lancasters were heavily modified to carry the huge weapons, and these were organized into Number 617 Squadron of the Royal Air Force's Bomber Command.

As Wallis was refining Upkeep, the Royal Air Force began operational planning for attacks on the three most strategically important of the Ruhr dams: Moehne, Eder, and Sorpe. Operation Chastise, as it was code-named, would be designed to hit all three dams under cover of darkness on the same night. Chastise would be executed during a full moon for the sake of visibility, and late in the spring so that the reservoirs would be full. This latter was important to ensure maximum water pressure against a damaged dam, and maximum volume for downstream damage to German infrastructure.

On the night of May 16, 1943, all but one of the 617 Squadron Lancasters under Wing Commander Guy Gibson took off from RAF Scampton in Lincolnshire. The bombers struck in waves from an altitude of 60 feet. Both the Moehne and Eder Dams were struck by at least two hits and crumbled under the pressure of their own reservoirs. The Sorpe Dam was damaged, but its core was not breached. The Germans were, however, compelled to partially empty the reservoir in order to repair the dam.

Eight of the 19 Lancasters were lost in the raid, but two major dams were destroyed. They would be rebuilt during 1943, but at a great cost in manpower and matériel.

Parenthetically, the Germans managed to recover one of the Upkeep bombs from a crashed Lancaster and attempted, without success, to reverse-engineer a copy.

Amazingly, the Upkeep weapon was never used again. There were plans to use it against the Modane Dam in Italy in January 1944, but this mission was canceled.

A spherical bomb known as Highball, which used the same "water bouncing" delivery as Upkeep, was tested extensively but never used in combat.

Operation Chastise made Number 617 Squadron one of the most famous squadrons in the annals of the Royal Air Force and went on to other glories. After the defeat of Germany in May 1945, it was assigned to the Tiger Force that Bomber Command was to send to the Far East to join the USAAF in the strategic offensive against Japan. The squadron transitioned to Avro Lincoln bombers in 1946, was disbanded in 1955, but reactivated in 1958 flying Avro Vulcan strategic bombers. Late in the century, now equipped with Tornado fighter-bombers, 617 Squadron saw action in the Gulf War. At the turn of the century, the legendary squadron was stationed at RAF Lossiemouth in Scotland, flying Tornado GR4s. Based on the actions of that one night in 1943, they are still known as the "Dambusters."

## Tallboy

Barnes Wallis emerged as one of the heroes of Operation Chastise and with a mandate to continue developing bigger and better ordnance. His next weapon was the Tallboy deep-penetration bomb. It was also known as the "Earthquake" bomb because it was designed to create underground shock waves in order to cause structures some distance from the point of impact to collapse.

Unlike the barrel-shaped Upkeep, Tallboy was a sleek weapon designed to be released from high altitude so that it would strike the ground at very high speed. Tallboy was 21 feet long with a diameter of 3 feet 8 inches. It weighed 11,855 pounds, including 5,200 pounds of torpex high explosives. When dropped from 20,000 feet it created a crater 80 feet deep and 100 feet across—and it could penetrate 16 feet of concrete. Its ability to deeply penetrate even the most hardened concrete and create an artificial earthquake made the Tallboy an excellent weapon for use against such targets as V-1 sites or U-boat pens.

As with Upkeep, 617 Squadron was assigned to deliver the Tallboys, and again, specially modified Lancasters were required. The only major technical problem came when the weapon picked up so much speed that it broke the sound barrier, creating supersonic shock wave that caused the weapons to veer off course. Wallis resolved this problem with a redesign of the Tallboy's tail fins.

The first Tallboy attack came on June 8, 1944. This was

two days after the Normandy invasion and the target was the Samur rail tunnel through which German supplies passed en route to the Normandy Front. Subsequent attacks in support of invasion forces were made over the following week, but when the Germans began attacking Britain with V-1s on June 16, the attacks shifted to the reinforced concrete V-1 launch sites.

The great German battleship *Tirpitz* (sister ship of the mighty *Bismarck*) was attacked with Tallboys in three separate waves, culminating in the November 12, 1944, sinking of the big ship, along with the heavy cruiser *Lutzow*. Also during the autumn of 1944, the Dambusters of 617 Squadron used Tallboys against dams. More than 850 were used against various targets before the end of World War II.

## Grand Slam

Following the success of Tallboy, Barnes Wallis was able to convince the Royal Air Force that he could and should built a *10-ton* "Earthquake" bomb. Actually, it would weigh a total of 11 tons.

The 22,000-pound Grand Slam was based on the design of the Tallboy but was much larger: 26 feet 6 inches long, with a diameter of 3 feet 10 inches. When its 9,135 pounds of torpex explosives were detonated inside 20 feet of concrete, the result was truly devastating.

The first Grand Slam was dropped on the Bielefeld railway viaduct on March 14, 1945, destroying two spans. In a subsequent attack on U-boat pens near Bremen, two Grand Slams penetrated over 23 feet of reinforced concrete before exploding, resulting in the collapse of the entire ceiling.

A total of 41 Grand Slams were dropped in the seven weeks leading up to the surrender of Germany. Plans were under way for the Royal Air Force Tiger Force to use them against Japan when a pair of bombs utilizing a different technology made that activity unnecessary. In the meantime, the USAAF evaluated the use of Grand Slams with the B-29 Superfortress under Operation Ruby, but none was used in combat by the Americans.

Though the U.S. Air Force later developed a 42,000-pound conventional bomb to be carried by the postwar Convair B-36 Peacemaker, the Grand Slam remains the largest conventional bomb that will probably ever be dropped in wartime. The Massive Ordnance Air Blast (MOAB) weapon, first tested in March 2003, weighs 21,500 pounds. The largest non-nuclear bomb in the world at the time, this U.S. Air Force bomb has been nicknamed "Mother of All Bombs," but Grand Slam still remains "Papa."

## Fx.1400 Fritz X

An extensively used antiship weapon, Germany's Fx.1400 "Fritz X" had been in service for just a few weeks in 1943 when it earned a notorious reputation as a "battleship buster," as it wrought havoc on the most heavily armored of warships. Given the damage it caused, the Fritz X is arguably the most potent antishipping guided weapon in the history of warfare.

As the designation suggests, the Fx.1400 was adapted from the Pc.1400, a widely used 1,400-kilogram armor-piercing bomb. Creating a "strap-on" guidance system for it was the idea of noted missile designer Dr. Max Kramer of Germany's Air Transport Research Institute, the Deutsche Versuchsanstalt für Luftfahrt (DVL). Also responsible for such weapons as the X-4 air-to-air missile, Kramer had the idea of turning ordinary bombs into guided weapons. This concept was the same as the one behind the American GBU-31/32 Joint Direct Attack Munition (JDAM), which made its debut in 1996, nearly 60 years after Kramer conducted his initial tests.

The radio-guided Fritz X was a winged 3,080-pound armor-piercing rocket with four stubby aluminum wings and a tail that ringed the aft end of its fuselage like the wing of the Douglas Roc. It was 10 feet 8 inches long, 22 inches in diameter, and had a maximum wingspan of just over 53 inches. The fact that it also had a rocket accelerator unit—actually a glorified flare—made it more sophisticated, at least in this respect, than the JDAM.

In operation, Fritz X had a range of about three miles, which permitted the launching aircraft to "stand off," away from any antiaircraft fire that might be present near the target.

Though Kramer's experiments were conducted between 1938 and 1940, the Luftwaffe would be slow in placing its initial production order, and the first Fritz X was not delivered until February 1942.

At one point, a production rate of 750 missiles *monthly* was discussed, but the overall total would fall well below twice this number. After the completion of testing over the Baltic Sea, the bomber squadron KG100, based at Istres in southern France, became the first unit operational with the weapon. Using Dornier Do.217Ks to air launch the Fritz X, KG100 began operations on August 29, 1943.

The decision to deploy the Fritz X against Allied shipping in the Mediterranean was an auspicious one. Less than two weeks later, on September 8, the Italians surrendered to the Allies, withdrew from the Axis, and changed sides. As part of this arrangement, the Italian fleet was to be integrated into Allied naval operations. On September 9, as the fleet steamed out of the big base at La Spezia on the west coast of Italy, KG100 struck, concentrating on the biggest vessels first. The Fritz X proved itself almost immediately with direct hits on the battleships *Roma* and *Italia*. The former took two hits, blew up, and sank. The latter was heavily damaged.

Over the coming weeks, the Fritz X became the scourge of the Allied invasion fleet anchored off Salerno, south of Naples. Here, numerous transports were sunk as well as many of their armored escorts. The Allies lost the cruiser HMS *Spartan*, the destroyer HMS *Janus* was sunk, and the cruisers USS *Savannah* and HMS *Uganda* were badly damaged. Meanwhile, the battleship HMS *Warspite* was so severely crippled that it was laid up for a year.

The Fritz X was also launched by Heinkel He.177A bombers, and it was also tried against high-priority land targets, such as bridges. As the Allies developed means to jam the guidance system of the Fritz X, Kramer retrofitted it with the unique wire guidance system that he developed for his X-4 and X-7 weapons (see chapters 6 and 11).

Amazingly, the Luftwaffe terminated Fritz X production in December 1944 after only 1,386 had been built. During the final months of the war, the last battle of the Fritz X was against the bridges spanning the Oder and Neisse Rivers that were the last obstacle to the Soviet drive against Berlin.

## AZON and RAZON

The American VB (Vertical Bomb) series of bombs used azimuth and range guidance systems to improve targeting accuracy. The VB-1 and VB-2 AZON (AZimuth ONly) utilized guidance in azimuth only, while the VB-3 and VB-4 RAZON utilized it in range (vertical trajectory) as well. Azimuth is defined as the horizontal angular distance from a reference direction—usually the northern point of the horizon—to the point where a vertical circle through a celestial body intersects the horizon, usually measured clockwise.

Like the JDAM weapons a half-century later, the VBs were simply standard-issue free-fall bombs retrofitted with a modular tail section replacing the standard fins. The odd-numbered weapons were adapted from 1,000-pound bombs, and the even-numbered weapons were modified 2,000-pounders. The smaller weapons were the most commonly used.

These weapons were also retrofitted with a simple guidance mechanism. For AZON, the tail unit contained a gyroscope that worked through the horizontal control surfaces to maintain the weapon in an upright position during its fall. A rudder was radio-controlled by the bombardier, who watched it as it fell toward the target. The tail unit also had a flare. Using the smoke trail of the flare, the bombardier could follow the bomb as it plummeted tens of thousands of feet.

AZON and RAZON were born out of the desire to create a class of highly accurate weapons that could be used against high-priority "point targets" such as bridges. The program was managed by the USAAF Air Matériel Command with input from a variety of sources. For example, the guidance system evolved from the work of George Philbrick of the Massachusetts Institute of Technology, who built an electronic-sight simulator for the National Defense Research Council that was used for fighter aircraft. Philbrick's Pilot Universal Sight System (PUSS) became the guided bomb training simulator used for AZON and later adapted for RAZON.

The two parts of the system were the mechanical and optical system, built by the Franklin Institute in Philadelphia, and the electronic analog computer/simulator, similar to the amplifier in the M-IX gun director, which was the product of Bell Telephone Laboratories (later Lucent Technologies) and the Bell-owned Western Electric. The RC-186 and AN/ARW-16 transmitters would be used to control the bombs, while the RC-185 and AN/CRW-2 through AN/CRW-9 (except AN/CRW-6) receivers were designed to fit within the bombs to receive the controlling data (downlink) and transfer this to the control surfaces.

In dropping the AZON bombs, the bombardier would line up the trajectory so that it appeared to pass through the target until impact. In clear weather, one bombardier could guide up to five VB-1s simultaneously. The bombardier "flew" the AZON like a radio-controlled model airplane, manipulating it with a joystick similar to that of a modern video game. Operationally, five separate downlink frequencies were used so that five bombardiers in the same formation could control five separate weapons simultaneously.

Learning to use the AZON was a complicated process for bombardiers, especially because the project was so secret that they were required to destroy the notes they took during their instruction in the system.

By setting several AZONs to the same frequency, one bombardier could theoretically put them all on the same target while watching just one. However, Air Proving Ground Command tests at Eglin Field in Florida showed that when several AZONs were dropped in one salvo, the results were not as good as they were in normal free-fall bombs. A direct hit for one bomb was probable, but the rest seemed to disperse more than uncontrolled bombs.

What had happened was that a free-fall bomb rolls as it falls. It drifts to the left, then it rotates and drifts the other way, correcting itself. Because the AZONs did not rotate, all the drift would be in one direction.

Another control problem that plagued AZON was that its radio receiver became confused if it picked up interference from the bomber's radar system or even from its ignition. Once confused, AZON was difficult to pull back onto course.

AZON and RAZON were being developed during 1942 and 1943 at the same time as work was proceeding on infrared and radar guidance technology. USAAF Commanding General Henry "Hap" Arnold favored the simpler AZON and RAZON because he feared that the more complex technology would not be ready in time to play a role in World War II. The U.S. Navy, meanwhile, did pursue radar technology in such weapons as the Bat antiship missile.

AZON matured more than half a year after Fritz X, and was first used operationally by the USAAF in February 1944. During that month, AZON was used to score direct hits on the Danube locks and on the Avisio viaduct in Italy south of the Brenner Pass.

The AZON was also widely used during World War II in Southeast Asia, where the USAAF 493rd Bombardment Squadron employed them to target bridges used by the Japanese in Burma. Because of the difficult terrain, resupply was dependent on a finite number of bridges, and these bridges were natural bottlenecks. A road crossing a single bridge might be the only link to a sizable geographic area, and once lost, a large force would be virtually isolated. Naturally, the bridges were heavily defended by antiaircraft artillery. This made destroying them a difficult mission—even a near suicide mission—for bombers with "dumb" bombs, but it was a task that was tailor-made for AZON. A reported 459 AZONs were dropped against point targets in Burma, and 27 bridges were destroyed.

Japanese antiaircraft gunners made the work difficult, though. Naturally, they targeted the bombers that came over rather than the fighter escorts. In April 1944, the USAAF started using this fact to their advantage. Lockheed P-38Js with "droop snoot" Plexiglas noses were brought in to escort the bombers. The bombers would simply release the AZONs and break away quickly. The bombardier that did the AZON directing work was actually watching through the Plexiglas droop snoot in a nearby fighter.

As bombardiers learned how to use AZON, it proved to be nearly 30 times as accurate as regular free-fall dumb bombs. However, USAAF planners were anxiously anticipating the replacement of AZON by RAZON. Like Fritz X, it was a more complex weapon that could be controlled in three dimensions, but therein lay the problem. It was easy for the bombardier watching from above to see the left-and-right movement of the bomb, but it was harder to perceive range from high above. For this reason, RAZON development took longer than its predecessor. It would not be ready for combat trials until the summer of 1945, about a year and a half after AZON went to war.

World War II ended before RAZON was deployed, but work would continue. Because of dramatic postwar budget cuts, the USAAF (U.S. Air Force after 1947) quickly did away with the battle-tested AZON program entirely. All eggs were now in the RAZON basket. By 1947, however, development problems with RAZON led to its being put on the back burner. As the system grew more complex, it also grew more fragile because of the increasing number of vacuum tubes in its electronic components.

The requirements of the Korean War breathed life into the RAZON program. Flying B-29 Superfortresses, each equipped with eight VB-3 RAZONs, the 19th Bombardment Group flew 21 sorties against bridges in North Korea in the autumn of 1950. The results were disappointing. They dropped 154 RAZONs, of which only 92 worked properly. Of these, 20 made direct hits on bridges, and 10 of the spans were destroyed. Because the latter were substantial steel structures, it took an average four 1,000-pound warheads to destroy one entirely.

The system failures in the RAZONs that didn't work were traced to such factors as corrosion, which had crept into the electronics at the bomber bases on humid Okinawa, and the absence of sophisticated testing and calibration equipment in the field.

The ultimate weapon in the VB family was the Bell VB-13 Tarzon (later ASM-A-1) that mated RAZON technology with a 12,000-pound bomb modeled after the Barnes Wallis Tallboy. Tarzon was introduced into the Korean War in the spring of 1951 to attack the Yalu River bridges. A reported 30 Tarzons were dropped and 6 bridges were destroyed.

## Japanese Balloon Bombs

On May 5, 1945, two days before the end of World War II in Europe, Reverend Archie Mitchell, of the Bly Christian and Missionary Alliance Church in Bly, Oregon, took his pregnant wife, Elsie, and five Sunday-school students on a fishing and picnic trip near Gearhart Mountain in the Fremont National Forest, 70 miles northeast of Klamath Falls, Oregon.

Mitchell pulled his car off the road at a point accessible to a nearby creek. As he was removing the picnic gear from the car, he heard 13-year-old Joan Patzke remark that she had found a huge object lodged in a tree. As the others moved in to take a closer look, there was huge explosion. Both Joan Patzke and Elsie Mitchell were killed, as were the other students—Edward Engen, Jay Gifford, Dick Patzke, and Sherman Shoemaker, all of them aged 11 to 14. Only Reverend Mitchell, who was farther away than the others, survived.

These six Oregonians were the first and only Americans

killed by enemy action within the continental United States during World War II—and the last for more than half a century, until the morning of September 11, 2001.

Ironically, the most successful operation aimed at bombing the United States during World War II was the most low-tech. One of the best-kept secrets of World War II, Japan's "Fugo" project was conceived as a reprisal for the 1942 Doolittle air raid on Tokyo. However, it did not get off the ground until November 1944, more than two and a half years after the raid.

Under the program, over 9,000 balloons made of laminated mulberry parchment paper or rubberized silk would be launched from Japan over a five-month period. Japanese meteorologists had discovered the jet stream and had calculated that balloons launched from their country could reach the continental United States in less than three days.

The balloons were about 32 feet in diameter, weighed about 150 pounds, and were filled with hydrogen. Each was designed to carry four to six small incendiaries and an explosive antipersonnel charge. The latter was later claimed to have been included to destroy evidence of the bombs, but it was one of these that was responsible for the deaths of the Mitchell party.

Each of the Fugo balloons was outfitted with approximately 30 6-pound sandbags that were released one at a time by an aneroid barometer trigger whenever the balloon dipped below 30,000 feet. It was estimated that after the last sandbag was detached, the balloon would be flying over the United States. An onboard battery ignited fuses to drop the incendiaries. The Japanese realized that the jet stream would carry most of the Fugo bombs over the heavily forested Northwest, so the incendiaries were intended to start forest fires, which were potentially devastating.

According to Japanese records, an attempt was made to

launch the Fugo operation in June 1944, but the first balloons did not have sufficient range and had to be redesigned. The Japanese began launching them again in October, which is well past the end of the fire season. Had the offensive begun in June, as planned, the results might have been quite different. As it was, the winter of 1944–1945 was particularly wet in the Pacific Northwest, and even by late spring, fire danger was low.

Most Fugo bombs landed in the Pacific Northwest—more in Washington than in any other state—but they are known to have landed as far away as Texas, Kansas, North Dakota, and Michigan. Some are reported to have reached Mexico.

In Utah, Box Elder County Sheriff Warren Hyde observed one of the Fugo balloons on February 23, 1945, as it was drifting low over the ground. When he attempted to catch it he was dragged for some distance. He finally wrestled it to a stop and turned the parts over to federal authorities.

Most balloon bombs did little if any damage. Aside from the Mitchell party, no one is known to have been killed or seriously injured—indeed, one boy in Washington actually turned a live bomb in to police.

The FBI and other law enforcement agencies had become aware of this secret weapon during the winter, but the veil of secrecy was not lifted by a first public announcement until about two weeks after the Oregon fatalities.

In August, after the Japanese surrender, the government formally confirmed that 230 of the balloons had been recovered. As many as half again more were discovered later. The last known find in North America came in 1955, when a 74th Air Rescue Squadron H-5 helicopter crew from Ladd AFB picked one up near Fairbanks, Alaska. Its ordnance was discovered to still be live after a decade of harsh weathering.

Ironically, in early 1945 one Fugo bomb knocked out power at the Hanford Engineering Works in eastern Washington, where uranium was being processed for the Manhattan Project.

Another ironic twist in the strange story concerns Reverend Archie Mitchell himself. He remarried and was serving as a missionary in Vietnam in the early 1960s. On May 30, 1962, while working with his second wife, Betty, at a hospital for lepers in the remote highlands about 150 miles north of Saigon, he and two other persons were abducted by the Viet Cong. As Betty Mitchell explained in a rare 1993 interview, "They just came in and took the three people they wanted and left. I never saw my husband again."

Today, a monument and a day-use picnic area mark the spot where the Mitchell party had their fateful encounter with Project Fugo. The monument was dedicated in 1995 on the fiftieth anniversary of the event. It is located 70 miles northeast of Klamath Falls and three and a half miles from the Corral Creek U.S. Forest Service Campground. The area surrounding the Mitchell Monument was donated to the Fremont National Forest by the Weyerhaeuser Corporation in 1998.

## The Bat Bomb

Many of the secret weapons of World War II explored unorthodox technology that still seems unconventional from our vantage point in the twenty-first century. Of all the American secret weapons that were actually funded and developed, perhaps the strangest was the so-called "Bat Bomb." Shortly after the United States entered the war, an Irwin, Pennsylvania, dentist named Lytle S. "Doc" Adams, developed the theory that *bats* could be used to destroy Japanese cities.

Doc Adams theorized that small incendiary devices could be attached to thousands of these small flying mammals, which could then be released by American bombers over Japan. Because bats are known to take up residence in the eves of wooden buildings, they would naturally position themselves—along with the attached miniature fire bombs—in a place where they could do the most damage. Adams imagined that a timer or temperature sensor could trigger the incendiary after the bat was in position. Each bat would give its life for the American war effort, and thousands of fires would erupt across Japan.

When routine bombing missions against Japanese cities finally began in 1944, the USAAF used high-explosive ordnance. It was not until early in 1945 that General Curtiss LeMay's Twentieth Air Force switched from high explosives to incendiaries. What LeMay figured out in 1945, Doc Adams had understood in 1941. Most Japanese housing construction was wood and paper, meaning that incendiaries were a far more effective weapon than high explosives.

Just as Albert Einstein was able to get his secret memo about nuclear weapons onto the desk of President Franklin Roosevelt, so, too, did Adams manage to get the ear of the president. After reviewing the Bat Bomb proposal, Roosevelt ordered the USAAF and the National Defense Research Committee to initiate a development program. In passing Adams' hypotheses along to General William J. "Wild Bill" Donovan, head of the office of Strategic Services (OSS), the president added a postscript the order, pencilling in the phrase that would warm the heart of any eccentric inventor—"This man is not a nut."

Under the code name Project X-ray, the Bat Bomb program was housed at Muroc Army Field (now Edwards AFB) in California's Mojave Desert. The bats themselves were Mexican free-tailed bats that were rounded up in caves located in the Texas hill country between San Antonio and Austin. These caves, such as Bracken and Frio, are home to the largest colonies of bats in the United States. In fact, Bracken Cave is today considered to be home to the largest concentration of mammals, of any kind, in the world. The current summer population estimate for this one cave is estimated at as many as 40 million bats.

Speaking of millions, the USAAF invested an estimated $2 million in the Bat Bomb program, designing, building and testing bomb casings in which the little mammals could be placed. As testing got underway at Muroc in 1943, a number of problems arose. One of the primary issues was how to carry the bats and to release them from the bomb casings without injuring or killing them. For example, it was discovered that the bats did not do well in the cold temperatures at high altitudes. Those who did not freeze to death were too groggy to escape from the casing and fly away. When they were carried at lower altitudes, it was hard for the bats to get out of the falling bombs, even when the bombs were slowed with parachutes.

When the bugs were worked out of these predicaments and the bats were successfully deployed, they proved to be unpredictable. For testing, a series of target buildings were constructed for the bats to "attack." However, some of the bats flew into the wrong buildings. The incendiaries went off, burning down unintended structures, as well as the intended target buildings. A general's staff car was also destroyed by the bats.

The Bat Bombs were scheduled to become operational early in 1944, with the first attacks on Japan beginning in March. Each B-29 bomber would be carrying more than 4,000 encased bats. However, the project is thought to have been terminated before any missions were actually flown.

Nevertheless, this writer has spoken with a Navy transport pilot who flew a "squeaking" cargo to the western Pacific around this time. When he asked what the sound was, he was told by the cargo handlers that it was "bats," but that he was not to ask any more questions.

In 1992, Jack Couffer, a member of the team that developed this strange secret weapon, told the story in his book *Bat Bomb: World War II's Other Secret Weapon*.

## The "Ultimate" Weapon

Most secret weapons are known to just a handful of people. Others, in order to be effective, must be revealed to the large numbers of people who will actually use them. Nuclear weapons were certainly among the former. Of the secret weapons of World War II that fall into the latter category, there is one that has probably been described as "ultimate" more often than any other American weapon—except nuclear weapons.

During World War II, the USAAF trained more than 45,000 bombardiers and then entrusted them with a weapon that they were sworn to secrecy to protect. It was the most valuable piece of equipment on any American bomber. Tens of thousands of people saw them every day, and their name—Norden—was part of 1940s American folklore. However, it was a federal crime to photograph them, and men risked their lives to keep them from being captured.

The Norden was just a foot wide and a foot and a half tall. It was so ordinary looking that it could be hidden in plain sight. If someone did not know what to look for, he would never have recognized the Norden as the ultimate weapon. The fabled Norden was not a bomb, but a means of delivering them.

## Norden Bombsight

The work of the artilleryman, like that of the naval gunner, has been an evolving science throughout the centuries large cannons have been used in warfare. By the First World War, the science of ballistics and the study of trajectory projectiles had been refined to a fine point. Mathematical formulas told gunners how to put shells on targets with chilling precision.

Just as with artillery, aerial bombardment began as a "aim-and-shoot" art. When aerial bombardment began its first widespread use in World War I, pilots simply lined up a target and released their bombs as they zoomed across it. The need for a precise method for aiming bombs was obvious. If they were dropped from too high an altitude, it was hard to see the target and wind drift often caused them to go astray. If a pilot went in low, he was exposed to ground fire.

Early attempts at creating bombsights were stymied by technical problems that few gunners had ever faced. Army artillery is fired from stationary guns, while naval gunners fire from platforms that usually move no faster than an automobile obeying the speed limit in a school zone.

Bombardiers, meanwhile, faced the task of aiming ordnance from vehicles traveling several hundred miles per hour and often bouncing up and down and sideways at the same time. Surface gunnery delivers a projectile that has its own momentum, while aerial bombs are propelled at a much slower speed, pulled toward their targets only by gravity. Thus, bombs are much more susceptible to the whims of wind currents that often flow in opposite directions at different altitudes, and change speed and direction invisibly.

Even today, with the computing power of microelectronics, creating a calculating bombsight is a complex task, but in the years between World War I and World War II, bombsight development was literally a hit-or-miss proposition.

The person who created the most sophisticated aiming device in history that did not use electronics was a man named Carl Lukas Norden. Born in Java in 1880, the son of Edward Norden, a Dutch trader, Carl apprenticed as an precision instrument maker in Switzerland before emigrating to the United States in 1904. He joined the research and development staff at the Sperry Gyroscope Company in 1911, where he would be recognized as a pioneer in the field of gyroscopically stabilized naval gun platforms. He resigned from Sperry in 1915 to strike out on his own, using his contacts within the U.S. Navy Bureau of Ordnance to line up work.

Ironically, the weapon that would account for the greatest offensive successes of the USAAF in World War II was created for the U.S. Navy. Because of his past performance on gyrostabilization, the Navy asked Norden to develop a bombsight for hitting maneuvering warships from the air.

Norden began work in 1921 and delivered his Mk.III model two years later, at which time he took on a partner, a former army officer named Theodore Barth. Together they formed Carl L. Norden, Inc. Barth served as front man, while Norden, a recluse by nature, worked at his drafting table. A little-known fact about the inventor of America's ultimate weapon was that he spent a great deal of his time during the 1920s and 1930s in Europe. His drafting table was located in Zurich.

By 1931, Norden had worked his way up to the Mk.XV,

a sophisticated gyro-optical device with a timing mechanism to tell the bombardier when to release the bombs. Provisions would be made to allow the bombardier to take lateral control of the aircraft from the pilot in order to line up the sight for the bomb run.

Both the U.S. Navy and the U.S. Army Air Corps (USAAF after 1947) were exceptionally pleased with the results the Mk.IV achieved. It was one of those rare technical innovations that truly took the state-of-the-art to a new level.

In 1935, the Air Corps' 19th Bomb Group, based at Rockwell Field near San Diego, achieved an unprecedented level of routine accuracy with the Norden, hitting within 165 feet of a target from altitudes up to 15,000 feet.

Accuracy continued to improve, culminating in the Norden M-Series Bombsight, delivered to the USAAF after 1943. If used correctly, it was capable of hitting within a 50-foot radius from an altitude of over 20,000 feet. This provided a level of precision up to eight times that of the contemporary British Mk.XIV bombsight. In 1943, it was estimated that the Royal Air Force was able to put 5 percent of its bombs within a *mile* of the aiming point under combat conditions. By contrast, the USAAF Eighth Air Force was believed to be able to put 24 percent of its bombs to within 1,000 yards of their targets. By 1944, using the Norden M, the USAAF was able to drop 40 percent to within 500 yards.

To use the Norden, the bombardier first set the course of the aircraft and the range to target. He calculated the latter by airspeed, altitude, and the wind. The fact that bombs tended to "trail" beneath a bomber rather than falling straight down also had to be figured in. The actual time of fall (ATF) was figured using a tachometer, and this was compared with a precomputed table that gave accurate ATF values depending on variables such as airspeed and altitude. This data was entered into the bombsight and the crosshairs were aligned on the target.

Because the bombsight had to be held steady, but an aircraft, especially a bomber under combat conditions, was always pitching, rolling, and yawing, a gyroscope was required in order to steady the bombsight. Bubbles such as those in a carpenter's level were used for this purpose, and the gyroscope was usually found to be able to do its job. The gyrostabilized optics permitted pilots to establish a vertical reference to the ground, necessary for aligning the course and measuring the drop angle for the bombs. If the bubbles were off by a degree, this translated to just over 200 feet of inaccuracy on the ground for every 10,000 feet of altitude.

Over the target, the pilot would take his hands off the controls and let the bombardier "fly" the bomber over the target through a C-1 autopilot slaved to the Norden Bombsight. If the correct settings were entered and it was properly leveled, the Norden Bombsight provided extraordinary accuracy. However, the precision was degraded by weather, especially cloud cover between the bomber and the target, and by the terrible combat conditions under which the bombardiers had to work.

The Norden Bombsight was also a beautiful piece of machinery, resembling a fine clock more than a weapon of war. Inside, it was filled with over 2,000 parts—from precision optics to a mass of intricate brass and steel gears with nearly microscopic teeth.

During World War II, the Norden company built 25,000 bombsights, and many more were built under license by other firms, including Sperry, Norden's former employer. They were used to equip the USAAF's fleets of B-17 Flying Fortresses and B-29 Superfortresses as well as many other types of bombers.

The Norden Bombsights were among the most complex analog instruments ever built, selling for $10,000 (nearly 10 times that in turn-of-the-century dollars) and worth the price for the amount of work that went into them. Check eBay to see how much a mint condition Norden sells for today.

By 1944, many people in the United States had heard of the fabled Norden, but no pictures had been published, and the bombsight was always covered when it was shown in a picture of an airplane. The bombardier was ordered to guard it with his life, and he always removed it from the bomber at the end of a mission. He carried it carefully in a leather case called a "football" and was instructed to destroy it in the case of a forced landing in enemy territory.

During the war, security surrounding the factories that built the Nordens was extraordinary, but, ironically, the most damaging espionage had occurred in 1938—before the war.

Major Nikolaus Ritter of the Abwehr (German military intelligence) had lived in the United States in the 1930s, where he successfully recruited a number of German Americans to be covert operatives. One of these was a man named Hermann Lang, who worked as an assembly-line inspector at the Norden factory. From Lang, Ritter— whose code name was "Dr. Rantzau"—obtained detailed drawings of the prewar version of the Norden Bombsight. These gave the Germans an idea of how it worked, but did not help them defend themselves against it. The Luftwaffe did not take the notion of developing long-range bombers seriously, so it did them little good in this respect as well.

After World War II, the Norden remained state-of-the-art until it was gradually replaced by radar bombsights that permitted bombardiers to "see through" cloud cover and to do their work at night.

In 1951, Carl L. Norden, Inc., was renamed Norden Laboratories, which merged with the Ketay Instrument

Company in 1955. In 1958, Norden-Ketay became the Norden Division of United Aircraft (United Technologies after 1971). The centerpiece of United Aircraft and United Technologies (which was associated with both United Airlines and Boeing until 1934) has always been Pratt & Whitney, which has been one of the world's largest makers of aircraft engines since before World War II.

Carl Norden himself, still a Dutch citizen, retired to Switzerland in the early 1950s and lived there in seclusion until his death in 1965.

# 4

## Secret Codes

As with the Norden Bombsight, the incredible importance of complex secret codes and code breaking demonstrates that the most secret and most important secret weapons of World War II were not really weapons at all.

One tries to use the word *ultimate* sparingly, but if the Norden Bombsight was the ultimate American weapon (until July 1945), then clearly Enigma and Ultra may have been referred to with such a superlative by the Germans and the British. The British were right in doing so, and because they were, the Germans, as we shall see, were *not*.

Of all the stories of the weapons and secrets of World War II, one of the most important is that of the German Enigma secret code system, and the British Ultra project that cracked it. In fact, Ultra was *so* secret that it was not known about for nearly three decades after the war. Ultra was so important that when former Group Captain Frederick William Winterbotham published his book *The Ultra Secret* in 1974, there were calls for a rewriting of the history of World War II.

Before Ultra, there had been Enigma, and it, too, was an astounding accomplishment.

## Enigma

Enigma (Greek for "puzzle") was a coding machine that was used to encipher German radio messages. It was a four-rotor typewriter that transformed one letter into another by a changing pattern of settings. This pattern was revised daily, and the Germans considered the system unbreakable—an "ultimate" code machine.

Mechanical encryption machines date back to antiquity, and in more recent times, Thomas Jefferson is said to have invented one. In the early twentieth century, electricity was plugged into the process. Between the last year of World War I and the early 1920s, several independently developed electromechanical encryption machines appeared. Among these were the devices invented by an American, Edward Hugh Hebern, Arvid Gerhard Damm of Sweden, Hugo Alexander Koch in the Netherlands, and a German named Arthur Scherbius. The latter was marketed commercially under the name Enigma. In 1927, Koch would sell *his* patent to Scherbius.

It was the Scherbius Enigma that would evolve into the Enigma machine used by Germany during World War II, but in the 1920s, it was sold to businesses wishing to keep transactions confidential. The German military first acquired a commercial Enigma machine in 1926, seven years before the Nazis came to power. They would continue to complicate and refine the system throughout World War II.

The Enigma had a keyboard like that of a typewriter or a personal computer. Inside, there was a series of circular rotors on a common axle that was turned from the front of the machine with a thumbwheel. The rotors could, in turn, be removed and their order shuffled. On the rotors were 26 cross-wired electrical contacts with the output contacts of one connected to the input contacts of the next. As a key was pressed, current from a battery passed through the rotors to illuminate one of 26 lightbulbs. At the same time, the first rotor rotated one position until it completed a full rotation of 26 positions. At that point, the second rotor began to advance, and so on. If the receiving machine was wired in the same way, then an encrypted message could be decoded.

In addition to the series of rotors, a series of 26 jacks and patch cords could be used to cross-connect the keyboard and rotors. This was said to increase the number of encoding variables from 2 or 3 billion to 10 quadrillion. This means that technicians who did not know the code could work 24 hours a day with a thousand Enigma machines, testing a key every 15 seconds, and not try every variable for 900 million years.

Because the Germans changed the code settings every day, even the possession of a captured Enigma machine would theoretically not be helpful. On top of this, each branch of the German military used separate Enigma settings. Thus, for example, the Kriegsmarine couldn't read Luftwaffe messages, and vice versa. During World War II, the Germans transmitted as many as 2,000 messages every day on Enigma—without any notion that the unbreakable code had been cracked soon after the war had begun.

## Ultra

The effort to penetrate the secrets of Enigma actually began in Poland, a nation that was wary of German military ambitions even before the rise of Nazism. The Polish intelligence services monitoring German military transmissions was able to tell when the Germans started using Enigma in 1926, and they figured out what it was. Using a commercial-model Enigma machine, mathematicians such as Marian Rejewski and Henryk Zygalski undertook the task of trying to break the ciphers. As the Germans had imagined, having an Enigma machine was essentially worthless, because no one had a clue as to how it was set and the variables were so many.

A breakthrough was achieved in 1933. A disinherited German nobleman obtained and sold some obsolete Enigma codes to Gustave Bertrand of the French secret service, who shared them with the Poles. In the course of several exchanges, Marian Rejewski managed to assemble copies of messages in both coded and uncoded form and was able to create a sort of Rosetta stone based on them.

Using the commercial Enigma machine, he tried unsuccessfully to work out the variables, finally discovering that the military Enigma did not use the typical typewriter keyboard layout that starts with $Q$ in the upper left. Though this achievement did not crack the Enigma code, it did get deep enough into the puzzle to drastically reduce the number of variables that stood in the way of doing so.

By 1937, the Polish team was able to work through the set of variables, which the Germans imagined would take a million years, in less than an hour. However, major upgrades by the Germans would soon put the Poles back to square one. It was still possible to calculate the *number* of variables, but it was no longer physically possible to try them all.

By July 1939, it was time to give up. From the few messages that they had been able to decipher, the Poles knew that their country was about to be invaded. At a clandestine, midnight meeting in forest near Pyry, Poland, Marian Rejewski and Henryk Zygalski handed everything they had on Enigma over to British agents.

As it turned out, the British had also been trying to break Enigma, but they had long since given up, calling the task impossible. The clueless British now had the clues they needed to take up the challenge again. Without the work of the Poles, Britain would certainly not have broken Enigma, and would probably have lost the war by 1941.

In August 1939, British code-breaking activity was secretly consolidated at a nondescript country estate north of London. The mundane civilian name of the place was Bletchley Park, but its "secret" designation was "Station X." The official descriptive designation was Government Code and Cypher School (GC&CS), but the initials were sacrilegiously translated by those who worked there as "Golf, Cheese and Chess Society" because many of the code breakers were chess masters.

One of the principal activities at Bletchley Park was the decoding of Enigma traffic. The decriptions came to be known as Ultra.

By the spring of 1940, Bletchley Park was making a great deal of headway in getting through the Enigma messages by looking for patterns that were repeated from day to day. Luftwaffe messages, for instance, were being routinely translated by the time that the Battle of Britain began in the summer of 1940. Kriegsmarine codes, however, defied decription for another year when the naval service added additional rotors to its Enigma machines.

The breakthrough in cracking the Kriegsmarine code came on May 9, 1941, when the German U-boat U-110 was forced to the surface and captured intact by the British destroyer *Bulldog*. Thinking that the U-110 was about to sink, the radioman made the fateful mistake of not destroying his Enigma machine. By the time the submarine did sink, both the radioman and his machine were in British custody.

Through Ultra, Bletchley Park was able to provide

warning of the Luftwaffe maximum-effort bombing campaign scheduled for August 15, 1940, and code-named
Adler Tag (Eagle Day). Bletchley Park was also able to
monitor German preparations for the Operation Sea Lion
invasion of Britain, including the good news of Sea Lion's
cancellation in September 1940.

The importance of the Ultra program to the British war
effort is often illustrated by the anecdote concerning a
message about an impending Luftwaffe raid on the city of
Coventry on November 14, 1940. As the story goes, Prime
Minister Winston Churchill was informed about the raid
several days ahead of time, but did not warn people in the
city to evacuate. Had he actually known of the impending
attack, he could have saved many of the lives that were
lost. The point of the story is that he made the difficult decision to allow Coventry to be bombed rather than risk re-
vealing that the British knew the German plans in advance.
In fact, it was later revealed that the Ultra decryptions had
not identified Coventry as the target for November 14. The
Royal Air Force, meanwhile, had a system of tracking German bombers by breaking into the radio beams that were
broadcast by the Luftwaffe as navigation aids. By the time
they had figured out that Coventry was to be the target on
that night, it was too late for an evacuation.

When the Colossus computer (see next entry) went on-
line in early 1944, the efficiency of the Bletchley Park code
breakers increased many fold. With the new machines, Ultra became an essential part of the planning and execution
of the June 1944 Operation Overlord invasion of Normandy. An indispensable part of invasion planning was to
create the false impression that the Allies were going to invade at Calais rather than Normandy. Through Ultra inter-
cepts, they were able to be certain that the Germans had
bought the ruse.

During World War II, more than 10,000 people—from

mathematicians to linguists—were employed at Bletchley Park. Among them were Alan Turing, who literally invented the modern electronic computer while there, and a man named Ian Fleming. After the war Fleming would go on to a career as a novelist, creating the world's most famous spy—James Bond. Fleming wrote the James Bond novels prior to 1974, so there is never even a hint of Bletchley Park in the stories.

Bletchley Park was closed down and dismantled by March 1946, with every crumb of evidence that it had been a code-cracking center removed. By 1991, the facility was deserted and facing demolition when the Bletchley Park Trust was formed to save and preserve it. The trust was ultimately successful, and today, Bletchley Park is open to the public as a museum.

## Colossus I

The world's first computer was a machine so secret that it remained unknown to the world for three decades, and, indeed, so secret that it was destroyed *almost* without a trace 16 years after it was built.

Despite possessing a German Enigma code machine, the British were faced with the necessity of performing millions of complex mathematical operations in a very short time, every day. The Enigma cipher machine was capable of being set up in a vast number of ways to encipher a message. On just a three-rotor machine this came to 150,000,000,000,000,000,000 possible settings. The code breakers had to find which one of this vast number of settings had been used before they could decipher a message.

In order to accomplish this, an entirely new calculating machine was needed. This machine was Colossus I, which is generally regarded as the world's first operational programmable electronic digital computer.

The theoretical mastermind behind Colossus was Alan Mathison Turing, a brilliant mathematician who developed the notion of applying algorithms to digital computers. Born in London in 1912, Turing was educated at Kings College in Cambridge and at Princeton University, and was later a fellow at both of those institutions as well as at the National Physical Laboratory and the University of Manchester. Also recognized as a pioneer in the field of artificial intelligence, he had theorized that it would be possible to create machines that could do many of the things that we take for granted in desktop computers today.

During the 1930s, he designed a theoretical mechanism called the "Turing Machine," which could execute any conceivable systematic calculating task. In doing so, he first expressed concepts we take for granted today, such as data input and output, digital memory, and coded programs. By 1938, he had actually started tinkering with building an analog mechanical apparatus to test his theory.

Recruited by the British government, Turing became one of the first people to join the Government Code & Cypher School staff at Bletchley Park in 1939. Working with such men as Max Newman and the great engineer Tommy Flowers, Turing began work on the problem of building a "thinking machine" capable of rapidly decoding Enigma. The machine that they eventually created would be many orders of magnitude faster and more capable than the German code machine.

Work on actual construction of the Colossus began early in 1943, and it was finally installed at Bletchley Park just after Christmas of that year. Operational testing began in January 1944, and the Colossus I was deemed a success. By the time of the Operation Overlord invasion of Normandy in June, it had been upgraded and rechristened Colossus II. Within a year, 10 such machines would be whirring through mountains of German code at Bletchley Park.

Each Colossus II occupied a separate room at Bletchley Park, and *occupied* was indeed the operative word, because the machines were huge. The main section stood over 7 feet tall, with two bays 16 feet wide and additional equipment adjacent to that. They could read 5,000 characters each second from a teletype printer.

Colossus II used photoelectric cells to read punched paper tape, much as did early computers that were in use as late as the 1970s. It was programmed with a cross-correlation algorithm through jacks and plugs similar to those then in use in telephone switchboards.

After World War II, as Bletchley Park was being closed down, all persons who had worked on the project were sworn to silence under the Official Secrets Act and eight of the super-secret Colossus II machines were completely destroyed. The remaining two were stored in London until 1960, when they, too, were torn down. Because the whole Ultra project, especially Colossus, remained so extremely secret, all the written data and diagrams related to their construction and operation were also destroyed in 1960.

Alan Turing went on to the National Physical Laboratory, where he continued to do theoretical work in the fields of digital computing and artificial intelligence.

Though the secret Colossus had been the first, many electronic computers arrived on the scene soon after the end of World War II. In 1946, the first U.S. government–funded computer, the 30-ton Electronic Numerical Integrator & Computer (ENIAC) went on-line. IBM introduced programmable memory in 1948, and the first commercially successful electronic computer, the Sperry Universal Automatic Computer (UNIVAC), was introduced in 1951.

In 1974, 20 years after the death of Alan Turing, the existence of Colossus was officially acknowledged. Many of the surviving people who had worked on the program three decades earlier, such as Dr. Tommy Flowers, were now permitted to discuss their work.

In 1991, as part of the campaign to save Bletchley Park from demolition by developers, Tony Sale at the Science Museum in London had the idea to rebuild a working example of a Colossus. Using the eight surviving 1945 photographs of Colossus plus circuit diagrams that some engineers had kept, in his words, "quite illegally, as engineers always do," he faced the daunting task of re-creating what had once been arguably the most complex machine in the world.

Sale transferred the two-dimensional photos to a three-dimensional computer drafting machine and worked with many of the original scientists to reengineer the hardware to the original specifications. He was also able to track down vacuum tubes similar to those used in 1943 and 1944. It took five years, but on June 6, 1996, the fifty-second anniversary of the Normandy invasion, the Duke of Kent came to the museum at Bletchley Park to ceremonially flip the switch to start the first Colossus machine in half a century.

## Navajo Code Talkers

If Colossus and the Ultra project were the harbingers of a new era in human civilization, the Navajo Code Talkers were an extraordinary idea that reached back to an earlier era of human civilization. The idea was brilliantly simple, but resulted in a means of communication that was utterly indecipherable by anyone unfamiliar with it. Because the Navajo language has no similarities whatsoever to any other language group in the world, there was no way that even a Colossus could decipher it!

The Navajo Code Talkers were one of the best-kept secrets of World War II, with much information about them not revealed until the 1960s.

The idea originated soon after Pearl Harbor with Philip Johnston, a World War I veteran and the son of a missionary who had worked with the Navajo people of the U.S. Southwest during the nineteenth century. Having grown up on a Navajo Reservation, Johnston was one of a handful of non-Navajos who spoke the language fluently. He was also aware that the Choctaw language had been used on a limited basis for message encryption during World War I.

Johnston set up a meeting with Marine Corps Major General Clayton Vogel a few weeks after the United States entered World War II. He arranged a series of demonstrations for Vogel, who commanded the Amphibious Corps of the U.S. Pacific Fleet, and his staff. At a time when it took an operator a half-hour to write three lines of code with an encryption machine, Johnston showed that a Navajo person could accomplish the task in less than half a minute.

Johnston further explained that the Navajo language was an extremely complex, yet unwritten, language. It had thousands of words and a complicated grammar, but it had no alphabet. The USMC staff had a chance to observe how its syntax and tonal qualities, not to mention its dialects, made it unintelligible to anyone without extensive exposure and training. Few people did. One estimate indicated that, at the start of in 1942, there were fewer than 30 non-Navajo persons who understood the language.

Vogel was impressed, and he recommended to the commandant of the Marine Corps that 200 Navajos be recruited to become what would be called "Code Talkers." These men would transmit encoded messages by speaking to one another on two-way radios in their own language.

To a non-Navajo who intercepted the conversation, it would be unintelligible.

In May 1942, the first 29 Navajo Code Talkers went to Camp Elliot (now Marine Air Corps Station Miramar) near San Diego to develop the code and to create a dictionary of equivalents for military terms that did not exist in the language. As new recruits completed boot camp, they memorized the dictionary and were sent to the Pacific Theater to be assigned to an operational Marine Corps unit. Here, they transmitted messages to Code Talkers in other units, discussing tactics and troop movements and conveying orders and other battlefield communications over radio and telephones. They also acted as messengers and performed other tasks.

Slightly more than 400 Navajo Code Talkers went overseas, serving at Guadalcanal, Tarawa, Peleliu, and Iwo Jima. They were active in every assault conducted by the USMC in the Pacific, operating with all six Marine Corps divisions, with Marine Raider battalions, and with Marine paratroop units.

In February 1945, at Iwo Jima, six Navajo Code Talkers assigned to the Fifth Marine Division worked around the clock during the first two days of the battle transmitting more than 800 messages without error. Major Howard Connor, the Fifth Division signal officer, observed that "were it not for the Navajos, the Marines would never have taken Iwo Jima."

In the dictionary that the Code Talkers created at Camp Elliot, the code was actually a variation on conversational Navajo. For example, when the Code Talkers transmitted a message, it came across as a series of seemingly unrelated Navajo words. The listener would first translate each Navajo word into its English equivalent. Then, using only the first letter of the English equivalent, he'd spell an English word. Most letters had more than one Navajo word representing them. For instance, the Navajo words *wol-la-chee* ("ant"), *be-la-sana* ("apple"), and *tse-nill* ("axe") all stood for the letter *A*. One way to say the word *Navy* in Navajo code would be *tsah* ("needle") *wol-la-chee* ("ant") *ah-keh-di-glini* ("victor") *tsah-ah-dzoh* ("yucca").

The dictionary also contained 450 frequently used military terms. For instance, *besh-lo* ("iron fish") meant *submarine*. *Dah-he-tih-hi* ("hummingbird") meant *fighter plane*. Among organizational units, *corps* was translated as *din-neh-ih* (meaning "clan"), *division* was translated as *ashih-hi* (meaning "salt"), *regiment* was translated as *tabaha edge* (meaning "water"), *battalion* was translated as *tacheene* (meaning "red soil"), *company* was translated as *nakia* (meaning "Mexican"), *platoon* was translated as *has-clish-nih* (meaning "mud"), *section* was translated as *yo-ih* (meaning "beads"), and *squad* was translated as *de-beh-li-zini* (meaning "black sheep").

Ships also had special terms. For instance, *battleship* was translated as *lo-tso* (meaning "whale"), *cruiser* was translated as *lo-tso-yazzie* (meaning "small whale"), *aircraft carrier* was translated as *tsidi-moffa-ye-hi* (meaning "bird carrier"), *minesweeper* was translated as *cha* (meaning "beaver"), *destroyer* was translated as *ca-lo* (meaning "shark"), *transport* was translated as *dineh-nay-ye-hi* (meaning "man carrier"), and *PT boat* was translated as *tse-e* (meaning "mosquito").

To someone who understood Navajo, these terms would be pretty straightforward, but for someone who did not, they would seem like gibberish. To understand a language, one looks at common root words for clues. For instance, a person who understands Italian can begin to decipher French or Portuguese, while a person who understands Norwegian can figure out Danish. However, Navajo, as we said, has absolutely nothing in common with any European or Asian language. The Japanese had code breakers who were fluent in English and European languages, but when they looked for linguistic clues in Navajo, there were none.

After World War II, Lieutenant General Seizo Arisue, chief of intelligence for the Imperial Japanese Army, bragged that his staff had cracked the codes used by the U.S. Army and the USAAF. He claimed that early in the Pacific war with Japan, his people had broken U.S. military codes with relative ease, but he admitted with chagrin that they never broke the strange code used by the USMC.

The master Japanese code breakers finally guessed that it might be a Native American language, and at one point a Navajo soldier who had been taken prisoner in the Philippines was forced to listen to the Code Talkers' transmissions. He was able to make out the words but—because of the encoding dictionary—not their meaning.

Because of their immense success during World War II, the Code Talkers were considered one of the most important secret weapons in the U.S. arsenal. For this reason, the USMC kept the lid of secrecy on the code and the activities of the Code Talkers, which were used again, on a limited basis, in the Korean War. The Code Talkers remained secret until their work was officially declassified in 1968.

Even after declassification, the work of the Code Talkers remained a little-known footnote of World War II. On September 17, 1992, 35 Navajo Code Talkers were invited to the Pentagon for a special ceremony commemorating the work of their small elite group. The 29 original Marine code talkers who developed the code were awarded Congressional Gold Medals by President George W. Bush on July 26, 2001.

Two months later, in response to the terrorist attack of September 11, the Navajo Code Talkers declared their "readiness and desire to support the president . . . and to provide assistance to our great and beloved country in this time of national emergency."

At the turn of the century, surviving Code Talkers were represented by the Navajo Code Talkers' Association (NCTA), headquartered in a small office at the Navajo Museum in Window Rock, Arizona, adjacent to the Window Rock Library. They usually meet on the first Saturday of the month at the Gallup Chamber of Commerce in Gallup, New Mexico. Though ill health was starting to plague their members, they were becoming increasingly popular as public speakers.

Ironically, their exploits would become more well known in the twenty-first century than they had been in the latter half of the twentieth. This was, in part, because of the 2002 movie *Windtalkers,* which dramatized the activities of Navajo Code Talkers on Saipan in 1944. The idea of the film is that the Code Talkers must be protected from falling into enemy hands. Nicholas Cage and Christian Slater portray Marines assigned to protect Code Talkers depicted by Roger Willie and Adam Beach. Willie is a Navajo from Colorado, while Beach is an Indian actor who grew up in Canada. Though not actually a Navajo, Beach won official approval from the Navajo Tribal Council to portray one. While Beach is an experienced actor, Willie was a novice chosen at an open casting call that he had attended just to accompany his nephew.

# 5

## Intermediate-Range Ballistic Missiles

Aside from nuclear weapons, intercontinental ballistic missiles (ICBMs), and the somewhat smaller intermediate-range ballistic missiles (IRBMs) would become the most feared of Cold War doomsday weapons.

Like nuclear weapons, the ballistic missiles designed to deliver them had their origin in World War II. However, while nuclear weapons were first created in the United States, ICBMs had their beginning in Germany. In fact, Germany was so far ahead of any other country in the technology of long-range missiles that for two decades after the war, German scientists would be an integral part of their development in both the United States and the Soviet Union.

Literally, ICBMs are ballistic missiles that have intercontinental range, or a range greater than 5,000 miles. IRBMs, so named only by comparison with ICBMs, have shorter range than ICBMs but a much longer range than any artillery piece. Before ICBMs came on the scene in the late 1950s, weapons such as the German V-2/A4 were the longest-range projectiles yet fired.

The mastermind of the German wartime ICBM program was a visionary engineer named Wernher Magnus Maximillian von Braun. He had always claimed that his real interest was in space travel, and in the 1960s, he would be the man who spearheaded the successful American effort to put human beings on the moon.

Von Braun was born in Germany on March 23, 1912, and received his doctorate in physics from the University of Berlin in 1934. His avid interest in rockets led him to study the work of American rocket pioneer Robert Goddard, who had invented the liquid-fuel rocket in 1926. By 1933, von Braun's work in rocketry landed him a job with the German army's Ordnance Department at Kummersdorf. Von Braun wanted a career in space exploration, but in Germany in the 1930s, the only people buying rocketry were the military.

In May 1937, the Ordnance Department, in cooperation with the Luftwaffe, established its rocket research station at Peenemünde on the Baltic Sea coast. Meanwhile, the army's rocket program was under the command of Captain Walter Dornberger, and von Braun was the program's charismatic star scientist.

Over the next eight years, von Braun and his team would develop a series of battlefield rockets used by the German army during World War II. These would culminate in the V-2/A4 program.

After the war, von Braun was taken prisoner by the U.S. Army, to whom he quickly offered his services. Under its Operation Paperclip, he and other key personnel were brought to the United States to develop long-range rockets as artillery.

Von Braun and his team developed the U.S. Army's Jupiter and Redstone rockets, the latter of which was used to launch the first American Earth-orbiting satellite, Explorer 1, on January 31, 1958. Von Braun also authored several technical books on space travel, including *Across the Space Frontier* (1952) and *Conquest of the Moon* (1953). In 1960, he and his scientific team were transferred to the National Aeronautics and Space Administration (NASA) and given the task of building a system capable of taking humans to the moon—the most challenging engineering project in history. Von Braun's team designed the huge Saturn 5 rocket. As tall as a 34-story building and capable of 7.7 million pounds of thrust, the Saturn 5 was the largest rocket ever built.

## V-2/A4

The grandfather of all IRBMs and ICBMs on both sides of the Iron Curtain was Germany's Vergeltungswaffe ("Vengeance Weapon") 2 (V-2), which was technically designated A4. Created by Werner von Braun for the German army, the A4 was adapted by the Soviet Strategic Missile Forces in the 1950s as the infamous "Scud," which became a household word during the 1991 Gulf War.

Developed and tested at the secret Peenemünde site on the Baltic coast, the V-2/A4 was so fast that once launched, it could not be intercepted. Because it was supersonic, it could not be heard. It just struck without warning, literally out of the blue. Because it was so secret, its victims did not know what was hitting them. For people living under threat of attack, it was the ultimate horror weapon of the war.

The world's first intermediate-range ballistic missile (IRBM) and the world's first fully operational liquid-fuel rocket, the V-2/A4 missile was 5 feet 6 inches in diameter, and 46 feet 1 inch tall when positioned vertically for launch. It had guidance fins at the base, which had a 12-

foot diameter. Its distinctive, finned appearance was extremely striking for its era and would influence two generations of science-fiction illustrators.

The V-2/A4 was fueled by a mixture of 75 percent alcohol and 25 percent water, with a liquid-oxygen oxidizer. These flowed into a single engine that delivered 55,000 pounds of thrust at launch, developing to 160,000 pounds at full burn. When launched, it achieved speeds of twice that of sound, or about 1,850 mph. Engine shutdown occurred a bit more than a minute after launch, after which the V-2/A4 continued in a supersonic glide to the target. The apogee of its trajectory would be at an altitude of 55 miles, and it could reach targets up to 225 miles away. In terms of speed and altitude, it was an extremely advanced vehicle.

The V-2/A4 missile itself weighed 6,278 pounds empty, with fuel adding about 19,000 pounds. In addition, the system carried a high-explosive warhead weighing just over 2,000 pounds. Had a small nuclear weapon been available, the V-2/A4 could have carried it. Guidance was by means of gyroscopes, although a radio beam was used for some later flights. All in all, it was a very ambitious and sophisticated weapons system.

It had taken 11 years to develop the V-2/A4 as a weapons system ready for combat. Back in 1933, Wernher von Braun's first experimental rocket—and the original ancestor of the A4—was predictably designated as the A1. It weighed 330 pounds and was powered by a small liquid-oxygen-and-alcohol rocket motor. The first A1 launch failed, but a year later, von Braun successfully launched a pair of 1,100-pound A2s—dubbed *Max* and *Moritz*—at Kummersdorf.

Over the next three years, von Braun carefully worked out the design for the A4 and constructed four 1,640-pound scale models, which he called A3s. In a February 1936 test launch, and in three subsequent tests conducted in December 1937, the A3 proved to be a failure. Undaunted, von Braun went back to the drawing board.

Beginning in 1938, Dornberger and von Braun proceeded on a dual development track, going ahead with a full-size A4 while at the same time testing a scale-model A5 vehicle. They had better luck with the A5 than they'd had with the A3, but were chronically delayed by a lack of official government enthusiasm for either project. The first launch of an A4 would not happen until more than two years after the start of World War II.

The German High Command, the Oberkommando Wehrmacht, regarded experimental weapons very cautiously in the early days, and the A4 was certainly among the more far-fetched. In March 1941, when Adolf Hitler downgraded the priority of any experimental weapon not likely to become operational in 18 months, the A4 moved to a distant back burner.

This first launch would occur at Peenemünde on March 23, 1942, but with less than stellar success. The missile crashed in the sea less than a mile away from the launch site. After a second failed attempt, the historic first successful launch of an A4 came on October 3, 1942, followed by a 120-mile flight.

Intensive testing continued through 1943, with dozens of launches at Peenemünde as well as many more at nearby Blizna in Poland. Despite missiles' less than 50 percent success rate, the official skepticism that had earlier dogged the program had evaporated. Hitler himself became enthralled with the A4 and dubbed it his "Vergeltungswaffe 2."

No sooner had the Führer embraced the project than it suffered its first major blow at the hands of its intended victims. Allied intelligence got wind of the missile tests in April 1943, and a major raid on Peenemünde by the Royal

Air Force on August 17 left the test facility in a shambles. The resulting delays meant that it would be more than a year before the newly christened V-2 would be ready for combat.

The operational debut of the V-2 came on September 8, 1944, with launches against Paris, which the Allies, had recently recaptured, and against London. The British capital bore the brunt of the ensuing V-2 blitz. The attacks on London served no purpose other than to terrorize its citizens, and the actual strategic effectiveness was minimal. However, the Belgian port of Antwerp was a truly strategic target. After October 1944, the V-2s were used to target this city when it became one of the chief arrival points for matériel bound for Allied forces in Europe.

The V-2s were originally intended to be launched from complex fixed sites that would include fuel manufacturing facilities. Construction on a number of these was begun in northern France, mainly in the vicinity of Cherbourg and Calais. However, the Allies captured these areas not long after the V-2s became operational, so they were never used. The German army would be forced to rely on mobile launchers known as Meillerwagens. Actually, the mobile scenario was more effective. The Meillerwagens were less susceptible to Allied air attack because they could be moved. The operational launches would occur from forested areas throughout northwest Germany as well as in the Netherlands.

From a weapon not taken seriously by the Oberkommando Wehrmacht in 1941, the V-2 was now a wonder weapon of the highest order. A vast underground factory— manned by slave laborers from concentration camps—was built in record time in the mountains near Nordhausen, and it has been reported that 10,000 V-2s were built or were in some stage of completion when World War II ended.

Records show that 5,789 V-2s were delivered and 3,225

were launched. Of the 1,359 that were directed toward England, more than 80 percent landed there, including more than 500 in London alone. The death toll from the V-2s is estimated at 2,754, 5 percent of the number of Britons killed in conventional bombing attacks. Though the ton of high explosives did considerable damage wherever a V-2 hit, few strategically important targets were struck because of guidance shortcomings.

Among the solutions to this problem von Braun and his team considered was the addition of a second set of fins in the upper part of the missile. Only two of the resulting vehicles, given the designation A4b, were test-fired.

The war ended with Soviet forces in possession of Peenemünde and the American capture of Nordhausen. Because of intense interest in the V-2 program, all the Allies were anxious to seize as many of the missiles as possible. Though it would be the Soviets and the Americans who would build massive postwar missile programs on the foundation of the V-2, it was the British who were first to conduct tests of their own.

The first postwar V-2 launch came on October 3, 1945, at Altenwalde, under the auspices of the British Project Backfire. Using German technicians, the British conducted a series of tests, mainly at Cuxhaven.

The Americans also collected unused V-2s, but chose to bring them to the United States. The Yanks also collected German technicians. Authorized by Secretary of War Robert Patterson, the U.S. Army's high-priority Operation Paperclip scooped up Wernher von Braun and much of his team as well as mountains of their files. Von Braun was anxious to be "captured" by the Americans, as he saw the United States as the place in the world where it was most likely that he could resume his dreams of space travel. He would not be disappointed.

The German scientists were sent to the U.S. Army's

White Sands Proving Ground in New Mexico, where they arrived in February 1946. It was here that the U.S. government had organized its Upper Atmosphere Research Panel, which included representatives from the military, other government agencies, and research institutions such as the Applied Physics Laboratory at The Johns Hopkins University. The first V-2 launch in the western hemisphere occurred at White Sands on April 16, 1946. On October 18, 1947, the Soviet Union conducted its first test launch of a captured V-2 at Kapustin Yar near Stalingrad.

In May 1948, the United States first successfully tested its "Bumper Wac," a two-stage rocket that used a Wac Corporal atop a V-2 for higher-altitude flights. On February 24, 1949, a Bumper Wac achieved an altitude of 250 miles, the highest ever reached by an object made by humans.

Had the Oberkommando Wehrmacht embraced the A4 program earlier, and had von Braun perfected its guidance system, the Vergeltungswaffe 2 might have been the wonder weapon that won the war for the Germans.

## A9/A10

The Bumper Wac was a postwar two-stage rocket that attached a smaller rocket as an upper stage to an V-2/A4. During the war Wernher von Braun had designed a massive rocket that would use the V-2/A4 as the *upper* stage atop an even larger rocket.

Unlike the Bumper Wac, which was used for atmospheric research, von Braun's vehicle would have been the world's first intercontinental ballistic missile. It was intended to attack New York City, rendering a level of destruction that would not be visited upon the city by a foreign entity for another 56 years. Indeed, late in its development, the A9/A10 program was conducted under the designation "Projekt Amerika."

The A9/A10 was a two-stage intercontinental ballistic missile that was capable of reaching the Eastern United States from European launch sites. The A9 upper stage was similar to the A4, while the A10 lower stage was much larger. Various A9 configurations were studied, but all were to have been within a few pounds and inches of the same size as an A4, and would have been shaped like an A4 or A4b. These would have been attached to the larger rocket with a sleeve or fairing. The engine would have also been essentially the same.

The A10 was originally conceived as a greatly scaled up version of the A4. Initially, it was to have been powered by a single very large alcohol-and-liquid-oxygen engine, but this eventually morphed into a nitric-acid engine with a cluster of combustion chambers feeding into a huge, common nozzle.

The A10 would have had a 13.5-foot diameter and been 66 feet high on the launchpad. The fins at the base would have spanned nearly 30 feet. It would have weighed 37,460 pounds empty and 152,000 pounds fueled. With the two vehicles mated, the A9/A10 vehicle would have been taller than an 11-story building, dwarfing the Atlas vehicle that took John Glenn into orbit a generation later.

Design work on the A9/A10 program began in 1940, two years before the A4 made its first flight, but it was formally suspended in 1943 so that the full resources of von Braun's team could be devoted to the A4, now V-2, program. In November 1944, however, the suspension was rescinded, and development resumed under Projekt Amerika. The intended 3,100-mile range was seen as sufficient to attack the United States from within Germany.

As with the existing V-2/A4 program, the Achilles' heel

of Projekt Amerika was guidance. One proposed solution
called for the A9 upper stage to be piloted. The pilot could
navigate by means of radio beacons provided by U-boats
in the Atlantic and abandon the vehicle before it struck the
target.

Work on Projekt Amerika was terminated early in 1945,
when it became apparent that Germany would be defeated
before any hardware could be tested.

## A11

Wernher von Braun conceived the A11 as a very large intercontinental ballistic missile capable of launching a
satellite into space. The A11 program developed in a
slightly later time frame than the A9/A10 project. Just as
the latter incorporated the A4 hardware, it was, itself, incorporated into the A11.

The A11 was to be a three-stage vehicle with the A9 and
A10 as the upper stages and a huge, squat first stage incorporating more than two dozen nitric-acid A10 engines firing simultaneously. It would have been more than 200 feet
in diameter at the base and possibly as tall as the gargantuan Saturn 5 that took Americans to the moon in the late
1960s and early 1970s. It was estimated to have weighed
nearly 2 million pounds.

If it had been capable of reaching orbit, the A11 could
have reached any point in America with ordnance. It was
never built, however, and von Braun himself abandoned
the concept to follow the track that eventually led him to
the Saturn 5.

**6**

## Tactical Artillery Missiles

As with air-launched weapons, the use of guided missiles as artillery was preceded by the use of unguided rockets. Such rockets work on a simple principle of burning a highly flammable substance in a combustion chamber with a single outlet. By directing the thrust generated in the combustion chamber, one takes advantage of Sir Isaac Newton's third law of motion, which states that for every action there is an opposite reaction. In other words, the object containing the combustion chamber will move in a direction opposite to the exhaust at a speed proportional to the amount of thrust generated.

The Chinese figured out this principle in the thirteenth century, and they are known to have used operational war rockets in 1232. The British Royal Navy used rockets developed by ballistics engineer William Congreve to bombard shore targets during the Napoleonic Wars and the War of 1812. Francis Scott Key's "Star-Spangled Banner" remarks on the "rockets' red glare" that he observed during the British bombardment of Fort McHenry.

As dramatic as they were, rockets were not really a practical weapon. As artillery improved, they became a "B-list" weapon at best. They were little used throughout the nineteenth century owing to their being less accurate than artillery while offering no improvement in range.

By World War II, ballistics engineers were ready to tackle the intertwined problems of aiming and guidance— and to develop weapons that could eclipse the capability of the best artillery. Of course, Wernher von Braun went a step farther in creating intermediate-range ballistic missiles that could travel hundreds of miles to strike targets in distant countries, but practical short-range artillery missiles were also in the works.

As with many other areas of missile development, Germany was the world leader in tactical artillery missile technology during World War II.

## Rheinmetall-Borsig Rheinbote

It was the artillery-manufacturing firm of Rheinmetall-Borsig that created what was arguably the most sophisticated and effective artillery missile deployed anywhere until the 1960s. Second only to the V-2/A4 in terms of range, the Rheinbote (Rhine Messenger) was the first multistage missile ever to become operational.

It was also the only four-stage operational ballistic missile. The modern Minuteman intercontinental ballistic missile, by comparison, has three stages. The four stages had a total length of 37 feet 5 inches, compared with the 46 feet 1 inch of the single-stage V-2/A4. In contrast to the 5-foot-6-inch diameter of the single-stage V-2/A4, the Rheinbote was pencil thin, with the top stage being just 7.5 inches in diameter. Each stage had six trajectory stabilization fins at its base, and the wingspan of the widest fins at the base of the first stage was just under 5 feet.

The Rheinbote was aimed rather than guided, but it offered a range of up to 135 miles and accuracy that generally matched that of the V-2/A4 with its problematic gyro. It was also very fast. At fourth-stage burnout, it reached a speed of Mach 5.6 (over 4,000 mph). When launched, the Rheinbote reached an altitude of nearly 50 miles before descending to the target.

The Rheinbote was used operationally during late 1944, joining the V-2/A4 in the bombardment of the Allied port facilities at Antwerp. A reported 200 were fired in this campaign.

## Ruhrstahl/Kramer X-7 Rotkappchen

Dr. Max Kramer of Germany's Air Transport Research Institute, the Deutsche Versuchsanstalt für Luftfahrt (DVL), was to small military rockets what Wernher von Braun was to intermediate-range ballistic missiles.

One of Dr. Kramer's major contributions was the invention of an ingenious wire guidance system for missiles. Rather than transmitting guidance by radio waves to the missile, commands were sent through wires like a telephone line. The weapon was literally *hardwired* to its controller!

Kramer also used wire guidance for his X-4 air-to-air missile, which was being developed at roughly the same time as the X-7.

The X-7 Rotkappchen (Little Red Riding Hood) was born out of a crash program initiated at the start of 1944 and aimed at developing a means of stopping Soviet tanks. By this time, the Red Army had geared up tank production to the point where the German army was on the verge of being overwhelmed. It didn't matter that the German Panther tank was superior to the Soviet T-34 (actually a very good tank) when the Panthers were outnumbered by T-34s.

By the end of the year, the X-7 was ready. It was a blunt contraption, 5.9 inches in diameter and 3 feet 1.4 inches long, with two short stubby wings spanning a half-inch short of 2 feet. Two guide wires were unreeled from bobbins located in wingtip pods. It was powered by a Wasag 109-506 diglycol-fuel rocket engine. The Rotkappchen weighed about 20 pounds at launch, with a warhead of about 5 pounds. It had a range of more than half a mile.

Though the wire guidance system broke new technological ground, operations probably broke a few wires as well. For this reason, other guidance systems were also tested and introduced. The Steinbock project fitted the X-7 with an infrared system, while electro-optical and television guidance systems were studied under the Peifenkopf and Pinsel programs. At the same time, television guidance was being used for air-launched missiles being developed in the United States, such as the Bat and the Roc.

A sizable number of X-7s, possibly several hundred, did eventually reach front-line troops, but are said to have been for "evaluation" purposes. Probably some of these were "evaluated" against Soviet tanks.

After World War II, the idea of using wire to guide antitank missiles languished for some time. Ironically, wire-guided antitank missiles would become standard equipment in the armies of the late twentieth century. Neither the Soviet Union nor the United States took up Dr. Kramer's idea until the 1950s, and no such weapon was used again in combat until the 1960s. France would be the first nation to create a postwar wire-guided antitank weapon. The Arsenal de l'Aeronautique dusted off Dr. Kramer's notebook in 1948 and created an all-new missile—albeit roughly the same size as the X-7—that went into production as the Nord 5200 series (SS-10).

The U.S. Army used the SS-10 as the basis for its first wire-guided missile, the SSM-A-23 Dart. The Soviet Union, meanwhile, developed the AT-1 Snapper and AT-3 Sagger, both of which were exported to Arab countries and used in the Middle East wars of the 1960s and 1970s.

Possibly the most successful wire-guided antitank missile in history is the American Hughes BGM-71, best known by the acronym TOW, which stands for Tube-launched, Optically tracked, Wire-guided. It entered service with the U.S. Army in 1970 and remained in the arsenal through the turn of the century. More than a half-million have been built, and they have been exported to or acquired by three dozen countries.

**7**

# Cruise Missiles

By definition, cruise missiles are airplanes that are designed to be flown without a pilot aboard, using autonomous or remote-control guidance. Tactically, the idea behind the cruise missile is obvious and straightforward. An armed but unpiloted airplane is used to fly to the target and simply impact it. In situations where a ground target is so heavily defended that an attacking aircraft has little chance of getting in and out safely, they offer an alternative.

A similar weapon is an aircraft that was originally designed to be flown by a pilot, but which was adapted to impact a target with or without a pilot aboard. These weapons are discussed in the following chapter.

Cruise missiles differ from intermediate-range ballistic missiles, medium-range ballistic missiles, and intercontinental ballistic missiles by virtue of the fact that they *cruise*.

IRBMs, MRBMs, and ICBMs are launched upward and travel in a high-angling arc before descending to their target at a steep angle like an artillery round. Cruise missiles have wings and fly like airplanes—in level flight—often for great distances. Compared with World-War-II-era technology, cruise missiles are relatively easier and more straightforward to produce and deploy than were intermediate-range ballistic missiles such as the German V-2/A4.

Among the earliest cruise missiles were the small and flimsy piston-engine pilotless airplanes developed during the First World War. In the United Kingdom, Harry Folland built a monoplane designated as AT (for "Aerial Target"), which was its "cover" identity. Meanwhile, Professor A.M. Low, also in the United Kingdom, experimented with television guidance and produced a radio-controlled rocket. In the United States, Dr. D.F. Buck built a piston-engine biplane designated "AT" (for "Aerial Torpedo"), while Charles Kettering of the Delco company built a similar vehicle that he called the Bug. The Bug was recoverable and had a range of over 60 miles. The U.S. Army Air Service ordered and tested large numbers of Kettering Bugs in 1918 and was planning to send them into combat when the war ended.

In the 1920s, Britain's Royal Aircraft Establishment built and tested the oddly named Larynx, a monoplane with a 100-mile range that was powered by a Lynx engine. Ironically, much of the testing took place in the deserts of Iraq.

Two goals in the development of cruise missiles—in World War II as today—are speed and guidance. Because an uncrewed aerial vehicle cannot actively defend itself from air defenses or interceptors, it has to be fast enough to reduce its chances of being hit. The Bugs and Larynxes were a nice start, but they were really too slow and vulnerable to be practical.

The guidance system was also critical. Because it was to travel greater distances than the projectiles of all but the largest of artillery pieces, the cruise missile could not be treated simply as such a projectile.

During and after World War II, the most successful cruise missiles were powered by jet engines because they are faster than piston engines and more suited to traveling long distances in level flight than are rocket engines.

Various forms of guidance systems were tried, including Professor Low's radio and television versions. During World War II, the Germans perfected the gyrocompass guidance technology that would be state-of-the-art for some time. During the 1950s and 1960s, numerous attempts to develop cruise missiles were hampered by the limitations of guidance technology. Finally, in the late 1970s, computer miniaturization and the much more sophisticated and accurate inertial navigation systems gave cruise missiles the long-sought pinpoint accuracy. In the 1980s, the United States deployed an arsenal of inertially guided cruise missiles—including the AGM-86 air-launched cruise missile (ALCM), the BGM-109 ground-launched cruise missile (GLCM or "Glickum"), and the RGM-109 Tomahawk.

Of course, at two points in history—in 1945 and in 2001—the guidance problem was solved by desperate pilots determined to go down in blaze of glory. The kamikaze weapons of 1945 are discussed in Chapter 8.

## V-1 (Fieseler Fi.103 Vergeltungswaffe 1)

The world's first operational cruise missile was the first of the German wonder weapons to receive Adolf Hitler's personal authorization to be designated with a *V* for Vergeltungswaffe (Vengeance Weapon).

The remarkable Fieseler Fi.103 brought together a radically new aerodynamic shape and the emerging technology of pulsejet engines. Pulsejets are jet engines that use a system of flap valves on the air intake to alternate bursts of air with a closed combustion chamber. This gives the pulsejet its familiar throbbing sound.

In Germany, the aerodynamicist Paul Schmidt had studied pulsejets since the late 1920s, but it was not until 1939 that the Reichsluftfahrt Ministerium (RLM, German Air Ministry) finally authorized a program to build them. This led to the Argus Ar.109/014, which had a thrust rating of 660 pounds at sea level. It would be another three years before a go-ahead was given for development of an operational pulsejet-powered cruise missile. Meanwhile, an airframe design by Robert Lusser at the firm of Gerhard Fieseler Werke received approval.

In June 1942, work began on the Fi.103, a torpedo-shaped vehicle with straight, stubby wings and tail plane. It was an inch shy of 27 feet long and had a wingspan of 17 feet 4.55 inches. It weighed 4,800 pounds fully loaded and had a range of more than 150 miles. The Argus gave it a speed of between 400 and 500 mph, depending upon altitude, which was faster than most Allied interceptor aircraft. Each missile carried an 1,870-pound payload.

As with many of Germany's wonder weapons, the Fi.103 did not have a high priority in the early days of its development, but when it caught the eye of the Reich's leadership in Berlin, it abruptly became the toast of the town. The Reich propaganda minister, Dr. Josef Goebbels, coined the appellation Vergeltungswaffe 1 to describe the Fi.103. Adolf Hitler embraced this colorful idea and soon Wernher von Braun's A4 became Vergeltungswaffe 2. Because the Fi.103 was a Luftwaffe program, and the A4 belonged to the army, there was naturally a good deal of intramural rivalry over which team would get their Vergeltungswaffe into action first. The V-1 would beat the V-2 by three months.

The V-1s were launched from a horizontal launch ramp constructed at an inclined angle and guided to a preprogrammed target using a gyroscopic/magnetic compass guidance system. It was not a very accurate system, but because V-1s were intended to be used against large cities, any hit within a 10-mile radius was considered acceptable.

The first unpowered test launch was conducted in December 1942 with a Fi.103 airframe being airdropped from a Focke-Wulf Fw.200 bomber. Subsequent flight testing was conducted at Peenemünde on the Baltic coast, and this led to full-scale manufacturing and the organizing of operational launch teams during 1943. Nearly 100 fixed launch sites for using the missiles against the United Kingdom were constructed throughout northern France, especially in the area near Calais.

Construction began in September 1943, and was soon detected by Allied photoreconnaissance aircraft. Analysts noticed the telltale "ski-jump" appearance of the V-1 launch ramp and compared this with similar ramps seen in reconnaissance photos of Peenemünde. From this, they were able to deduce the purpose of the huge bunkers.

Allied bombing raids against the "ski-jumps" began in December 1943 under Operation Crossbow, the operational code name for strikes on both V-1 and V-2 sites. The attacks caused delays for the Germans. It also led to the rethinking of the fixed-base concept for the V-2s. However, work continued on the more numerous V-1 fixed sites.

The first operational launch of the V-1 against the United Kingdom came on the night of June 13–14, 1944—a week after the Operation Overlord invasion of Normandy on D day. Had it not been for the Allied bombing raids and the repair work required, it is estimated that the V-1s would have been capable of massive attacks as early as February or March 1944—but this was small consolation after the Allies arrived in Normandy.

Unlike the V-2, which arrived silently at supersonic speeds, the V-1 announced its arrival with the strange wobbling warble of its pulsejet engine. It was not the sound of the V-1 that struck fear into the hearts of Londoners—it was when the sound suddenly stopped. This was because the engine cutout signaled the impact of the missile just a few seconds later.

Though Londoners adopted silly popular nicknames for the V-1, such as "Doodlebug" and "Buzz Bomb," it quickly became one of the most feared terror weapons of the war. The frightening sound just added to the horror.

Because they were so fast, the V-1s were harder to stop than conventional bombers, although the Royal Air Force Fighter Command gradually developed techniques for shooting them down or stopping them. The Buzz Bombs could outrun Supermarine Spitfires, so Britain's new Gloster Meteor jet fighters were pressed into service because they could match the missile's speed.

One technique that proved useful was for the interceptor pilot to slip his wingtip beneath that of the V-1 and gently flip it over. This confused the guidance system and the Buzz Bomb went out of control and crashed. Despite the best efforts of the Royal Air Force, more than half of the V-1s that survived technical glitches at launch and actually reached England did so unmolested.

The V-1 created a major crisis for the Allies. The Germans had intended them as terror weapons to destroy the morale of the British people, and they were having that effect. When no missiles were used before or during the Overlord landings, Allied leaders believed that the air offensive they had conducted since December had neutralized them. Now this was shown to be untrue.

The Allies soon estimated that unchecked, the Germans could produce 3,000 V-1s monthly and support a daily launch rate at each of the nearly 100 sites. British Prime

Minister Winston Churchill requested that Allied commanders "take all possible measures to neutralize the supply and launching sites subject to no interference with the
essential requirements of the Battle of France."

At one point, Churchill even suggested that the Allies
break their self-imposed ban on the use of poison gas in
order to attack the V-1 sites. Stopping short of such an extreme, they decided on June 18, 1944, that Crossbow targets should have a higher priority for Allied bombers than
anything "except the urgent requirements of the battle."

As the larger sites came under attack, the Germans re-
sponded by installing simpler prefabricated launchers.
These were initially spared when photo interpreters mistook them for decoys. After a short lull in V-1 activity in
July while the switch to simpler sites was made, the Luftwaffe was able to resume a full-scale "Buzz Bomb Blitz"
in August.

For nine months, from June 1944 until the last one fell
on March 29, 1945, it is calculated that 3,531 Buzz Bombs
reached the United Kingdom, with 2,420 hitting greater
London. Beginning in October 1944, after the Allies recaptured the port of Antwerp in Belgium, an estimated 5,600
V-1s would strike the city, although they did little substan-
tive damage to the port facilities. The V-1s are estimated to
have killed 6,184 people in Britain alone, and to have seriously injured nearly 18,000.

On the other side, the Royal Air Force Bomber Command and the USAAF Eighth and Ninth Air Forces would
fly 68,913 missions in support of Operation Crossbow and
drop 122,133 tons of bombs on both V-1 and V-2 sites.
This represented 6.8 percent of the total bomb tonnage
dropped in Europe during World War II. For the 13 months
ending in August 1944, 15 percent of Allied bomb tonnage
was directed at missile sites. This was an enormous pro-

portion when compared to all the other requirements at the time.

Ultimately, the fixed sites in northern France were never put completely out of business until Allied ground troops physically captured the area at the end of the summer of 1944. After that, the Germans switched to launch sites in Holland and Germany that posed less of a threat to the United Kingdom. The Luftwaffe also converted a number of Heinkel He.111 bombers to V-1 carriers, and these were used to air-launch approximately 1,200 Buzz Bombs.

It is calculated that as many as 10,500 V-1s were launched by all means, and Allied records show that slightly fewer than 4,000 were shot down or destroyed by air defense forces. Total production is estimated to have reached an incredible 29,000 units, with some estimates suggesting as many as 32,000. Either number would place the V-1 in the top half-dozen most numerous winged vehicle types of all time. Part of the key to the huge production numbers was the extremely simple plywood-and-sheet-metal construction.

A safe manufacturing location was also important, and Hitler's Vergeltungswaffen got the best. Both V-1s and V-2s were manufactured in the vast underground factory complex at Nordhausen, while V-1 production also took place at the heavily reinforced Volkswagen factories at Fallersleben and Schönebeck.

When the war ended, the Allies captured many V-1s at these and other locations, and some were used as the basis for further developments, such as the American JB-2.

In summarizing the effectiveness of the V-1, General Dwight Eisenhower candidly admitted that it could potentially have forced a cancellation of Operation Overlord—and hence have changed the course of World War II and possibly world history. Said Eisenhower: "I feel sure that if [the Germans] had succeeded in using these weapons over a six-month period, and particularly if they had made the Portsmouth-Southampton area one of the principal targets, Overlord might have been written off."

## Northrop JB-1 and JB-10 Bat

Germany was not the only country to develop cruise missiles during World War II. In the United States, the USAAF had begun work on jet-propelled pilotless aircraft even before the details of the German V-1 were known, or before that weapon had become operational. Like the German V-1, the Northrop JB-1 was flight-tested in both piloted and nonpiloted configurations.

The aircraft originated in late 1943 under the highly secret USAAF Project MX-543. John Knudsen "Jack" Northrop, president of Northrop Aircraft of Hawthorne, California, had been a proponent of "flying wing" aircraft, and had flight-tested his first piston-engine flying wing, the N-1M, in 1940. For Project MX-543, Northrop proposed a jet-propelled flying wing to be powered by a General Electric B-1 turbojet engine.

The B-1 itself is an interesting story. It came about when the General Electric J-31 jet engine, which was in development for the Bell XP-59, the first USAAF jet fighter, proved too heavy for the Northrop missile. To solve the problem, General Electric heavily modified its B-31 turbosupercharger—which was widely used to boost high-altitude performance on piston engines—into a turbojet engine that was designed to produce 400 pounds of thrust. Just as the pulsejet engine of the V-1 earned it the nickname "Buzz Bomb," the B-1 turbojet had a peculiar squeal that gave it the appellation "Thunderbug."

The revolutionary Northrop flying wing and the innovative turbojet were mated and delivered under the USAAF designation JB-1 for "Jet-propelled Bomb, First." The official name, "Bat," is a reference to the shape of the wings, but the Thunderbug name would be widely used unofficially. The first one, designated simply as JB-1, was an unpowered vehicle intended for aerodynamic glide tests. Initially, a dozen of the powered JB-1As were built.

Both JB-1 and the JB-1A had a wingspan of 28 feet 4 inches and were 10 feet 6 inches long. The powered JB-1A weighed 7,080 pounds and had a pair of B-1s. It carried a pair of 2,000-pound bombs in pods clustered next to its engines.

The first piloted JB-1 glide tests occurred in 1944 over Muroc Army Air Field (now Edwards AFB) in the Mojave Desert of California with Northrop test pilot Harry Crosby at the controls. The first flight of the powered, but unpiloted, JB-1A occurred at Eglin Field in the Florida Panhandle on December 7, 1944. The JB-1A was launched from a pair of rails laid across the sand dunes—very much like the launch rail that the Wright brothers used at Kitty Hawk in 1903. It had been three years to the day since Pearl Harbor and six months since the German V-1 became operational.

Technically, the makeshift B-1 did not work as well as was hoped. The USAAF had, by December 1944, gotten hold of some V-1s and decided to use the pulsejet engine rather than the small turbojet. Only one JB-1A was completed, but Northrop converted others on the assembly line to pulsejet power under the designation JB-10. During flight testing, which began in April 1945, the JB-10 demonstrated a range of 200 miles and a cruising speed of 400 mph.

If the invasion of the Japanese home island had gone ahead as planned during the winter of 1945–1946, the JB-10 would have played an important role. When the Japanese surrendered in August 1945, however, the JB-10 program was terminated with just 24 missiles having been completed. In January 1946, Northrop began work on the B-62 Snark, its first postwar cruise missile. Unlike the Thunderbug, Snark would have a conventional aircraftlike fuselage and would not be a flying wing.

The original JB-1 has been restored and is now on display at the Western Museum of Flight in Hawthorne, California.

## Republic JB-2/KVW-1 Loon

The second missile designated under the USAAF jet-propelled bomb series was the Republic JB-2. Unlike the JB-1, however, it was not an American original, but a reverse-engineered copy of the notorious German V-1.

Within days of its first use on the night of June 13–14, 1944, the V-1 had become synonymous with the notion of diabolical German secret weapons. Of course, the Allies were anxious to lay their hands on this secret and the wonder weapon technology that it represented.

As soon as a V-1 was captured intact in August 1944, it was rushed to the United States. Republic Aviation of Farmingdale, Long Island, was picked to build the "American Buzz Bomb" under the JB-2 designation. The Ford Motor Company was given a contract to build the reverse-engineered pulsejet engines. By the beginning of 1945, JB-2s had been built and flight-tested and were ready for production.

Like the Northrop JB-1A and JB-10, the JB-2s were test-launched at Eglin Field in Florida using launch rails on the dunes, but they were also successfully launched from the air from a Boeing B-17 bomber.

As was the case with Germany's Luftwaffe, the USAAF put a very high priority on cruise missile development as soon as flight testing demonstrated that the weapon worked. The JB-10 was earmarked for rapid development with an eye toward mass production by the end of the year. The initial order called for 1,000 JB-2s, but additional orders reportedly pushed the number as high as 75,000, with the Willys-Overland company—makers of the famous "Jeep"—brought into the program as a "second-source" manufacturer. Like the JB-10, the JB-2 was seen as an important weapon in the upcoming Battle of Japan. However, when the Japanese surrendered before an invasion was necessary, the previously urgent JB-2 program was terminated.

Approximately 1,200 JB-2s had been built when World War II ended, but none are believed to have been actually used in action. Some were transferred to the U.S. Navy, where they were redesignated as KVW-1 and named "Loon." The latter were first tested at the Navy's missile facility at Point Mugu on the Southern California coast. Both JB-2s and Loons were used for test and research purposes through the end of the 1940s.

## Other JB-Series Secret Weapons

The JB-1/JB-10 and the JB-2 cruise missiles were the principal weapons in the USAAF jet-propelled bomb series of secret weapons. However, as the sequence numbers imply, there were seven others. Only two, the JB-3 and the JB-4, were actually built. These would remain more secret and become less well known, mainly because they were not so widely used. Of the seven, only the JB-7 was actually a cruise missile, but all are mentioned here to keep weapons of a common prefix together.

Built by Hughes Aircraft, the JB-3 was 625-pound air-to-air rocket that was named "Tiamat," after the five-headed dragon of Sumerian mythology. The JB-4 was a pulsejet-powered, 5,000-pound rocket with a range of about 75 miles that was developed by the USAAF itself.

The JB-5 and JB-6 would have been short-range rockets, the JB-7 would have been a cruise missile with a 400-mile range, the JB-8 was to have been an antiaircraft missile, and the JB-9 an artillery missile. The "JB" designator was officially discontinued in 1946, and all the latter missile types were superseded by other postwar programs.

## 8

## Aircraft as Cruise Missiles

Just as cruise missiles are aircraft that are purposely built to be unpiloted, cruise missiles can be created by modifying an aircraft that was originally designed to have a human pilot. It's all a matter of the guidance system. An aircraft could be retrofitted with an autonomous or preprogrammed guidance mechanism, such as the gyrocompass system of the World-War-II-era German V-1 or the American JB series cruise missiles. A simpler way would be for the pilot to fly the aircraft to the final bomb run, aim it at the target, and simply bail out.

The latter presupposes that saving the life of the pilot is an important element in the design of the vehicle. Obviously, a human pilot would be the best possible means of guiding the aircraft into impact with the target, but most armies do not deliberately plan to kill their own personnel. While the term *suicide mission* is often used to describe the extremely dangerous missions that are occasionally necessary in wartime, it is rare that the actual death of the participants is part of the mission planning.

The deliberate planning for the systematic use of multiple crewed aircraft for what were literally designed as suicide attacks has occurred in two notable instances. In both cases, religious fanatics convinced human pilots into flying such airborne suicide missions with the promise that they would go to heaven. In 1945, desperate Japanese warlords cloaked themselves in Shintoism and sent dupes to their death under the doctrine of the kamikaze. In 2001, cunning al-Qaida gangsters cloaked themselves in Islam and sent dupes—along with innocent passengers—to their death under the doctrine of jihad.

In 1945, the Japanese used existing aircraft for suicide attacks, but they also created a specific aircraft whose only purpose was a suicide attack. The Yokosuka MXY7 Ohka was one of the most grisly secret weapons of the war. It is hard to imagine a society that could consciously design, build, and deploy a weapon such as the Ohka, but in war, mankind is driven to some rather barbaric extremes.

## Yokosuka MXY7 Ohka

It was one of the most macabre machines ever designed— an airplane that existed to kill its own pilot. In 1944, as the Japanese Empire was sensing the end, the fanatic samurai who ruled the code by which the Japanese fighting man lived and died, concocted the ruthless doctrine of kamikaze (divine wind), which literally involved pilots crashing their airplanes into American ships.

The kamikaze attacks were first encountered during efforts to recapture the Philippines in July 1944, and reached their crescendo during the invasion of Okinawa in April 1945. They would have been the first line of defense against the Allied invasion of Japan itself had this invasion become necessary.

Initially the kamikaze attacks were conducted in aircraft designed for other purposes—fighters, bombers, and even rickety biplane trainers. The doctrine reached a new level of madness, however, in April 1945, when the Yokosuka MXY7 Ohka (Cherry Blossom) made its ghastly debut at Okinawa.

The Ohka was essentially a rocket-propelled flying torpedo with 2,646 pounds of high explosive in the nose and a human being to guide it into the target. Ironically, this desperate creation was the only nonpropeller-driven aircraft to see widespread service with Japanese forces during World War II. It was 19 feet 11 inches long, with a wingspan of 16 feet 9 inches. The gross weight was 4,700 pounds, with over half of that being the explosive warhead. The power plant was a cluster of three Type-4 short-duration (three to four minutes) rockets, delivering 1,760 pounds of thrust. In its final moments—which consisted of a steep dive from which it was neither designed, nor intended, to recover— the Ohka could reach speeds of nearly 600 mph. This made it particularly deadly to Allied shipping, and very hard to shoot down.

Designed at the Imperial Navy's big Yokosuka complex on Tokyo Bay during the summer of 1944, the Ohka was built by a variety of Japanese manufacturers, including Dai Ichi Kaigun, and the firms of Fuji and Hitachi, whose products—albeit of a different nature—are still familiar to consumers today.

Of the total 852 Ohkas that were built, 755 were of the Model 11 type. Other variants included the jet-propelled Model 22, which had a longer range and carried a 1,320-pound bomb in addition to its internal payload. The Model 43 was essentially a training form of the Model 11, with the warhead replaced by a second cockpit and with a landing skid so that this craft—unlike the Model 11—could be recovered. One wonders what must have gone through the minds of the people who trained others to fly the Ohka.

A typical Ohka mission began with the pilot being bolted into the cockpit sans parachute and airlifted to within roughly 20 miles of his target by a carrier plane, which was typically a Mitsubishi G4M "Betty" bomber. The plane was thus carried because the MXY7's engines and simple aerodynamic design did not permit it to take off from a runway under its own power. Furthermore, except for the handful of Model-43 trainers, the Ohkas were incapable of landing.

After being released from the carrier plane, the pilot would start the engines and have three to four minutes to find his target, which was usually American ships. The Americans called the Ohkas "Baka Bombs" (Fool Bombs), and they were as deadly as they were insane. In their first deployment, off Okinawa on April 1, 1945, an Ohka hit and severely damaged the battleship USS *West Virginia* (BB-48), a survivor of Pearl Harbor. On April 12, an Ohka was responsible for its type's first ship sunk, as the destroyer USS *Mannert L. Abele* (DD-733) went down off Okinawa. The making of the Ohka was a macabre act of desperation, but it failed to affect the war's final outcome.


## Early American Efforts

Prior to World War II, both the U.S. Navy and the USAAF had used small aircraft as radio-controlled, pilotless drones for aerial gunnery targets. In 1942, both services began to experiment with converting similar small aircraft to radio-controlled flying bombs. The U.S. Navy used their "TD" (for Target Drone) designation for its flying bombs, while the USAAF created a new designation, "BQ" (for Bomb, Guided). Collectively, the TDs and BQs were the generation of aerial vehicles that would evolve into cruise missiles.

The first American flying bombs were adaptations of small aircraft. The Fleetwings BQ-1 and BQ-2 were each one-of-a-kind experimental contraptions, while the BQ-3 was a Fairchild AT-21 trainer packed with 4,000 pounds of explosives. It was the only member of the first generation of "flying bombs" capable of carrying more than a ton, but only one was built, and it was used only for testing.

Interstate Aircraft & Engineering of El Segundo, California, built a large number of small, single-engine flying bombs. These included the Navy's TD2R and the USAAF's BQ-5, as well as a larger aircraft ordered by the Navy as TD3R and the USAAF as the BQ-6. Interstate's biggest seller was the TDR/BQ-4, of which the Navy alone bought nearly 200.

## Aphrodite and Anvil, the Big "BQ Bombs"

The fact that they were slow and limited to a payload of one ton or less clearly limited the usefulness of America's first generation of flying bombs. The bomb load of a fast-attack bomber such as an A-20, an A-26, or even a P-47 fighter-bomber was greater than that of the BQ weapons, and these aircraft were faster. However, the idea to use BQ weapons still remained alive in the minds of military planners. Meanwhile, the JB weapons (see Chapter 7) were still not fully developed. As late as 1944, modified piston-engine drones were seen as representing a shortcut to an American cruise-missile capability.

In 1944, having rejected smaller aircraft as ineffective, the USAAF and U.S. Navy jointly decided to turn full-size heavy bombers into flying bombs. These weapons were secret then, and even today, few details of their operations are common knowledge. They are known to have been used in the European Theater and are believed to have been intended for use in the Pacific.

Approximately 25 to 27 Boeing B-17F and B-17G Flying Fortress heavy bombers were field-modified in England and redesignated as BQ-7 under the USAAF Project Aphrodite. All their gun turrets were removed, and the flight decks were reconfigured as open cockpits to permit an easy escape for the pilot and copilot. The 10-man crew was cut to just 2. The planes were then packed with 20,000 pounds of impact-fused Torpex explosives.

The BQ-7s could be radio controlled after takeoff, with a ground-based controller "flying" them by means of a television camera in the nose that sent back real-time imagery of where the aircraft was headed. In this sense, they were operated like the RQ-1A Predator pilotless aircraft that were seen as technological marvels when they were operated over Afghanistan more than a half-century later. Because the range of the television signal was so short, however, the operator was shifted from the ground to an accompanying aircraft. The BQ-7 could be controlled from a distance of 11 miles.

In addition to the Flying Fortresses, at least two (but possibly more) Consolidated Liberators were also converted and redesignated as BQ-8. Designated as B-24 by the USAAF and PB4Y-1 by the U.S. Navy, the Liberators had a longer range and a slightly greater payload capacity than the Fortress. The Liberators were converted under a program known as Project Anvil, which is not to be confused with Operation Anvil, the original name for the August 1944 Allied invasion of southern France. (After it was planned, but before it occurred, this operation was renamed Dragoon by Winston Churchill.)

Like the BQ-7 Aphrodites, the BQ-8 Anvils were stripped down and packed with Torpex. The total payload of 25,000 pounds made the Anvil aircraft the biggest non-nuclear "punch" of any missile in history. Like the BQ-7, the BQ-8 used a radio/television guidance system. In both systems, this was complicated by the television receiver and the radio controller being in two separate aircraft.

BQ-7 and BQ-8 operations were reserved for high-priority targets that were heavily defended and very "hardened." These included German V-1, V-2, and V-3 sites in France that were protected by many feet of reinforced concrete. The specific missions were reportedly flown under a variety of operational code names, including Batty, Castor, Perilous, and Aphrodite. The missions were, indeed, considered perilous, and the crews that flew them were volunteers.

The BQ-7 missions were flown from the USAAF base at Fersfield in southern England by the 562nd Bomb Squadron, assigned to the 388th Bomb Group. The two known BQ-8s were former U.S. Navy PB4Y-1s, and were flown by the Navy's VB-110 bomb squadron based at Blythburgh, England. At least eight BQ-7s were expended in actual missions, as were the two known BQ-8s.

The first of the latter missions was flown on August 12, 1944. The target is believed to have been the V-3 secret weapon site at Mimoyecques, near Calais. The pilot was Lieutenant Joseph Patrick Kennedy, the son of the former U.S. ambassador to the United Kingdom, and the older brother of John F. Kennedy, the future American president. Reportedly, Elliot Roosevelt, the son of President Franklin D. Roosevelt, was present that day aboard one of the accompanying aircraft.

Apparently, when Kennedy set the fuses in preparation for abandoning the BQ-8, they misfired and the Torpex exploded in midair. This was the first violent death in a series of such that would plague the Kennedy family for over half a century.

Three weeks later, on September 3, the second BQ-8 mission successfully obliterated a German base in Heligoland.

## German Misteln

Like the Americans, the Germans adopted the notion of using bombers packed with explosives as cruise missiles. The German approach to guidance and delivery was more compact and involved physically attaching the bomber to the controlling aircraft. Conceived by Siegfried Holzbauer, a test pilot with the Junkers company, the concept was adopted by the Reichsluftfahrt Ministerium (RLM, German Air Ministry) in 1942 under the operational code name Beethoven.

Known as "Mistel" (Mistletoe), the weapon involved a piloted fighter being attached atop the uncrewed bomber in a "huckepack" (piggyback) configuration. Other nicknames included "Vater-und-Sohn" (father and son), as the term *Mistel* (the plural is *Misteln*) came to refer only to the bomber portion.

Various aircraft combinations were tested, but the combination that was deemed operational was a Messerschmitt Bf.109F or Focke-Wulf Fw.190A fighter atop a twin engine Junkers Ju.88A bomber. The Ju.88 had its flight deck and forward fuselage replaced by a cumbersome nose probe, and its controls were transferred to the fighter.

The bomber would be packed with 8,380 pounds of explosives. Like America's BQ-7 and BQ-8 flying bombs, the Misteln would be used against heavily defended, high-priority targets. Unlike the American concept, however, the Luftwaffe imagined using their secret weapons in mass assaults rather than in single attacks.

The Luftwaffe placed an initial order for 15 Misteln,

which were secretly tested in 1943. The tests included the sinking of a target ship, an old French ocean liner.

The new weapons were earmarked for operations in the event of an Allied invasion of northern France. The first mission, flown on June 24, 1944, nearly three weeks after D day, was a failure, but another attack by four Misteln soon after succeeded in hitting four Allied ships. Although the latter were damaged, they did not actually sink.

Despite the bomber's limited success, the Luftwaffe expanded their order to 75 Misteln and planned a raid against the British Royal Navy's super-base at Scapa Flow in Scotland. This massive assault was to have been launched from a field in Denmark and would have involved 60 Misteln along with escorting aircraft. Planned for December 1944, it was put back to January 1945, scrubbed because of bad weather, and never rescheduled.

Luftwaffe planners turned to the Eastern Front. They conceived a major Mistel attack on Soviet industrial targets under the code name Eisenhammer (Iron Hammer). It was to have been a grandiose maximum effort involving 100 Misteln launched from bases in East Prussia. Training began in January 1945, with the mission penciled into calendars for March. By then, however, East Prussia had been occupied by Soviet forces, which were driving toward the Oder and Neisse Rivers. Once those were crossed, they would be at the gates of Berlin.

The Oberkommando Wehrmacht (German High Command) then decided to use the Misteln in an effort to destroy the Oder and Neisse bridges, as well as those across the Rhine in the west. As such, this powerful secret weapon was never used for the massed attacks originally planned.

Though they were employed far more sparingly than the V-1 cruise missiles, the Misteln were more accurate than V-1s, and they saw more action than the American BQ

Bombs. Of the estimated that 250 Mistel combinations were completed, only 50 were captured unused at the end of the war.

## Fieseler Fi.103 Reichenberg

As a cruise missile, the Fi.103 earned a place among the pantheon of World War II's most notorious weapons under the designation V-1. Reich propaganda minister Dr. Joseph Goebbels—with the smiling approval of Adolf Hitler himself—picked it as the first in the series of weapons that were given a *V* for Vergeltungswaffe (Vengeance Weapon).

The estimated 10,050 of the unpiloted V-1 variant that were launched overshadowed the mere handful of Fieseler Fi.103 aircraft that were built to be flown by a person. The pilot would aim the missile at the target and then bail out of the aircraft.

The idea apparently originated independently with two well-known people from entirely different backgrounds. On one hand, there was Hauptman Otto Skorzeny, the famed SS special-operations commander. On the other was Hanna Reitsch, the great woman test pilot whose credentials included flight testing such high-performance aircraft as the Messerschmitt Me.163 rocket-powered interceptor.

In 1944, the project received official Luftwaffe sanction under the code name Reichenberg, and a development contract was issued to the German Glider Research Institute (Deutsche Forschungsinstitut für Segelflug, DFS), which handled rocket-powered projects as well as gliders. The piloted versions were simply V-1 cruise missiles with DFS-added cockpits and controls. Known as Reichenberg I, these aircraft would not be ground-launched, as were the V-1s, but air-launched from Heinkel He.111 bombers.

Flight testing began in September 1944 at the Laerz test

center. This involved unpowered, piloted Fi.103s air-launched and landed on the runway using a skid similar to that used on the Me.163 rather than wheeled landing gear. Hanna Reitsch herself made several of the early flights. Both landing the Fi.103 and operating the canopy in order to escape proved to be very difficult, even for a skilled pilot.

In the meantime, an operational squadron (*geschwader*), KG200, was formed with an eye toward getting the Fi.103 into action. However, most pilots viewed such operations as suicidal, and KG200 was unofficially known as the "Leonidas Staffel," after the Spartan king who fought a suicidal battle against the Persians at Thermopylae.

DFS constructed four versions of the aircraft, including the two-seat Reichenberg II and the Reichenberg IV, which was to have been the operational variant. The total number reached 175, but it is believed that no Fi.103 Reichenbergs were ever used in combat.

## Daimler Benz Cruise-Missile Projects

Known primarily as a builder of surface vehicles and of piston engines for aircraft and surface vehicles, Daimler Benz contributed several proposed aircraft to the lore of manned missiles.

The company had previously produced a series of designs of huge airborne aircraft carriers, large multiengine aircraft (see Chapter 19) with enormous wings that were designed to carry other manned aircraft. Among these were small swept-wing aircraft powered by turbojet engines. Operationally, the larger aircraft would have carried five or six of the smaller "parasite" jets, which would be air-dropped near the target. The pilot had only to line up the target in his sights, dive on it, punch out using an ejection seat, and *hope* that he would survive. Though the latter was considered unlikely, these parasite craft were technically not regarded as "suicide planes."

Though Daimler Benz had no experience building jet aircraft, it designed at least two distinct types of small parasite jets for the big aircraft carriers. One version looked like a swept-wing V-1 and was 42.5 feet long with a wingspan of 29.5 feet. The BMW 018 turbojet engine was to have been mounted atop the aft fuselage like the pulsejet of the V-1 or the Fi.103 Reichenberg.

Another Daimler Benz parasite looked rather like a Messerschmitt Me.262 with a single engine mounted beneath the rear fuselage. It was to have been 30 feet long with a wingspan of almost 28 feet. It was to have been powered by a Heinkel Hirth 011, which represented the second generation of German jet-engine technology after the familiar Junkers Jumo series.

No Daimler Benz manned missile is believed to have been built before the war ended.

**9**

## Air-to-Surface Guided Missiles

Attacking ground and air targets from the air with unguided rockets was not new to World War II. During the First World War, the French, notably Lieutenant Y.P.G. Le-Prieur, used flimsy and barely reliable rockets adapted from fireworks to attack German balloons and airships. Because such vehicles were filled with very volatile hydrogen gas, virtually any hit turned the gasbags into torches. In World War II, somewhat more sophisticated, albeit still unguided, rockets were widely used by the various air forces involved, primarily against ground targets.

Meanwhile, secret efforts were under way on both sides to create a better weapon. Unguided aerial rockets were essentially little more than sophisticated projectiles. Like a machine-gun round or a cannon shell, they were delivered by simply aiming and firing. They also had the hitting power of a cannon shell. What if a rocket had a more sophisticated guidance system? What if it had the hitting power of a *bomb*?

Of course, far more complex ballistic missiles and cruise missiles were also being secretly developed during

World War II, but what was sought here was a better, but still relatively straightforward means of hitting surface targets from the air.

Many of the cruise missiles discussed in the previous two chapters were air-launched, but the missiles that are the subject of this chapter are distinguished by their smaller size, shorter range, and tactical application. The air-launched missiles considered below were developed to strike targets within a radius of about 15 miles, or essentially within line of sight.

The technology pioneered in these secret weapons of World War II is still being used in the twenty-first century in much more well-known weapons. The air-to-surface guided missiles of World War II are the tactical ancestors of the likes of today's McDonnell Douglas AGM-84 Harpoon antiship missile and the Hughes AGM-65 Maverick, the television guided "tank buster" that was used so effectively in the Gulf War and the Balkans during the 1990s. These American weapons all began with the Bat.

## ASM-N-2 Bat

While the Germans led the world in most phases of missile development throughout World War II, the American Bat glide bomb was an exception. It was one of the most advanced missiles used in World War II or for decades thereafter.

Unlike many such weapons, the missile's airframe was developed not by private industry but by an in-house government effort headed by the Bureau of Standards and the Navy Bureau of Ordnance in close collaboration with the Massachusetts Institute of Technology.

The project, originally known as Dragon, began in early in 1941—before the United States entered World War II—

as an antiship missile that would use the emerging technology of television for guidance systems. The Dragon was superseded in 1942 by the Pelican, an antisubmarine weapon concept that arose from the U-boat menace. The threat that German U-boats posed to shipping in the North Atlantic was one of the paramount concerns of American military planning.

By 1943, the U-boat hazard had lessened considerably, and the missile was again an air-to-surface weapon guided by a radar homing system. It emerged in 1944 as the ASM-N-2, meaning "Air-to-Surface Missile, Navy." While its blunt nose and stubby wings did not make it look like those fuzzy denizens of the night, it was one of a number of aerial weapons systems to receive the appellation "Bat."

The ASM-N-2 was an inch short of 12 feet long and had a wingspan of 10 feet. It weighed 1,880 pounds, of which 1,000 were the explosive warhead. The radar homing guidance system was developed by Western Electric, which later became Bell Labs, and still later Lucent Technologies.

The Bat was air-launched from Consolidated PB4Y-2 Privateers, four-engine heavy bombers that each carried a pair of Bats on racks attached to its wings. Bats were first used against Japanese ships off Borneo in May 1945, and were quickly found to be very potent weapons.

They were probably the most effective air-launched antiship weapons used in the Pacific Theater, claiming, among other vessels, a Japanese destroyer at a range of 20 miles. Bats were also used successfully against land targets, including bridges in Burma and other Japanese-held territories.

Hugh L. Dryden of the Massachusetts Institute of Technology, who won the Presidential Certificate of Merit for the development of the Bat, went on to serve as director of the National Advisory Committee for Aeronautics (NACA) from 1947 until 1958. When NACA became the

National Aeronautics and Space Administration (NASA) in 1958, Dryden served as deputy administrator through 1965.

## ASM-N-4 Dove

Like the Bat, the Dove was a U.S. Navy Bureau of Aeronautics project to designated under the ASM for air-to-surface nomenclature. Whereas the ASM-N-2 was designed from the ground up as a new aerial vehicle, the ASM-N-4 Dove was essentially a 1,000-pound bomb to which electrically operated wings and a guidance system were added. Developed by Eastman Kodak, the Dove's gyroscopic guidance system used an elementary heat sensor as a homing device. Unlike the Bat, the Dove was not widely used.

## McDonnell LBD-1/KSD-1 Gargoyle

During World War II, secret projects were often cubbyholed to keep them away from prying eyes in other departments. Parallel development of similar projects often took place, and in the case of the U.S. Navy, parallel designation systems for glide-bomb programs evolved. At the same time that the Bat and Dove were designated under the joint service ASM system, other glide bombs used the U.S. Navy's LB (later KS) for bomb-carrying glider nomenclature.

The first of this group would be the McDonnell LBD-1 (later KSD-1) Gargoyle antiship missile, which also had the distinction of being the first missile built by the McDonnell Aircraft Company. Though it was an insignificant maker of airplane parts during World War II, the St. Louis company would eventually evolve (as a component of the McDonnell Douglas Corporation) into the largest maker of military aircraft in the United States and the originator of the Harpoon antiship missile.

The swept-wing, butterfly-tailed Gargoyle was 10 feet 1 inch long, with a wingspan of 8 feet 6 inches. It weighed 517 pounds empty but carried twice its own weight—1,000 pounds—in explosives.

The Gargoyle was first flown in March 1944 with a small rocket engine attached. Beginning in December, a series of tests demonstrated that when dropped from 27,000 feet, it had a range of 5 miles. When the war ended, McDonnell and the Navy were still trying to sort out a usable guidance system.

## Pratt-Read LBE-1 Glomb

Like the converted airplanes discussed in Chapter 8, the Pratt-Read LBE-1 Glomb (Glider Bomb) was an attempt to create ordnance using an existing airframe. Whereas the weapons of Chapter 8 were converted aircraft, the Glomb was loosely based on existing aircraft—the LNE-1 training glider manufactured by Pratt-Read of Eddystone, Pennsylvania.

In 1942, the U.S. Navy considered buying large numbers of Glombs, so in addition to LBE-1s built by Pratt-Read, Piper would have built them under the designation LBT-1, and Taylorcraft as LBT-1. Though the craft's altitude performance would have been an operational plus, only three XLBE-1s are known to have actually been built and none are known to have survived the war. Secret weapons were easier to destroy than to reclassify. In 1952, a civilian-operated LNE-1 set a world altitude record for unpiloted vehicles.

## Gorgon

Late in World War II, the Naval Air Development Center (NADC) began work on a new family of air-launched, propelled guided missile. It was named Gorgon, after the daughters of Ceto and Phorcus of Greek mythology—Spheno, Euryale, and Medusa—known collectively as Gorgons because of their snake-infested hair.

Though they were not actually completed during World War II, Gorgons rate a mention because the name often comes up in discussions of wartime missiles. Brewster Aeronautical of Johnsville, Pennsylvania, had made the Navy's famous F2A Buffalo fighter aircraft before and during the war, and had been contracted to build the Vought Corsair. However, quality-control problems led to a cancellation of its orders in 1944. The NADC took over the factory and built Gorgons.

The first one, the turbojet-powered KUN-1 Gorgon I, appeared in 1946 and evolved into the rocket-propelled NU2N-1 and the CTV-N Gorgon II, which included the CTV-N-4 Gorgon IIC, which was intended to be surface-launched. After building the early Gorgons itself, the Navy turned to private industry. The Martin Company built the Westinghouse turbojet-powered PTV-N-2 Gorgon IV and the XASM-5 Gorgon V, which was powered by the very fast Marquardt ramjet engine. No Gorgons are known to have been used in combat, and the program was terminated in 1953.

## McDonnell AQM-60 Kingfisher

Like the Gorgon, the McDonnell AQM-60 Kingfisher anti-ship missile was not tested until after World War II. However, it deserves to be mentioned because it evolved directly from the wartime Gargoyle project. Both had the distinctive V tail and a 1,000-pound warhead, but the Kingfisher's nose was much longer. Unlike the rocket-propelled Gargoyle, the Kingfisher had a jet engine. It was tested by the U.S. Navy though the late 1940s. Two decades later, McDonnell would merge with Douglas, and from McDonnell Douglas would come the AGM-84 Harpoon, the ultimate turn-of-the-century air-launched antiship missile.

## Douglas MX-601 Roc

Like McDonnell, with whom it would merge in 1967, the Douglas Aircraft Company began building guided missiles during World War II. Such work had begun as early as 1940 under secret Project MX-601. This program included the development of the Roc family of four air-launched missiles that were extremely advanced for their day. The weapons were similar in appearance, with a distinctive circular wing that ringed the torpedo-shaped fuselage like a large doughnut. They differed primarily in their guidance system.

Named for the enormous bird of Arabian mythology, the radar-guided Roc I was acquired by the USAAF under the vertical-bomb designation VB-9. The VB-10 Roc II, which appeared in 1943, was similar, but used a television guidance system. It was one of the first weapons to successfully exploit the emerging technology of television for guidance systems. Such work was then being done at RCA, which had acquired the patents of Hungarian inventor Kalman Tihanyi, an early pioneer in the field of practical television applications. The VB-11 Roc III was an infrared-guided weapon, while the VB-13 Roc IV was guided visually by a weapons-system operator.


## Henschel Hs.293/Hs.294

Like the American Bat, the Henschel Hs.293 and Hs.294 were air-launched missiles widely used during World War II in an antishipping role. Like the Fritz X glide bomb, they were among Germany's unheralded wonder weapons. The series was also the first-ever guided-missile type to be mass-produced.

Henschel took an early lead in the field after 1940, when it hired missile virtuoso Dr. Herbert Wagner away from the rival Junkers firm. His early work included the Hs.291 project, which had evolved into the guided Hs.293 glide bomb by the summer of 1940. By the end of that year, he had mated the Hs.293 to a small Walter 109 rocket engine, and had developed a multichannel radio control system that would permit a weapons-system operator to "fly" as many as 18 missiles simultaneously.

The Hs.293 was 12 feet 6 inches long, with a wingspan of 10 feet 2 inches. It had a launch weight of 2,300 pounds and a range of up to 20 miles. As with the Douglas Roc, there were several versions, differentiated by their guidance system. The He.293A was the original radio-guided version, the He.293B was wire-guided, and the He.293D was an experimental version with a television guidance system. Later variants included the delta-winged Hs.293F and the Hs.293G "dive-bomber" version that impacted its target vertically. The Hs.293H variant was used as an effective air-intercept weapon, being air-launched against Allied bomber formations.

The He.293 became operational with the bomber squadron KG100 in France during the summer of 1943, being air-launched from a variety of aircraft types, including Dornier Do.217s and Heinkel He.111s. On August 27, one was used to sink a small British patrol vessel. This was the first ship in history to be lost to a guided missile.

Although the He.293s never took out any vessels as large as those claimed by the Fritz X glide bombs, they claimed at least five destroyers and many transports. Like Fritz X, the He.293 was used mainly in the Mediterranean Theater but also saw service against high-priority land targets during the final weeks of the defense of Germany.

The Hs.294 evolved from the Hs.293C project. It was a twin-engine missile with a sharply pointed nose that was capable of diving beneath the surface of the sea, thus hitting ships beneath the waterline. Two variations on the Hs.294 concept that were armed with fragmentation warheads included the twin-engine Hs.295 and the single-engine Hs.296.

## Blohm und Voss Bv.143

While Germany earned a reputation for creating some very leading-edge aerial weaponry during World War II, the Bv.143 glide bomb made by the great ship and seaplane maker Blohm und Voss was clearly not among them. In retrospect, these secret weapons should have had their secrets *deliberately* leaked as misinformation!

Making its debut in 1942, the Bv.143 was an antiship weapon that was accelerated by a rocket engine. It was sleek, streamlined vehicle, 19 feet 7.5 inches long, with a wingspan of 10 feet 3.25 inches and a launch weight of 2,326 pounds.

It was an early attempt to create a sea-skimming missile

that could escape detection by flying just seven feet off the surface of the water. Rather than using a remote sensing device to achieve proper altitude, it used a cumbersome spring-loaded "feeler" arm to detect the surface of the water beneath it. When it "felt" the wave tops, the rocket engine would ignite for a five-mile dash. As might have been predicted, all the Bv.143 flight tests failed and the project was terminated in 1943.

### Blohm und Voss Bv.226/Bv.246 Hagelkorn

Like the Bv.143, the Hagelkorn (Hailstone) was a sleek glide bomb that looked fast and dangerous. It was a better weapon, and was more widely used, than its predecessor, but the secrecy of the program meant that little in the way of operational data survived World War II.

At 11 feet 7 inches, it was shorter than the Bv.143 and weighed just 1,600 pounds, but it had a broader wingspan of 21 feet. Strangely, the wings and tail were made of cast concrete over a steel core. Despite this obviously low-tech approach to wing design, it had a maximum glide range of more than 100 miles.

Ordered under the designation Bv.226, the Hagelkorn was revised on the drawing board and delivered under the designation Bv.246, beginning in 1943. As with the American McDonnell Gargoyle, the Hagelkorn suffered from having reached production without a firm idea of what sort of guidance system it should use. During extensive airdrop tests using Heinkel He.111H and Focke-Wulf Fw.190As as "mother ships," the Luftwaffe tried various guidance concepts. These included radio control and infrared devices. Finally, the Hagelkorn was retrofitted with the primitive Radiesch (Radish) radar homing system that made it a technological ancestor of the American AGM-88 HARM antiradar missile that was widely used in the 1980s and 1990s, notably during Operation Desert Storm.

Production of the Hagelkorn ended abruptly in February 1944 after delivery of 1,100 units, but the weapon remained in service until most of the supply had been expended.

## I-Go

As we mentioned earlier, an interesting aspect of World War II weapons development in Japan was that new technology was generally developed on parallel and competing tracks by both the Imperial Japanese Army and Imperial Japanese Navy. Both, for example, produced families of antiship missiles. Like Germany, Japan had such programs in development by 1942.

The Japanese Imperial Army program was a series of weapons designated as "I-Go," meaning "Plan 43," indicating a planned initial operating capability in 1943. Coincidentally, I-Go would also be the operational code name of the Imperial Japanese *Navy*'s April 1943 aerial campaign against Allied shipping and air bases at or near Guadalcanal and New Guinea.

The first weapon in the series, I-Go 1A, was a radio-controlled, 19-foot wooden airplane with a wingspan of 11 feet 9.75 inches. Powered by a rocket engine, it weighed 3,086 pounds, of which 1,764 pounds were high-explosive warhead. I-Go 1A was developed internally by the Imperial Japanese Navy's Rikugun Kokugijutsu Kenkyujo (Air Technical Research Institute) at Tachikawa.

In 1942, the program was handed off to Mitsubishi for further development and eventual production. Test drops from aircraft began in the summer of 1944 and guided flights followed during the autumn, but the weapon was never mass-produced and probably was not used in combat.

The slightly smaller I-Go 1B reached the test phase at about the same time as its predecessor, and about 180 pre-production weapons were made. These were apparently expended in extensive testing during the winter of 1944–1945. It is believed that no production-series I-Go 1Bs were built, and none were used in combat. They were 13 feet 5 inches long, with a wingspan of 8 feet 6 inches. Their total weight was 1,499 pounds with a 661-pound warhead.

The 11.5-foot I-Go IC was a planned third member of the family that was intended to be guided by a complex guidance system employing a vibration sensor. The Imperial Japanese Army never fully worked the bugs out of this sensor, which was to have homed in on the vibration of antiaircraft guns aboard ships. The I-Go 1C was still in development when the war ended.

In retrospect, I-Go would have been a potent weapon that could have substituted for kamikazes. The weapons were smaller than aircraft, and, therefore, harder to hit with antiaircraft gunfire. Because they were built of radar-absorbing wood rather than radar-reflecting metal, they were "stealth" weapons that would have been hard to defend against.

## Funryu 1

In 1942, the Imperial Japanese Navy undertook development of a guided antiship missile at its main base at Yokosuka near Yokohama. Like the American Glomb, which was being designed at exactly the same time, the Funryu 1 (Raging Dragon) was a radio-controlled, air-launched weapon. While the Imperial Japanese Army missile program is fairly well documented, little information about the Funryu survived the war. It is known, however, that it carried an 882-pound warhead and that it was test-launched using Mitsubishi G4M "Betty" bombers.

The Raging Dragon appellation was also applied to a series of solid-fuel surface-to-air rockets. The Funryu 2 and 4 are discussed in Chapter 10.

## 10

## Surface-to-Air Missiles (SAM)

Pioneered during World War II, surface-to-air missiles evolved into one of the most important military missile types in the postwar world. In Vietnam, for example, more American aircraft were lost to enemy surface-to-air missiles than to enemy aircraft. In the 1991 Gulf War, as in Operation Enduring Freedom a decade later, enemy surface-to-air missile sites were in the top tier of the target list when American and coalition bombers went to war. Destroying them was of the highest priority.

World War II began with antiaircraft guns as the only surface-to-air weapon. These included heavy-caliber machine guns and such artillery weapons as the German 88mm gun and the U.S. Navy's five-incher. Machine guns and artillery shells were fast, potent, and cheap. Surface-to-air missiles were much more expensive and harder to use and offered no advantage unless an extremely accurate guidance system could be developed. In that case, accuracy at a longer range would make then a step beyond antiaircraft artillery, which had to be visually aimed from the ground.

An interesting footnote to the World War II surface-to-air missile deployment was that they were nearly all launched from rails mounted on modified antiaircraft *gun* mounts.

When the war began, surface-to-air missiles were simply a theoretical possibility. Germany, which eventually did more work in the field than any other nation, might have taken an early lead, but did not. The first German design studies emerged as early as 1941, but at that time, Allied air attacks on Germany were a rare nuisance and the Reichsluftfahrt Ministerium (RLM, German Air Ministry) showed little interest in the concept.

It was not until 1944 that serious development work got under way on surface-to-air missiles and their guidance systems in any country. However, while guidance systems for air-to-ground weapons were successfully developed, guidance for missiles going the other way proved impossibly elusive.

By 1945, at least a half-dozen projects, mainly German and American, were coming *close* to achieving what had been unimaginable in 1939, but they were still not quite there. The war would end without a single guided missile having shot down an enemy aircraft.

## Little Joe

Because the U.S. mainland was never seriously threatened by air attack, and because the USAAF had relative air superiority over most battlefields where the U.S. Army was engaged after 1944, that service never undertook a serious surface-to-air missile program during World War II.

The catalyst for the U.S. Navy's first such program was the sudden appearance of Japanese kamikazes. These attacks startled the U.S. Navy and resulted in an emergency program that was initiated in-house during the summer of 1944. The Naval Air Matériel Command quickly began work on a radio-controlled missile powered by a solid-fuel rocket engine. It was given the designation KAN-1, with the prefix indicating that it was radio-controlled and the suffix that it was to be built by the Naval Aircraft Factory. The nickname "Little Joe" was apparently derived from its size. The KAN-1 was to be 11 feet 4 inches long, with a diameter of 22.7 inches.

The first missiles were built in record time, and soon the KAN-1 evolved into the slightly more sophisticated KAN-2. Testing of the 1,210-pound, rail-launched missile was under way by early winter. Manufactured by Aerojet, the main engine offered 1,000 pounds of thrust, which was augmented by three small cordite rockets. Apparently the smoke trail from the Little Joe interfered with the vision of the person trying to control it. Conversely, this would have made it easy for the kamikaze pilot to see it coming. This and other problems led to Little Joe being canceled in favor of the Lark program in February 1945.

## Lark

For the U.S. Navy, development of a surface-to-air missile capability was a high-priority emergency program. At the same time that the U.S. Navy's Naval Air Matériel Command began working on the Little Joe, a second development team was working on what was known as the "Little Lark." The hope was that at least one project would evolve into a usable weapon. Actually, neither did. Little Joe was abandoned, and its competitor was not ready before the war ended.

Developed under the name Lark, with the adjective dropped, the missile was an inch shy of 14 feet in length, with an 18-inch diameter. It had a wingspan of 6 feet, with its four wings arranged in a cruciform pattern. A more sophisticated weapon than Little Joe, the Lark had a range of four miles, double that of its predecessor. Power was supplied by a Reaction Motors liquid-fuel rocket engine. Guidance was by radio, and various control surface arrangements, involving aileron configurations in the wings and tail, were studied.

When the war ended, the Lark had still not gone into production, but the program showed enough promise that it was kept going at a time when the majority of aircraft and missile programs were terminated.

Developed internally by the U.S. Navy through VJ day, the Lark program was then turned over to Fairchild Aircraft, who created a new guided missile division to develop the weapon. The Lark entered flight testing under the designation CTV-N-9, and such tests continued until the early 1950s.

## Project Bumblebee

By the spring of 1945, it was clear to U.S. Navy planners that the Little Joe and Lark were not going to be useful in the emergency effort to use missiles against kamikazes. While Lark continued, the Navy brass decided to began work on a parallel project to develop a second-generation ship-launched surface-to-air missile capability.

Though the name sounds like it might have been that of a small wartime missile, Bumblebee was actually a secret *program* to develop the technology for a future weapon. While the emergency effort that produced Little Joe and Lark cut a lot of corners in the interest of haste, Bumblebee was intended as a project that would take whatever time was necessary to develop a supersonic surface-to-air missile second to none.

Begun by the U.S. Navy Bureau of Ordnance in January 1945, Project Bumblebee envisioned a full research-and-development program undertaken by the bureau in conjunction with the Applied Physics Laboratory at The Johns Hopkins University in Baltimore. The hardware production would be turned over to private industry under the auspices of the bureau's Section T. While none of this hardware was ready for field use before the end of World War II, the Section T program led to the U.S. Navy's first family of postwar missiles, all named with a word beginning with *T*.

The first Bumblebee missile was the Talos, whose development program began in March 1945. The prime industrial contractor would be the Bendix company, with McDonnell Aircraft as the airframe subcontractor. Developed under the designation SAM-N-6, the Talos finally became operational as the RIM-8 aboard the USS *Galveston* in 1958.

The 21-foot Talos became the standard shipboard air defense missile for the U.S. Navy. Carried by ships worldwide, especially in war zones, the Talos was the first and only U.S. surface weapon to shoot down an enemy aircraft during the Vietnam conflict. On May 23, 1968, a Talos downed a MiG-21 over the Gulf of Tonkin. After a second MiG was downed by a Talos, the North Vietnamese Air Force never strayed near the ships of the U.S. Fleet.

The Talos missiles remained aboard the U.S. Navy's guided-missile cruisers until the 1980s, when they were gradually converted for use as MQM-8 target drones.

The later Bumblebee missiles, all of which originated after World War II, were the Bendix/McDonnell SAM-N-8 Typhoon, the Convair Terrier, and the Convair Tartar. Both of the Convair (later General Dynamics) missiles started out under the designation SAM-N-7, but were redesignated as RIM-2 and RIM-24 respectively. Like the Talos, they remained in service for three decades.

## Brakemine

During the infamous Blitz, the vicious German air campaign against on British cities during the latter half of 1940, antiaircraft weapons were a high priority for Britain's war planners. However, surface-to-air missiles were never a high priority in the United Kingdom during World War II, and the only such program to reach the hardware stage was consistently underfunded. Called Brakemine, this missile was first proposed in 1942, but not approved for development until April 1943.

The radio-guided Brakemine was 6 feet 7 inches long, with a wingspan of 2 feet 9 inches and a diameter of 10.5 inches. During the design stage, the wing layout started as four wings in a cruciform pattern, but later evolved into two wings arranged like those of an airplane. The power plant was a cluster of six rockets in the aft section of the fuselage. As with most contemporary surface-to-air missiles, it was rail-launched, with the launcher adapted from an antiaircraft gun mount.

The design was finally accepted in February 1944, and testing began seven months later. Initial engine failures led to a redesign of that section, and the Brakemine program moved slowly. As with the later American surface-to-air missiles, it did not reach operational use during World War II, but continued in development after the war ended.

The bugs were finally worked out, but the Brakemine program was terminated in 1947. Unlike the American World War II surface-to-air missile programs, which continued to evolve, the postwar British surface-to-air systems would not have their roots in the wartime Brakemine.

## Funryu 2

The Imperial Japanese Navy applied the Funryu (Raging Dragon) appellation to a series of solid-fuel-guided rockets. The first of these is discussed among surface-to-air missiles (see Chapter 9). The Funryu 2 was a cruciform-winged antiaircraft missile powered by a solid-fuel rocket motor.

Secret design studies began in 1943, and little more of the Funryu 2's history is known other than that some flight tests occurred. The rocket was 7 feet 3 inches long, 11.8 inches in diameter, and its wingspan was an inch short of 3 feet. It weighed 816 pounds, including a 110-pound payload, and is believed to have had an operational intercept altitude of over 16,000 feet.

## Funryu 4

Aside from its basic mission, the Imperial Japanese Navy's Funryu 4 was unlike the Funryu 2 in nearly all respects. It was twice as large, weighing 4,189 pounds. It was 13 feet 1.5 inches long, almost 2 feet in diameter, and had a wingspan of about 30 inches. The Funryu 4 was powered by a liquid-fuel rocket engine based on a German Walter HWK-509—the engine that powered the Messerschmitt Me.163—that was delivered to Japan secretly by U-boat. The Funryu 4 was late in coming and had yet to be flight-tested when the war ended.

## Enzian

One of Germany's memorable secret projects, the Messerschmitt Enzian (Gentian Violet) was a subsonic surface-to-air missile based on the design of Messerschmitt's Me.163 Komet rocket-propelled fighter. While it was similar in proportions to the Komet, it was smaller, being 7 feet 10.5 inches long, with the span of its stubby, straight wings 13 feet 1.5 inches. Made of wood, it weighed 3,968 pounds, including a 661-pound warhead.

Flight testing began at the Karlshagen research center in 1944, with the rail-launched Enzian powered by four Schmidding 109-553 rocket engines delivering over 15,000 pounds of thrust. At least 10 tests of the Enzian 1 through Enzian 3 prototypes were flown. This round of testing led to the Enzian 3B and Enzian 4 preproduction missiles, of which about 60 were built. Roughly half of these were test-flown, demonstrating a range of more than 15 miles. This was promising, but a maximum target altitude of less than 8,500 feet would have made the missile ineffective against high-flying Allied strategic bombers.

The program was officially terminated in January 1945, although Messerschmitt went on to propose a swept-wing Enzian 5 a month later. A miniature Enzian 6 was also suggested as an antitank weapon.

## Feuerlilie

Like the U.S. Navy's first surface-to-air missiles, the German Feuerlilie (Fire Lily) began as an in-house project that was later farmed out to industry. The Luftwaffe and the Reichsluftfahrt Ministerium (RLM, German Air Ministry) did the general design work on the concept and assigned the project to Rheinmetall in 1942. Germany's first surface-to-air missile, the Feuerlilie was a radio-controlled, liquid-fuel rocket that was 15 feet 9 inches long and 21.7 inches in diameter. It had a futuristic appearance, with swept, aft-mounted wings that spanned 8 feet 2.5 inches.

Feuerlilie testing began in May 1944 and lasted at least four months. It achieved a speed of over 500 mph and a range of more than 4 miles, but the project was not developed into an operational weapons system. After the war, the Allies evaluated examples of the Feuerlilie, and one example is on public display at the Royal Air Force Museum at Shropshire in England.

## Rheintochter

Like the Feuerlilie, the Rheintochter (Daughter of the Rhine) originated in 1942 and was developed by the Rheinmetall-Borsig company. Separate versions of essentially the same vehicle were developed for the German army and for the Luftwaffe, which assumed control of antiaircraft defenses of German cities in 1944.

The army's Rheintochter I was 20 feet 8 inches long, with a diameter of 21.25 inches and the wings spanning a maximum of 7 feet 4 inches. Built later, the Luftwaffe's Rheintochter III was similar, but 4 feet 4.5 inches shorter.

The Rheintochter had fourteen separate wings that were were grouped the three distinct sections. There were four sharply swept wings in the tail, six in the midfuselage, and four short, movable fins near the nose.

The seven rocket engines it contained delivered an aggregate of 165,300 pounds of thrust, propelling the Rheintochter to almost supersonic speed. Tests, which began at Libau in August 1943, demonstrated a range of almost 25 miles. The operational altitude of nearly 20,000 feet would have been adequate to hit most Allied bombers, but it was less than that promised by the Henschel Hs.117 Schmetterling surface-to-air missile, which is discussed below.

The Rheintochter I tests ended in the autumn of 1944

after more than 80 flights. Meanwhile, the Rheintochter III was in the works; at least six were delivered by the end of the year, and at least five were tested in December 1944.

At this point, the Rheintochter program was abruptly terminated, and the Luftwaffe relied on antiaircraft artillery for ground-based air defense through the end of the war.

## Taifun

The simplest surface-to-air missile system seen in Germany during World War II was certainly the innovative Taifun (Typhoon). It was also the cheapest, owing to the fact that it had no guidance system. Given this, it is paradoxical to note that the missile reportedly demonstrated a high degree of accuracy up to about 25,000 feet. Perhaps this was because it was designed to be launched into bomber formations in braces of 30 missiles. The Taifun was 6 feet 4 inches long and 4 inches in diameter, with tail fins spanning 8.7 inches. The launch weight was 46.3 pounds, including a 1-pound explosive charge.

## Wasserfall

Created by Wernher von Braun's missile development team at Peenemünde, the Wasserfall (Waterfall) was, in many ways, like a scaled-down A4 (V-2). As such, it was probably the most complex of all the surface-to-air missiles tested during World War II. It was smaller than the A4, but of similar shape and also powered by liquid fuel. It was 25 feet 8.5 inches long, almost 3 feet in diameter, and its four tail fins spanned 8 feet 3 inches. It had a launch weight of 7,716 pounds, of which 320 pounds was the explosive warhead and 198 pounds was an explosive charge designed to destroy the missile if it missed its target. The single engine delivered 17,635 pounds of thrust.

Unlike most other surface-to-air missiles, which were rail-launched at a steep angle, the Wasserfall was launched vertically like the A4. It had a range of 22 miles and an intercept altitude of well above 50,000 feet. This was more than enough to hit any Allied strategic bomber, but unlike the A4, it was never used operationally.

After many delays—including the deaths of key personnel in British air raids—the Wasserfall was first successfully tested in February 1944. Over the course of the next year, there were at least three dozen test flights, and an underground production facility at Bleichrode was in the planning stages. However, the Wasserfall program was terminated in February 1945.

## Henschel Hs.117 Schmetterling

During World War II, the ultimate German surface-to-air guided missile was the Henschel Hs.117 Schmetterling (Butterfly). While less complex than the Wasserfall, the Schmetterling was the winner in the race to be the surface-to-air guided missile that came the closest to operational readiness of any in the German arsenal. Though ordered into production, it never quite made it.

In 1941, the firm of Henschel Flugzeugwerke undertook surface-to-air missile studies that culminated in the Hs.297 project. Since there was no official interest in surface-to-air missiles, the proposal languished on the shelf at the RLM until 1943.

Having been ordered to dust off the concept, Henschel came up with the Hs.117 Schmetterling. It was an airplane-shaped vehicle with a cruciform tail and two long, narrow

Schmidding liquid-fuel outrigger engines above and below the fuselage. These were designed to drop off during flight, leaving the BMW 109-558 main engine. With all three engines firing, the top speed would be 680 mph.

The Schmetterling was just over 14 feet long, with a diameter of 14.75 inches and its stubby wings spanned 6 feet 6.75 inches. It weighed up to 980 pounds at launch, including a 55-pound warhead.

The first Schmetterling was launched at the Karlshagen test facility in May 1944. Over the next seven months, numerous ground launches and airdrop tests demonstrated a range of 20 miles and an effective altitude of over 30,000 feet. Various guidance alternatives included radio control—with an operator having a 10-power telescope and a joystick control—and a radar-control option using Wurzburg radar for night and poor-weather operations.

The first operational training unit was activated in September 1944, and the Schmetterling was officially ordered into production three months later. The order called for a monthly manufacturing rate of 150 by March 1945, rising to 3,000 by the end of the year. Of course, for the Luftwaffe, 1945 would last only until the first week of May, and the grand plans for Schmetterling production and deployment never got off the ground.

## 11

## Air-to-Air Guided Missiles

Today, air-to-air missiles are a staple of modern aerial combat. In World War II, as in World War I, virtually all the aircraft shot down in air-to-air combat fell to gunfire. In all the wars that took place during the last quarter of the twentieth century, virtually all air-to-air kills were accomplished by guided missiles.

During World War II, unguided rockets, such as the German R4M and the American high-velocity aerial rocket (HVAR), were developed, but mainly for ground-attack use. Occasionally, though, they were used in aerial combat. After the war, HVARs and folding-fin aerial rockets (FFARs) became common air-to-air armament for interceptors.

If you were close enough to simply "aim and shoot," then guns or rockets were fine. At longer distances, interceptor pilots craved a guided missile. However, guided missiles were an elusive technology—because they needed to be *guided*. In order for them to be worth the expense, they needed the kind of highly accurate guidance system that did not appear until after the war.

The American Hotshot program of 1946 evolved into

the radar-guided AIM-7 Sparrow, which is still in use in the twenty-first century. The AIM-9 Sidewinder was created in the early 1950s specifically to target jet aircraft using a heat-seeking sensor, and it is still in service. During World War II, radar guidance was in its infancy, while a heat seeker would obviously be impractical for hunting piston-engine aircraft.

The United States actively considered air-to-air guided missiles during the war, but only in Germany was hardware actually produced.

### Henschel Hs.298

The world's first air-to-air missile, the Hs.298 used radio-command guidance, although a wire-guided version was also developed. Though more than 300 were built and test-launched from Ju.88 and Fw.190 aircraft over the Karlshagen test facility, it is not believed that any were actually used operationally. The program was officially terminated in December 1944.

The airplane-shaped Hs.298 bore some resemblance to Henschel's Hs.293 air-to-ground missile, but was about half the size. It was six feet six inches long, with a wingspan of four feet four inches. The launch weight of 209.5 pounds included a 55-pound warhead.

### Ruhrstahl/Kramer X-4/Rk.344

As noted previously, Dr. Max Kramer of Germany's Air Transport Research Institute, the Deutsche Versuchsanstalt für Luftfahrt (DVL), was an important figure in the field of missile development during World War II. His remarkable fin-stabilized X-4 is generally regarded as the first practical air-to-air missile. It was similar in overall appearance to Kramer's Fritz X "smart bomb," but much smaller. It weighed 132 pounds and carried a 44-pound proximity-fused warhead.

The X-4 had the appearance of a postwar science-fiction rocket, with four swept wings, spanning 22.6 inches, arranged in cruciform shape, as well as four small control fins. It was 6 feet 6 inches in length, the same as the Hs.298, a size apparently governed by operational considerations such as the type of aircraft that would carry it. The X-4 was tested aboard Ju.88 and Fw.190 fighters and was intended to be used as an operational air-intercept missile for aircraft such as the Me.262 jet fighter.

Like Kramer's X-7 artillery missile, the first X-4 missiles were controlled by two thin copper guidance wires that were unrolled from spools contained in pods at the wingtips. Wire control was selected primarily because, compared with radio remote control, it was seen as practically jamproof.

During the flight tests, there were no damaging effects from static electrical charges accumulating on the wires, but mechanical difficulties arose as the wire played out from the bobbins in the missile, so similar bobbins on the parent aircraft were designed to dispense wire simultaneously from both ends. When this scenario proved impractical, an acoustic homing system known as Pudel was developed.

Basing its work on the same fundamental principles as the Kranich acoustic proximity fuse, Pudel used a carbon microphone that homed on the sound of the aircraft engines. This data fed into a single-stage amplifier that was relay-mounted to the longitudinal axis of the fuselage. As the X-4 rotated, the output of the microphone would be constant if the missile was homing directly on target. With no modulation output there would be no steering corrections. If the missile was not aimed directly at the target, the modulation frequency would change, and this data would go to the control surfaces to change the course of the missile. Steering was by means of rake spoilers located in the tail fins.

The BMW 109-548 rocket motor was fueled by a nitric-acid-and-triethylamine mixture and delivered an initial thrust of 330 pounds. The Schmidding solid-propellant engine was also proposed and tested.

The first X-4 test flight occurred on August 11, 1944, and by year's end Ruhrstall produced approximately 1,300 under the designation Rk.344. Had the engines for the production series not been destroyed in the bombing of the BMW plant at Stargard, the missile would have been ready for operational units by early 1945. Though work continued on refining the acoustic guidance system, the program never got back on track.

After World War II, the X-4 attracted a great deal of attention from Allied technical analysts, although there was no serious effort to manufacture the missile. Most of the captured X-4s were scrapped, but a number still exist. Surviving examples are on public display in England at the Royal Air Force Museum in Shropshire and in the United States at the National Air and Space Museum Garber Facility in Silver Spring, Maryland, and at the U.S. Air Force Museum near Dayton, Ohio.

# 12

## Mega-Artillery

Myriad types and designs of artillery pieces were used during World War II. Among the more well known were weapons based on the famous "French 75"—a basic 75mm design dating to the World War I era—and the legendary German 88mm gun, which was adapted for uses from field artillery to antiaircraft artillery and also used as a tank gun.

The war also saw the combatants utilize the largest artillery pieces ever fired in wartime. As was the case with many other types of hardware, the Germans led the way, and the Americans followed. During World War I, the Germans had pioneered mega-artillery through the use on land of mobile guns that were on the scale of those used aboard battleships.

The debut of the large German guns in World War I came in August 1914 during the opening phase of the war as the German army attempted to execute an abbreviated version of the von Schlieffen plan for the defeat of France. First used to reduce the defenses of the Belgian city of Liege were the 420mm (16.5-inch) "Big Bertha" railway guns. They were so named by the British for the daughter of Friedrich Krupp, whose legendary arms-making company manufactured the weapons. Used later against the French fortress city of Verdun, the Big Berthas fired shells weighing more than a ton. Because of their size, they were a cumbersome weapon, requiring a full day for assembly and a dozen railway cars for transport. In order to position them for firing, it was often necessary to build a dedicated section of railway line.

The ultimate German rail gun of World War I had been a 380mm (15-inch) weapon that was more accurate than the Big Berthas. Known to the Germans as the Kaiser Wilhelm Geschutz, these guns were better known as the "Paris Guns" because they were used to drop shells into the French capital during the spring and summer of 1918. Hidden in the forest of Crécy, these three guns were never located by the Allies while they were operational, and were successfully evacuated before the area was recaptured. They lobbed more than 300 shells, killing 256 people, but their success was more psychological than tactical.

## American Megaguns

Through most of World War II, the U.S. Army fielded both 75mm and 105mm guns in large numbers, but the largest artillery pieces in widespread use by the U.S. Army were the 155mm M1 "Long Toms." In addition to the towed Long Tom, there was a 155mm M12 self-propelled gun that used an M4 tank chassis. The United States also fielded an 8-inch (203mm) gun in small numbers.

The largest operational fieldpiece deployed by the U.S. Army in World War II was the very heavy 240mm howitzer. Weighing a staggering 80 tons, these huge guns began reaching the front in significant numbers early in 1945.

By VE day, 15 of the 238 field artillery battalions in the European Theater were equipped with 240mm howitzers. In the Pacific, 5 out of 53 field artillery battalions had the gun by August 1945.

In the early 1950s, 20 of the 240mm guns were rebored to 280mm to become the T131 "Atomic Cannon." These weapons were intended to be used to fire a nuclear shell more than seven miles. The 280mm Atomic Cannon fired its first live nuclear weapon, known as Test Shot Grable, on May 25, 1953, in Nevada. Soon thereafter, the U.S. Army deployed its Atomic Cannons to Germany to face the Warsaw Pact. After a decade of remaining on alert in Europe, they were retired, and the last one was taken out of service in 1963.

## Anzio Annie and Her Sisters

Having built the definitive "big guns" of World War I, the German arms maker Krupp was called upon to create such weapons in anticipation of World War II. Perhaps the best known of Krupp's World War II big guns was the 280mm K5 (Kanone 5) cannons. In turn, the two most famous K5s were probably "Anzio Annie" and her sister, the "Anzio Express," who proved themselves an unwelcome surprise to Allied forces on the Anzio beachhead south of Rome early in 1944.

Known to the Germans as "Robert" and "Leopold," these two weapons were each supported by 24 railcar wheels and mounted on tracks that led in and out of mountain tunnels. When a gun was ready to fire, it was rolled out. When the firing was completed, the gun was returned to the safety of the tunnels and out of sight of aerial reconnaissance.

"Annie" was eventually captured and is now on display

at the U.S. Army Ordnance Museum at the Aberdeen Proving Ground in Maryland.

Krupp delivered the first K5 in 1936 and produced a modest 28 units through early 1945. Deeply rifled, with 12 quarter-inch grooves, the K5s fired a 565-pound shell nearly 40 miles. Rocket-assisted shells that were tested later in the war extended the range to more than 50 miles. The 120mm rocket-propelled Pfeilgeschoss (Arrow Shell) developed at Peenemünde gave it a range of almost 100 miles, but this ammunition was not widely used.

## The Channel Gun

A contemporary of the Krupp K5 was the Krupp K12, a 211mm railway gun designed during the late 1930s. Based on the 1918 Paris Gun, it fired a 237-pound projectile. The K12 was initially tested in 1937, and the first of two guns entered service in 1939. They were used operationally from the autumn of 1940 through the spring of 1941 to bombard southern England, especially in and around Dover, from locations in northern France.

The cumbersome, 300-ton weapons were obviously susceptible air attack, and were withdrawn. Though they had a theoretical range of more than 70 miles, they probably fell short of 60 miles, but that was more than adequate to throw a shell across the English Channel.

## World's Largest Mortars

Dwarfing nearly every mortar or field gun in use during World War II, Germany's 600mm Gerat 041 "Karl" mortars were the largest mobile mortars ever deployed. They were nicknamed for General Karl Becker, who conceived them as a "bunker-busting" weapon. Similar to the deep-penetration weapons in use today, the 2,776- to 3,476-pound shells were designed to penetrate 8 feet of reinforced concrete before exploding.

The Karls were mounted on a tanklike chassis and weighed over 120 tons. Though they were nominally self-propelled, they were carried on heavy transporter vehicles and used their own motive power mainly for final positioning before firing. The Rheinmetall firm built six Karls, and these were deployed together as a unit in June 1941 during Operation Barbarossa, the invasion of the Soviet Union. They were used as a siege weapon in a number of actions on the Eastern Front, including the attacks on Brzesc (Brest-Litovsk), Lvov, and Sevastopol.

Beginning in 1942, the Karls were retrofitted with longer range 540mm barrels. These could be interchanged with the 600mm barrels depending on the availability of ammunition.

In August 1944, as the Allies were in the process of liberating northern France, Adolf Hitler ordered that Paris be destroyed. He specifically insisted that a Karl mortar be sent to the French capital to hasten the annihilation of its world-famous monuments. Hitler loved Paris and had coveted it, but if he could not own it, he felt that no one should. He realized that a single barrage from a Karl could pulverize the City of Lights and render it virtually unrecognizable.

A Karl was sent. However, there were serious logistical problems inherent in moving such an incredibly huge and bulky object over heavily used rail lines that just happened to be under constant attack by the largest tactical air force the world would ever see. The big weapon finally reached northern France, but by that time, the German garrison in the city had surrendered and the Karl could not get within range.

At least two Karls survived the war. So, too, of course, did Paris and her monuments.

## World's Largest Cannons

According to both folklore and fact, Adolf Hitler had a fascination for very large guns. As such, he is known to have waxed rhapsodic about the monumental 800mm (31.5-inch) cannon that came to be known as "Schwere Gustav" (Heavy Gustav).

The project was initiated by Krupp in 1937, and was ordered by the German army with an eye toward operational availability by 1940. In preparation for attacking France's Maginot Line, Germany needed a gun capable of penetrating 3 feet of steel, 20 feet of concrete, or 100 feet of densely packed earth. The result was the gun that the *Guinness Book of World Records* confirms as the largest ever built.

Designed by Erich Müller and named for company president Gustav Krupp, the gun would have a 100-foot barrel that fired projectiles that would be the largest artillery shells ever manufactured. The high-explosive shells each weighed 10,580 pounds, while the concrete-penetration rounds each weighed 15,650 pounds. Mounted on what amounted to a pair of 20-wheel reinforced railcars, the entire gun unit weighed nearly 3 million pounds!

In 1940, when the German armies invaded France, the Maginot Line was bypassed, not bombarded, and there was no need for Gustav. This was probably just as well, because the gun was not completed until 1941, and the entire unit was not ready until 1942.

After tests on the Baltic coast near Rügenwald, the behemoth was deployed to the Eastern Front, where it was used in reducing the Soviet fortress city of Sevastopol.

During the siege, the gun successful pulverized every target assigned to it. Although it could fire just 14 shots a day because of the complicated reloading procedure, 2 or 3 were sufficient for most targets. The concrete-piercing projectiles ultimately proved capable of penetrating 264 feet of reinforced concrete.

After firing four dozen rounds into Sevastopol, Gustav was returned to Germany for refurbishment, and it was later redeployed to Leningrad. Meanwhile, a second, identical gun was built, this one being dubbed Dora, after Dora Müller, wife of the designer. Dora is believed to have also been used at Sevastopol and possibly during the 1944 Warsaw Revolt. Work on a third gun was reportedly begun but never completed.

The big guns had a range of about 30 miles, but use of the Pfeilgeschoss (Arrow Shell) would have theoretically extended the reach to about 120 miles. However, such a shell was almost certainly never fired by either Gustav or Dora.

Because of the complexities associated with moving and using them, the 800mm guns saw very little combat. They were so heavy that they required two sets of railway track and the efforts of 1,500 men to lay a special roadbed for the rails. The gun crew alone numbered about 500 men.

By war's end, both guns had been disassembled and parts of them were recovered by the Allies.

## Pfeilgeschoss (Arrow Shell)

The German army's aerodynamic research laboratories at Peenemünde are best known for the development of guided missiles, especially the A4 (V-2). However, because Peenemünde had what was possibly the best wind tunnel in the world, the German army also did other ordnance work here. Most important of these activities were those related to the remarkable Pfeilgeschoss (Arrow Shell).

The Arrow Shell program began in 1940, envisioned as a rocket-propelled projectile designed to be fired from special smoothbore versions of standard German-army artillery pieces. The original Arrow Shell was designed to be fired from a version of the famed 280mm K5 railway gun that would be bored out to 310mm.

The first Arrow Shells were dartlike projectiles, 75.2 inches long and 120mm in diameter, with four fins (310mm across) at the tail and a 310mm sabot or discarding ring around the middle of the shell at its center of gravity. This ring would fall away outside the gun muzzle when fired. In turn, the accelerating shell would reach a velocity of 5,000 feet per second and obtain a maximum range of nearly 100 miles.

Probably no more than two K5s were converted to accept the Arrow Shells, and these did not become operational until 1944. One of these guns was used operationally against the U.S. Third Army during the Battle of the Bulge, firing from a distance of 78 miles.

There was also an antiaircraft version of the Arrow Shell that was designed for the 105mm antiaircraft gun. It could reach extremely high velocity so as to shorten flying time and eliminate aiming errors. The gunners were able to aim, fire, and hit without having to worry about the speed of the aircraft and the altitude. During tests, these shells demonstrated a muzzle velocity of 3,500 feet per second. However, these amazing weapons were never placed into production. By the time the antiaircraft Arrow Shells were tested, German industrial capacity was collapsing under the weight of the same bombing raids against which Arrow Shells might have defended.

## V-3 (Vergeltungswaffe 3) Hochdruckpumpe

The lesser-known third of Hitler's vengeance weapon series, the V-3 Hochdruckpumpe (High-Pressure Pump) was actually a massive multichambered 150mm gun, 490 feet long, with a range of more than 100 miles. Located at Miedzyzdroje in Poland and at Mimoyecques near the French city of Calais on the English Channel, the V-3s were was intended to lob 300-pound shells for up to 100 miles. The V-3 in France would have been capable of striking London, 95 miles away.

The Hochdruckpumpe had a conventional breech at the rear and six auxiliary chambers just in front of the breech that fired fin-stabilized shells at a muzzle velocity of some 5,000 feet per second.

The idea behind the Hochdruckpumpe was to increase acceleration of a projectile in the gun barrel by reducing or eliminating the effect of the compression of air that naturally occurs ahead of the projectile. This was done by creating a near vacuum within the barrel and constructing six angled lateral chambers containing electrically detonated explosive charges behind the moving projectile.

The U.S. Army had unsuccessfully tested the concept during the nineteenth century, and rocket pioneers Willy Ley, Hermann Oberth, Max Valier, and Baron Guido von Pirquet retried it in the 1920s. These German and Austrian scientists had initially imagined using a Hochdruckpumpe as a means of firing a projectile to the moon.

The firm of Saar Roechling developed the idea of the electrically operated side chambers early in World War II, and a 20mm scale model was successfully test-fired at Miedzyzdroje during the spring of 1943. The Oberkommando Wehrmacht (German High Command) apparently was not enamored with the weapon, but when Adolf Hitler and Armaments Minister Albert Speer became aware of it, they were extremely enthusiastic. Hitler dubbed it "Vergeltungswaffe 3" and ordered 50 of them built in France.

Under Operation Wiese, a five-gun V-3 emplacement was to be installed at Mimoyecques, France, with a second one planned for nearby Piheu-les-Guines, which was never built. Excavation work began at Mimoyecques in September 1943 under the management of the Todt Organization, which was then in charge of the construction of the Atlantic Wall. Many of the workers were imported from the concentration camps in Eastern Europe, but also included were German coal-mining crews who were experienced in digging deep shafts.

Work continued throughout the winter on a series of tunnels, rooms, and ammunition dumps connected by a subterranean railway. A dedicated electrical-generation plant was also built to provide the power to fire the auxiliary chambers.

The guns were to be installed in a subterranean bunker in a hillside and positioned at a fixed upward angle of 50 degrees. The six lateral tubes on each barrel were, themselves, angled at 45 degrees. These were spaced at 11.9-foot increments along the barrel in such a way that there would be relatively easy maintenance assess. The V-3 installation would then be protected by concrete on all sides, including 18 feet above.

Allied aerial reconnaissance in September and October 1943 identified the site as a potential target. This led to USAAF Ninth Air Force bombing raids in November, but work continued underground.

Live firings of a full-scale, 150mm V-3 at Miedzyzdroje are believed to have begun early in 1944, but these tests were unable to do much better than a range of about 50 miles—about half of what was expected. The firms of Krupp and Skoda were both called upon to design and build better projectiles for the experimental weapon, and this took time. Among the other problems were that the auxiliary chambers had a tendency to fail under the pressure of three or four firings. Repairing or replacing these took yet more time. In May 1944, however, the V-3 program was set back by the destruction of one of the guns when it apparently blew up during firing.

Meanwhile, the hundreds of workers at the Mimoyecques site attracted the attention of the French Resistance. They passed the information to the Allies in Britain, where intelligence analysts correctly deduced that the site was still active and that it housed a major weapons system.

Allied bombers attacked both sites during the spring of 1944, but the damage to the underground facilities was minimal. The turning point came on July 6, 1944, when the Royal Air Force Number 617 "Dam Busters" squadron attacked at Miedzyzdroje with their six-ton Tallboy penetrator bombs. One Tallboy seems to have scored a nearly impossible direct hit, dropping straight through an open gun barrel shaft, while others falling close by created devastating concussions. Damage was so extensive that the facility was deemed not worth repairing.

Also during the summer of 1944, the Allies stepped up air attacks against German offensive sites in northern France, including V-1 launch facilities as well as the V-3 site at Mimoyecques. These raids involved the U.S. Navy as well as the USAAF, under Project Aphrodite and Operation Anvil (see Chapter 8). When Lieutenant Joseph P. Kennedy Jr., the elder brother of the future president, was killed on August 12, 1944, he was bound for an attack on Mimoyecques.

One month later, when the Germans abandoned the facility, it was nearly completed, but the Hochdruckpumpe guns had not yet been installed. British engineers systematically dynamited the Mimoyecques facility on May 9, 1945, two days after the end of the war in Europe. Despite this, the massive concrete bunker complex was impossible to destroy. It is still visible and can be visited.

The retreating Germans used Hochdruckpumpe technology—and possibly components of the actual V-3 guns originally earmarked for installation at Mimoyecques—to construct two such weapons in or near Luxembourg. It is believed that these may have been used during Operation Wacht am Rhein, the Ardennes offensive in December 1944 that resulted in the Battle of the Bulge.

# 13

## Strange Artillery

As impressive as they remain today, and as impressive as they were when they were first unveiled, the German missiles and big guns seem ordinary in comparison with some of the other strange secret weapons that the Wehrmacht had under development during World War II.

These little-known but technologically imaginative inventions are rarely discussed in the annals of more conventional weapons systems. As unusual as it may seem today, the Germans envisioned using air, sound, and electricity as offensive or defensive weapons. There was even a bizarre "Sun Gun," discovered by American troops, that appears to have been a prototype of a weapon that was to reflect and focus solar energy into a beam that could be used to down Allied aircraft. A similar principle would later be employed in the generation of solar electricity.

## Compressed Air Weapons

The Germans pursued the use of compressed air as a point-defense weapon against low-flying enemy aircraft during World War II in a number of interesting projects. One cannon designed to fire a stream of compressed air was actually built.

In this weird weapon, an explosion of a critical mixture of molecular hydrogen and oxygen fired a burst of compressed air and water vapor through an angled barrel. Tests showed that such a vaporous "projectile" could inflict damage to fixed targets, but tests done on moving targets, such as low-flying airplanes, are unknown. At least one such cannon was installed as an air defense measure at a bridge, but it was apparently never used.

The vortex gun, or *Turbulenzgewehr,* was a strange German compressed air weapon that was designed to knock aircraft out of the sky by creating an artificial tornado. It consisted of a large mortar barrel that was partially buried in the ground. It fired a slow-burning explosive projectile that, in tests, created a forward-moving explosion; this led to the formation of strong turbulence. The range and effectiveness of the gun was limited because the "hurricane" dissipated quickly and before it could move far enough to strike a high-flying airplane.

## Electromagnetic Guns

Once a popular ploy in science fiction, the use of electromagnetically propelled projectiles was the subject of experiments conducted by the Germans during World War II. The Siemens company examined a solenoid-type gun. In order to ensure an adequate supply of electricity—50,000 tons of coal per month would be needed to generate the power—it was built into a hillside near the Lille coalfields in France. The Siemens gun was designed to attack London from a range of 155 miles with 450-pound shells. In 1943, Albert Speer, the Reichsminister for armaments, canceled this project when it was deemed impractical.

A year later, the Gesellschaft für Geratbau proposed a multibarreled, 20mm antiaircraft gun with a linear electric motor that could fire 6,000 rounds per minute. Tests confirmed a muzzle velocity of 2,000 meters per second. However, the amount of electricity required was immense, and attempts to develop a new condenser to rectify the situation were never successful.

The prototype weapon was captured in Bavaria by American forces. Postwar studies showed that the gun, while theoretically functional, was impossibly expensive to operate because of power requirements.


## High-Decibel Sound

Ever since Joshua brought down the walls of Jericho, the idea of sound waves as an offensive weapon has been on the backlist of the unusual methods of warfare. During World War II, the Germans actually created a device to exploit this principle.

Designed by Dr. Richard Wallauschek, the Stichhaltiger Cannon (Sound Cannon) consisted of large paraboloid reflectors connected to a chamber composed of several sub-units firing tubes that fed a mixture of methane and oxygen into the combustion chamber. Here, the two gases were ignited in a cyclical, continuous explosion. The length of the firing chamber itself was exactly a quarter of the wavelength of the sound waves produced by the ongoing explosions. Each explosion initiated the next by producing a reflected, high-intensity shock wave, and so creating a very high-amplitude sound beam.

The noise, a single continuous note, was so great, and of such an intensity of pressure, that humans would be killed at a distance of 150 feet and incapacitated for up to a quarter of a mile. Laboratory tests using animals demonstrated that the concept worked, and at least one such weapon was built. It was captured by American forces.

In 2001, this writer proposed that such a weapon might be useful in attacking and destroying al-Qaida terrorists hiding in caves in Afghanistan. Whereas high-decibel sound waves eventually dissipate in an open battlefield environment, they would be focused and even amplified (by echo effect) if directed into a cave. Unlike high explosives, which would potentially destroy evidence, sound waves would do little, if any, material damage. Because verification of specific enemy killed was seen as an important aspect of the operation, this fact was important. Whereas explosives can be defended against within caves by means of baffles and blast doors, high-decibel sound would reach more deeply into the cave.

## Intense Cold

One of the strangest and most improbable secret weapons German scientists were rumored to have studied was a munition that, when exploded, produced intense cold rather than intense heat. Chemically, this is related to what is known as an endothermic reaction, such as photosynthesis, in which heat is converted to chemical energy. The opposite is an exothermic reaction, a chemical reaction that results in the release of heat.

This weapon is not to be confused with the well-known—but incredibly dangerous—physics experiment that shows how freezing water can be used to create a crude bomb. If water is sealed in a metal container and frozen, the ice will eventually reach critical pressure, at which point the metal container will fail catastrophically and explode. Of course anyone who has had water pipes that have frozen during cold winter months has experienced this phenomenon.

The idea that the Germans apparently had in mind was to explode their mystery munition and create sudden, intense, subfreezing temperatures. These conditions would theoretically extend to as much as a mile from ground zero and last long enough to kill every living thing in the blast zone—while leaving buildings and equipment intact. Such is the tactical theory of the postwar neutron bomb.

This secret project—if it was real—remained secret until some years after World War II. In the 1950s, there were reports that the Soviet Union was seriously evaluating the German data on the project.

# 14

## Supertanks

Used during World War I largely as a tactical experiment, tanks had become an essential part of modern armies by the late 1930s. Most military planners understood that they were useful, but most countries would not fully realize to what extent until World War II.

In Germany, tanks were taken very seriously. Their true potential in warfare was graphically illustrated by the German Blitzkrieg attacks on Poland in 1939 and against Western Europe in 1940. Fast-moving, well-armed Panzerkampfwagen II and III tanks spearheaded the German armies and were the single-most-important surface weapon in the German conquest of nearly all of Western Europe. Not only were the Panzer IIs and IIIs fast, they were capable of operating on most kinds of terrain and they were impervious to gunfire from most infantry weapons.

However, the Blitzkriegs of 1939–1940 would teach different lessons to different parties. To nations such as the United States and the Soviet Union, the lesson involved the use of massed armor. The Germans, meanwhile, gravitated toward bigger and better tanks, and the adaptation of the legendary "German Eighty-Eight" 80mm cannon as a tank gun. In addition to tanks, the Germans also developed a variety of "self-propelled guns." Like tanks, self-propelled guns are mobile, tracked vehicles, but unlike tanks, their main gun is in a fixed, rather than a swiveling, turret. Many used the Eighty-Eight as main armament, but some used even larger weapons.

During World War II, the Soviets produced the durable yet powerful T-34 tanks in very large numbers, while across the Atlantic, American industry churned out tens of thousands of M4 Sherman tanks. If the Soviets and Americans had a secret weapon with regard to tanks, it was their ability to produce very large numbers of them very quickly.

On the other hand, the German armor of the latter part of the war was defined by smaller numbers of the remarkable Panzerkampfwagen IV Panther and Panzerkampfwagen V Tiger families of tanks. Both mounted 88mm guns and both, especially the Tiger, were superior to the T-34 or the Sherman in an even match. However, many factors, including constant pressure on German industry by Allied airpower, meant that neither the Panther nor the Tiger would be available in the numbers required to maintain the advantage in armor that Germany had enjoyed early in the war.

For the Americans, the Panthers and Tigers could be defeated by Shermans through the latter's maneuverability and large numbers. The United States had a heavy tank in the pipeline, but it would not be until the final months of the war in Europe that a few of the bigger M26 Pershings, with their 90mm gun, reached the battlefield.

## Lions and Tigers and Bears

The largest tanks fielded in significant numbers by the Axis during the war were the Panzerkampfwagen V Tigers, which were developed by the Henschel company and manufactured by both Henschel and Porsche. They weighed more than 50 tons, compared with 15 to 23 tons for Panzerkampfwagen III and 35 tons for the American Sherman. Tigers mounted the legendary 88mm gun, while the Panzer III carried a 37mm or 50mm gun and the first generation of Shermans were armed with a 75mm gun. With the 88 and 4 inches of forward steel armor plate, the Tiger was a formidable vehicle. First introduced on the Eastern Front in the autumn of 1942, the Tigers played an important role in that theater as well as on the Western Front. However, there were fewer than 2,000 Tigers built, compared with 6,000 Panthers, 35,000 T-34s, and 50,000 Shermans.

A rival design to the Tiger, also with an 88mm gun, was a 68-ton monster designed by Dr. Ferdinand Porsche, who would turn to his famous line of smart little sports cars after the war. Like Adolf Hitler, Porsche was an advocate of very large tanks. However, when Hitler and his staff evaluated the two tanks side by side in August 1942, the Tiger was selected for mass-production over the competing Porsche machine, which was then known as the "Ferdinand," after its creator.

Hitler was unwilling to walk away from the Porsche tank entirely, and he ordered that a few of them be produced for use on the Eastern Front. Nearly 100, now officially named "Elefant," were delivered in 1943 as self-propelled guns. They had forward armor that was eight inches thick and were built using a Tiger chassis.

Despite its weight and complexity, the Tiger was an extraordinary weapons system, and its successes led German military planners to think even bigger. First was the 75-ton

Tiger II, or King Tiger, which made its operational debut late in 1944, and of which nearly 1,000 were built.

A parallel development was the 80-ton "Jagdtiger" (Hunting Tiger) version of the Tiger II, which carried a 128mm antitank gun in a fixed turret. These huge vehicles were first used during the Battle of the Bulge and later during the defense of the Reich. Apparently, only 77 were built, too few to make a difference.

The Tiger family were the largest operational tanks widely used in World War II, but the Germans had even larger tanks on the drawing boards, and a few would make it into action. These projects were true "secret weapons."

In November 1941, Krupp began work on a tank that was ultimately intended to succeed the Tiger—which had been designed by the rival Porsche firm. In keeping with the German practice of naming tanks after large felines, it was to be called Löwe (Lion), the king of beasts.

The Panzer VII studies were based on predictions that the Soviet Union was developing super-heavy tanks and a weapon larger than a Tiger was needed to counter them. In fact, the heaviest Soviet tanks to serve in the war would be the 50-ton Josef Stalin family of tanks. The first of these tanks, the IS-1, carried an 85mm cannon, although the later variants designated as IS-2 and IS-3 mounted 122mm guns.

Two Panzer VIIs were designed. The "Light" Lion (Leichte Löwe) weighed 76 tons and had 5.5-inch front armor. Armament under consideration included both 88mm and 105mm guns. The Heavy Lion (Schwere Löwe) weighed 90 tons and carried a 150mm cannon, although a 105mm weapon was also considered. Power was to be supplied by a 1,000 hp Daimler Benz engine adapted from that used by the fast navy patrol boats known as Schnellboots.

Original plans called for both types of Lion to be produced, but Adolf Hitler intervened. Owing to his love of the large, the Leichte Löwe was canceled in March 1942, and work proceeded on the Schwere Löwe only. By the end of the year, however, the entire project was terminated in favor of the even larger Maus (see below). The Löwe and the Maus would be just two stops on Hitler's quest for an "indestructible" tank.

At the same time that the Lion was under development, the Oberkommando Wehrmacht (German High Command) was also planning for a pair of bears—the Bär (Bear) and the Brummbär (Grizzly Bear).

The Bär was to have been a 120-ton self-propelled gun mounting a 305mm mortar capable of throwing a 770-pound shell 6.5 miles. The project was initiated by Krupp in March 1943, with the suggestion that a Tiger-tank chassis could be used as the basis for the vehicle. However, the Bär was never actually produced.

## Grizzly Bear

The Sturmpanzer IV Brummbär (Grizzly Bear) was a large self-propelled vehicle based on the chassis of the 25-ton Panzer IV medium tank. The idea behind it was the need for a 150mm gun platform as an infantry support weapon. Though smaller than the Bär, the Brummbär actually saw service.

The idea for the weapon originated in the summer of 1941, but it was nearly two years before the first operational Brummbärs entered service with the 216th Sturmpanzer Division.

The first of the initial production series of 60 Brummbärs had their baptism of fire at the Battle of Kursk—the largest tank battle in history—in July 1943. They were also used in combat near Kharkov later in the year.

Operationally, the Brummbär proved clumsy and top-heavy. The light chassis mounting the extremely heavy gun with a withering recoil made it unstable. Late in 1943, a redesigned version with a lower, lighter 150mm gun was introduced. A total of 80 examples of this second series was delivered. A further redesigned Brummbär made its debut in 1944, and production continued through March 1945. Approximately 300 Brummbärs of all types were delivered.

Brummbärs eventually equipped four Sturmpanzer Divisions and served in Italy and Western Europe as well as on the Eastern Front. In February 1944, the 216th Sturmpanzer Division was transferred from Russia to Italy, to defend against Allied forces coming ashore at Anzio and Nettuno, and remained there until the war ended. The 217th Sturmpanzer Division took part in the Battle of Normandy during July 1944 and in the Battle of the Bulge in December 1944.

Units of the 218th Sturmpanzer Division were used in the massacre of the Warsaw Uprising of 1944, as well as in the defense of the Reich. The 219th Sturmpanzer Division saw action in Hungary and Czechoslovakia until April 1945, when its last Brummbär was knocked out of action.

## Maus

Despite its name, the Maus (Mouse) was a 188-ton supertank mounting a 128mm gun. It was the largest tank ever to see combat, with an armored skin that averaged more than seven inches in thickness. Designed by Dr. Ferdinand Porsche, the Maus was on the opposite end of the size spectrum from his sports cars. It would have dwarfed any other vehicle on the battlefield. Since it was too heavy to use on most bridges, it was designed to ford rivers underwater using an electric drive.

The idea for this huge tank surfaced in June 1942, after the German armies had been fighting on the Eastern Front for a year. Originally known as the "Mammut" (Mammoth), the project soon took on the amusing unofficial nickname "Mauschen" (Little Mouse) and later became known as Maus. It superseded the Löwe project (see above) by the end of the 1942, but it would be August 1943 before metal was cut for a Maus prototype.

The first Maus chassis was completed in December 1943 and delivered to Böblingen for tests the following month. In the meantime, there had been an ongoing debate over which gun to mount in the turret. Porsche had designed the Maus for a 150mm gun *and* a 105mm gun, but various other weapons were considered. These included a 127mm naval gun and various 128mm cannons. In January 1943, it was decided to equip the Maus with turret-mounted 128mm and 75mm guns. Plans remained alive, however, for future variants with 150mm—and even 170mm—guns.

A further variant of the Maus that was considered during the last year of the war was the E.100 Flakzwilling. (The *E* stood for "Entwurf," meaning "design" or "rough draft," and the name impled a twin-barreled antiaircraft weapon.) Indeed, the Flakzwilling vehicle would have used a Maus chassis to mount a turret equipped with a pair of 88mm antiaircraft guns.

By March 1944, a second chassis had been delivered and Porsche had two more in the pipeline. Because of the problems inherent in so large a vehicle, however, it would be June 1944 before the first turret was mounted. Apparently, this was the only operational turret ever to equip a Maus. The first prototype was fitted only with a mock-up, and no further chassis were completed.

Meanwhile, the immense size of the tank necessitated the building of auxiliary equipment. This included underwater apparatus as well as a special heavy-duty railcar to transport the "Mice." Indeed, no other available vehicle was capable of pulling or carrying a Maus.

In October 1944, the German army began testing the second Maus prototype near Berlin at the Kummersdorf proving ground. In April 1945, as Soviet forces approached Berlin, the massive prototype—and possibly its sister ship as well—was still located at the facility. As legend has it, the massive machine actually engaged the Soviet tanks. In any case, it was not destroyed, although this fact remained a Soviet military secret for nearly half a century.

For decades, the Maus remained an enigma, known more from rumor than from hard evidence. American forces captured some Maus components at the Krupp factory, but it was widely believed that no complete Maus survived World War II.

Soviet forces, however, did, in fact, capture the completed Maus, and it was secretly transported to Kubinka, near Moscow, for evaluation. Here it remained, unknown to the outside world, until the 1990s. It is now on public display.

## Ratte

The Krupp Projekt 1000 (P.1000) Ratte (Rat) involved far more than building an enlarged variation on the Maus—which, of course, was being developed by Krupp's rival, Porsche. The name Ratte, which Krupp adopted toward the end of 1942, had actually been used informally to refer to Porsche's Maus project. The idea behind the Ratte seems to have been to outdo Porsche in a field of weaponry that thrilled Adolf Hitler. The Führer would not have been disappointed.

The Ratte was to have been an enormous vehicle. Its chassis would have been 114 feet long, compared with 30 feet for the Maus and 20 feet for the Tiger. It would have been 46 feet wide, wider than a four-lane highway. However, it would have been able to operate on a highway. Its weight, more than 1,000 tons, would have pulverized any paved road. In fact, its two guns *each* weighed almost as much as an entire Tiger tank.

These two guns were intended to be a pair of 280mm naval cannons in a turret modeled after the turret of a Graf Spee–class battleship. The shells would have been more than four feet long, and the armor would have varied between eight and ten inches. The Ratte was meant to be a true land battleship.

The huge tank would have been powered by eight Daimler marine engines delivering 16,000 hp. Even with this power, the Ratte would have been ponderously slow. While a specially designed railcar was necessary to transport the Maus, the Ratte could not have been carried by any other vehicle unless it had been partially disassembled.

Because of the vehicle's weight, the crew would have had to choose their route carefully. Highways, sand, and marshland were ruled out. However, if such a tank got to within 25 miles of the front, it would have been a fearsome weapon and virtually impervious to fire from any other tank.

No Ratte was ever built, and it is not known whether any actual hardware was ever manufactured.

## World's Largest Tank

Just as the Ratte dwarfed the Maus, the Ratte was dwarfed by the machine that Germany's armaments minister, Albert Speer, referred to simply as a "monster." Krupp's Projekt P.1500 was a self-propelled gun that was the largest armored land vehicle ever seriously considered.

The idea was to utilize the 800mm "Schwere Gustav" (Heavy Gustav) railway gun in a tracked vehicle. The power would be provided by four U-boat-sized diesel engines. It would have weighed approximately twice as much as the Ratte, or more than 4 million pounds. As such, it would have probably been the slowest self-propelled weapon on any battlefield.

The P.1500 was never actually built, and, as with the Ratte project, its deployment would have presented a number of interesting problems. First of all was the need for sufficient surface area on the vehicle's tracks to support its vast weight. Next, of course, was the corollary problem of choosing a roadway that could support this weight. It would have been too heavy for soft earth and would have pulverized pavement.

There was also the issue of carrying a supply of 8-ton rounds of ammunition and loading the shells in the 200-ton gun. The crew would have to have been sizable, and there would have to have been armor protection for the internal scaffolding required for manipulating the rounds for loading. Finally, one can only imagine what was necessary to absorb the recoil of such a gun in a tracked vehicle.

For a man who was obsessed with very large weapons, the P.1500 probably afforded Adolf Hitler with some happy moments of perverse pleasure.

## 15

## Super-Submarines

In World War II, as in World War I, the Germany navy
started out with a small, but technologically advanced, surface fleet that sat idle and unused during the second half of
the conflict. Meanwhile, the German submarine fleet in
both wars proved to be one of the most effective weapons
deployed by any of the German armed services.

Known as U-boats (from the German *Unterseeboot,*
meaning "undersea boat"), German submarines were the
most successful of the war, claiming 14.4 million tons of
Allied shipping. By comparison, the second-place U.S.
Navy submarine fleet sank 5.3 million tons of mainly
Japanese vessels.

The Germans also suffered the most losses, with 821
U-boats sunk, compared with 52 submarines lost by the
U.S. Navy. Of the U.S. Navy submarine personnel who
went to sea, 22 percent never returned, the greatest loss
rate of any American service in World War II. The Germans, meanwhile, lost 63 percent. It was a nasty business,
but the German navy, the Kriegsmarine, was determined to

see German technology rule the undersea world of the Atlantic. For a time it did. This control of the seas waned by 1943, but had things gone differently with the rest of the war, the "secret weapons" taking shape in German shipyards in 1945 might have restored that primacy.

In World War II, Germany produced the most advanced submarines yet seen. As with many of Germany's World War II "wonder weapons," these super-secret, super-submarines reached service too late to show their full potential. However, as with German developments in jet aircraft technology, German submarines would influence the postwar evolution of submarine technology for several decades.

The Germans' Axis partner was also a major player in the submarine war. While the Imperial Japanese Navy undersea force took second place to that of the U.S. Navy in the Pacific Theater for most of the war, the Japanese are remembered for having built the largest submarines. Indeed, the I-400 class were more than submarines, they were submersible aircraft carriers!

## Type XI "U-Cruisers"

The inclination of the Kriegsmarine to treat the U-boat service as its favorite is illustrated by the its having considered creating submersible capital ships. With four 127mm guns in two armored turrets, these vessels could have functioned as a capital ship while on the surface. Meanwhile, six torpedo tubes would have made them deadly attack boats while submerged.

Like a surface cruiser, the Type XI U-Cruiser would also carry its eyes in the sky, an Arado Ar.231 reconnaissance floatplane that was stored in a watertight container while the ship was submerged. The ships were to have been 377 feet long and weigh nearly 7,000 tons. They were to have had a crew of about 110 men—double the complement of a typical U-boat.

Four Type XI ships were ordered in 1937 and 1938 and were assigned the hull numbers U-112 through U-115. Construction had begun in Bremen by early 1939, but the Kriegsmarine officially canceled the Type XI program before the outbreak of war in September.

For many years, it was understood that the partially completed Type XI ships were cut up for scrap. In 1988, however, stories began to circulate that a submarine that was attacked—and possibly sunk—off Cape Cod near Nantucket on August 25, 1944, was a Type XI ship. As the story went, it had been secretly completed and was being used for clandestine operations.

What sorts of operations are unknown. One scenario suggests that the secret vessel was intended to be used to evacuate Adolf Hitler from Germany if his life was in peril. Conversely, another scenario suggests that the last mission of the mystery ship had something to do with the conspiracy to overthrow Hitler.

The Nantucket sinking is believed to have been of the U-boat that is known to have departed from Gdansk (then Danzig) on July 20, 1944, the same day that the attempt to assassinate Hitler failed. This scenario supposes that the Type XI boat was carrying a secret negotiating team to the United States for the purpose of striking a deal on an armistice. It has also been suggested that the ship carried documents and valuables that certain people, perhaps German corporate leaders, wanted to remove from Germany for safekeeping.

A conspiracy theory circulating on the Internet at the turn of the century linked the mysterious purpose of the July–August 1944 U-boat mission to Princess (later Queen) Juliana of the Netherlands. She was vacationing on

Cape Cod at the time of the July 20 coup attempt and left for Canada on August 26. The Dutch royal family was in exile in Canada during World War II and made occasional visits to the United States. Meanwhile, Juliana's German-born husband, Prince Bernhard, was believed to have had ties to German industrial entities and to the German government itself.

In 1993, Edward Michaud, the skipper of a vessel participating in the Massachusetts Water Resources Authority, became interested in the mystery of the sunken U-boat. Using sonar, he located the sunken vessel and undertook a detailed survey of the site. His work confirmed the size and shape of the vessel as consistent with the dimensions of a Type XI ship.


## Hellmuth Walter

No mention of the success of German submarine technology is complete without mention of marine engineer Hellmuth Walter. Submarines, like surface ships, use diesel engines while under way on the surface. Because combustion engines require air for combustion, they can't be used underwater, so a submarine must switch to electricity when submerged. Batteries eventually run down and must be recharged. To do this, a submarine must go back to the surface and remain there for hours. In essence, the submarine must maintain two completely different types of engines.

In the 1950s, nuclear reactors would be adapted for submarine propulsion, but such technology was unimaginable when Walter began his theoretical work in the 1930s.

Walter was employed at the Germaniawerft shipyard in Kiel when he conceived the idea for a closed-circuit propulsion system that used hydrogen peroxide and oil to fuel engines that promised to be lighter and more compact than the combination of two engine types. When he proposed his plan to the Kriegsmarine in 1934, it was promptly rejected as preposterous, but he was persistent. Three years later, he made another pitch, this time to Captain Karl Doenitz, a rising star in the U-boat community who would go on to command the entire U-boat fleet during World War II. Doenitz realized that Walter was onto something, and he finally convinced the high command at the Kriegsmarine to give Walter a try.

In 1939, construction of a U-boat fueled by Perhydrol (a stabilized form of hydrogen peroxide) was authorized. Under a blanket of secrecy, Germaniawerft constructed the V80 experimental submarine in Kiel, and it was launched in April 1940. The results were astonishing. The V80 proved to be the fastest submarine in the world, reaching speeds in excess of 23 knots while submerged. At that time, 10 knots was considered satisfactory.

Despite the promise of the Walter technology, the construction of the first four "Walter boats" was not authorized until January 1942. It would seem that a crash program to develop this new secret weapon was warranted, but the Kriegsmarine balked, fearing that the technology might not work in a large, operational submarine. Seven Type XVII Walter U-boats were built, but a pair of very large Type XVIII boats were ordered, then canceled (see below).

The war ended before any of the Walter boats saw combat, and all the boats that had been completed were scuttled. The concept would probably have matured within two years. Had the Kriegsmarine embraced the Walter idea in 1934, or even as late as 1939, the story of the Battle of the Atlantic would have been different.

## Type XVII

These were the initial class of operational Walter boats based on the engine design of Hellmuth Walter (see above) that used Perhydrol to achieve high speed and a range of 2,500 miles on the surface or 500 miles submerged. Ordered in January 1942, the Type XVIIA included four 128-foot vessels with a displacement of 250 tons. Germaniawerft built U-792 and U-793 in Kiel, while Blohm und Voss built U-794 and U-795 in Hamburg. The even-numbered vessels were commissioned in November 1943, the others in April 1944. In test runs, they reached an amazing 25 knots while submerged. They also demonstrated a range that was in excess of that achieved by diesel and electric U-boats. However, they were not used operationally.

Meanwhile, three 136-foot, 310-ton XVIIB Walter boats were constructed. Given the hull numbers U-1405 through U-1407, they were all the work of Blohm und Voss and were commissioned in December 1944, February 1945, and March 1945. Like the XVIIA boats, they never saw action.

In order to keep them out of enemy hands, all seven were scuttled at the time of Germany's surrender. However, the Allies took an interest in the heretofore secret Walter engines, and two were raised. U-1406 was taken to the United States for evaluation, and U-1407 was operated by the Royal Navy as HMS *Meteorite* through 1949.

## Type XVIII

This class was to have been the oceangoing operational attack U-boats based on Hellmuth Walter's Perhydrol engine. Walter himself proposed the 235-foot, 1,480-ton

Type XVIII, and construction of two was authorized in January 1943. These boats, U-796 and U-797, were laid down at Deutsche Werke in Kiel, but canceled in March 1944 before they were completed.

A further Walter boat that was ordered but not produced was the Type XXVI. It was an oceangoing vessel with 10 torpedo tubes arranged in the "Schnee Organ" configuration—four in the bow and six aft. Blohm und Voss was ordered to build 100 (U-4501 through U-4600) at Hamburg, but only the first four were laid down before the war ended.

## Schwertwal

A little-known Walter-engined miniature submarine, the SW-1 Schwertwal (Grampus) was perhaps the fastest Perhydrol-powered underwater craft ever built. Capable of 30 knots submerged, it was built as a one-of-a-kind prototype that apparently did not lead to a production series. It was scuttled at the end of the war, but raised by British marine engineers during the summer of 1945. It was subsequently broken up.

## Type XXI

The Type XXI U-boats represented the ultimate oceangoing undersea weapon of World War II, but like many of Germany's last-minute wonder weapons, they were too late. Unlike the Walter boats, they were produced quickly and in significant numbers, but they did not enter the Kriegsmarine fleet until the war was practically over.

A key design element that made for their potential effectiveness was their submerged range of 325 miles, which would have allowed them to evade Allied shore-based patrol aircraft. They were big, 252 feet long overall, and they were fast, making 17 knots submerged and nearly 16 knots on the surface.

A hydraulic torpedo reload system permitted reloading of all six tubes in under 10 minutes. This was less time than it took to load a single tube in an earlier U-boat such as the Type VII.

As many as a thousand Type XXI boats were to be built, but only 118 were commissioned. Of these, 41 were built in Bremen by Weser and 30 by Schichau in Danzig (now Gdansk). The rest were built in Hamburg by Blohm und Voss.

The first one, U-2501, was laid down in April 1945 and launched just two months later. By the end of August, six Type XVIII boats had been launched. The last two Weser-built boats were U-3529 and U-3530, both of which were laid down in November 1944 and launched in late March 1945. The last three laid down were the Schichau boats U-3040, U-3041, and U-3044. Laid down in December 1944, they were also launched in March 1945.

While virtually the entire Type XXI fleet went to sea for crew training duty, it is believed that only U-2511 undertook a combat patrol, and this did not occur until March 1945. The Type XXI embodied a great deal of unrealized potential, but ironically, it became an important operational type only after the war. The Soviet Union used the boat as the basis for their famed "Whiskey"-class boats, 235 of which became operational in the 1950s.

## Type XXIII

Smaller than the oceangoing Type XXI, the "coastal" Type XXIII was also part a new generation of long-range

U-boats that were faster submerged (12.5 knots) than on the surface (9.7 knots). They were 114 feet long, displaced 275 tons, and had a submerged range of 120 miles.

Though 61 boats were commissioned, only 6 served on actual combat patrols. Of the total, 48 were built by Deutsche Werft in Hamburg, and the remainder by Germaniawerft in Kiel. The first one was U-2321, launched on April 17, 1944, and the last was U-4712, launched a year and two days later. The Kriegsmarine had ambitious plans to manufacture as many as 500 Type XXIIIs at shipyards in France, Italy, and even Russia, but the occupied territories slipped away and the type was produced exclusively in Germany.

U-2324 made the first combat patrol by a Type XXIII boat, departing Germany on January 29, 1945, after spending the better part of a year on training duty. Between January and May, four of the six operational Type XXIIIs sank or damaged five ships, totaling 14,601 tons. These included the last two ships sunk by the Kriegsmarine in the war—a pair of British freighters sunk by U-2336 inside Scotland's Firth of Forth on May 7, the day that the war ended.

Of the 20 Type XXIIIs that surrendered to the Allies, most were scuttled at sea under Operation Deadlight. However, the British Royal Navy operated U-2326 and U-2353 as N35 and N37, and U-4706 became the Norwegian submarine *Knerten*.

## Type XXVII Seehund

The ultimate German miniature submarine of World War II was the Type XXVII, also known as the Seehund (Seal). The Kriegsmarine imagined a fleet of more than a thousand Seals but built just 285 and commissioned only 138.

Designated with hull numbers between U-5001 and U-5269, they were delivered between September 1944 and April 1945. Production peaked with the 70 delivered in December 1944.

The Seals had a crew of 2, displaced 17 tons, and carried 2 externally mounted torpedoes. They had a range of 300 miles at 7 knots surfaced and 63 miles at 3 knots submerged. Between January and April 1945, the Seal fleet made 142 patrols, sinking or damaging 11 ships, totaling 18,384 tons.

## Seeteufel

Probably the strangest miniature submarine built in Germany during World War II was the Seeteufel (Sea Devil), which was equipped with the chassis of a tank. This would theoretically allow it to crawl across the bottom of a lake or harbor at depths of up to 70 feet. It was 47 feet long, displaced 35 tons, and carried a crew of 2. Work on this project began at Lübeck in March 1944, but apparently only the prototype was completed by the end of the war, and it was scrapped. Reportedly, the Soviet Union developed a similar craft after the war.

## Manned Torpedoes

Sometimes the simpler forms of technology are the most effective. The notion of using a person to direct a torpedo is an obvious—if dangerous—means of destroying enemy ships that could not easily be approached by a submarine.

Both Germany and Japan used manned torpedoes during World War II, but while Japan was straightforward about the torpedo's pilot being on a suicide mission, the

Germans designed their system so that the pilot could, theoretically, escape.

German manned torpedoes were actually pairs of torpedoes, with the pilot in one and the explosives in the other. The pilot would fire the ordnance and then try to escape. Apparently about half the time, pilots actually did get away. Nevertheless, manned torpedoes accounted for more shipping damage than Type XXI U-boats, mainly in and around invasion beaches.

The first major type of manned torpedo was the 2.75-ton Neger, of which approximately 200 were built, beginning in March 1944. The second was the 3-ton, 27-foot Marder, of which more than 500 were in service from July 1944 through the end of the war. Invented by Richard Mohr, the Neger had a range of 48 miles at 4 knots. The Marder had similar performance, but could also dive to depths of 100 feet. This gave it an advantage over the Neger, which lay vulnerable on the surface. Once a Neger was spotted, it was an easy target.

The Marder was expected to be succeeded by the Hai (Shark), a 36-foot torpedo with a range of 63 miles and an attack speed of 20 knots. However, because of control problems, the Hai did not develop beyond the prototype stage.

The Neger first saw action offshore from the Normandy beachhead in June and July 1944. A "school" of 24 Negers based near Honfleur successfully attacked the invasion fleet on July 5, sinking the minesweepers HMS *Magic* and HMS *Cato*. However, only 9 of the torpedoes escaped destruction. Two days later, 21 Negers attacked again, sinking the minesweeper HMS *Pleiades* and damaging the Polish cruiser *Dragon*. No Negers survived this assault.

Marders entered action against the Allied flotilla off the Normandy coast near Courseulles-sur-Mer on the night of August sinking a Liberty ship, a minesweeper, and the de-

stroyer HMS *Quorn*. However, 41 of the 58 attacking torpedoes were destroyed. The final Marder attack at Normandy came on the night of August 16, when 42 torpedoes
sank 3 ships, including an obsolete French battleship. Only
16 Marders escaped.

In September 1944, Marders based at Ventimiglia in
Italy were used unsuccessfully against Allied forces engaged in the invasion of southern France. A subsequent air
attack destroyed the Marder base, closing an interesting
and desperate chapter in the annals of seaborne attacks.

## Japanese Submersible Aircraft Carriers

The idea of carrying observation aircraft aboard subs was
not unusual during World War II, but the use of submarine-
carried aircraft as offensive weapons was. The Imperial
Japanese Navy planned extensively for such operations,
building nearly 40 such vessels in six classes, although
these were used quite sparingly.

The most dramatic of these operations came on the
morning of September 9, 1942, in first of the only two confirmed air attacks on the continental United States during
the war. The 2,500-ton submarine I-25 surfaced west of
Cape Blanco, near Port Orford, Oregon, and launched a
small, single engine Yokosuka E14Y1 floatplane piloted by
Chief Flying Officer Nobuo Fujita.

Fujita's mission was to start a forest fire in the densely
wooded Oregon Coast Range, and he did manage to drop
incendiary bombs on Mount Emily, about 10 miles northeast of Brookings. Unfortunately for Fujita, rains—for
which the Oregon coast is renown—had dampened the forest and no fire was started.

Fujita returned to the submarine without incident, but
shortly thereafter, the I-25 came under attack from USAAF

bombers. It managed to escape and to launch Fujita on a second attack on September 29. No damage was done in either air attack, but the I-25 did sink two tankers off the Oregon coast with torpedoes.

In 1942, the Imperial Japanese Navy began construction of the I-400–class Sen Toku submarines. With the exception of the German Kriegsmarine's Type XI U-Cruisers (which may or may not have been completed), the I-400 vessels were the largest submarines yet built. They were 60 percent larger than any American World War II submarine and larger than most postwar attack subs still in use in the twenty-first century. Today's ballistic missile subs are, of course, much larger.

The 5,200-ton I-400 vessels each carried *three* seaplanes that were designed to attack high-priority targets, including the Panama Canal and the West Coast of the United States. They were designed with immense fuel tanks that gave them a range of more than 37,000 miles, or roughly one and a half times around the world. There were 8 torpedo tubes, plus a 5.5-inch deck gun and numerous 25mm antiaircraft guns. The ship's complement was 145 crewmen, although 213 were found aboard when I-400 was captured in 1945.

Imperial Japanese Navy plans called for a dozen ships in the class. Though several had been laid down, only two were commissioned, the I-400 and I-401. The I-402 was completed, but converted into an submarine refueling vessel. The smaller I-12–class subs were designed to carry a pair of floatplanes.

In the I-400 and I-401, the three Aichi M6A1 Seiran (Storm in a Clear Sky) floatplanes were designed to be folded and packed into a 115-foot, barrel-shaped hanger located aft of the conning tower. These were compact, high-performance single-engine aircraft designed to carry torpedoes as their primary offensive armament. Theoretically, each Seiran could be unpacked and made flight ready in less than 10 minutes.

Late in 1944, I-400 and I-401, along with a pair of I-12–class boats, were organized into an offensive unit under the command of Captain Tatsunosuke Ariizumi. Among the operations considered were an attack on the Panama Canal and a series of biological warfare attacks against the population centers of the American West Coast. These, like similar biological attacks Japanese forces conducted against Chinese cities, would have involved the release of vermin infected with such agents as rabies, bubonic plague, cholera, and typhus, all of which had been isolated for weapons use by Japan's notorious Unit 731 (see Chapter 25).

The biological warfare attack on the United States, thought to have been code-named "Cherry Blossoms at Night," was reportedly canceled on March 26, 1945, by General Yoshijiro Umezu, the chief of the army general staff. He feared that such a scenario would have escalated into a retaliation from the United States that Japan could not have survived.

The attack on the Panama Canal was, however, authorized. In fact, a full-scale replica of the Gatun Lock complex was constructed at Toyama Bay for the pilots to practice on. On July 23, 1945, the I-14 (under Commander Tsuruzo Shimizu), the I-400 (under Commander Toshio Kusaka), and I-401 (under Commander Shinsei Nambu) departed from Japan. They were to take widely separated routes and rendezvous at sea three weeks later to coordinate their air attack.

Within those three weeks, while the huge subs were at sea, dramatic events were unfolding. After the two nuclear attacks in early August, Emperor Hirohito broadcast the order on August 15 for all Japanese forces to lay down their arms. The commanders of the subs considered continuing the mission, but finally obeyed the emperor's command. All the seaplanes and torpedoes were jettisoned, and all the documents relating to the Panama Canal mission were destroyed.

The vessels turned for home and were intercepted east of Honshu on August 28 by the U.S. Navy. In an interesting twist of history, I-14 was taken over by Commander John S. McCain Jr., the son of carrier task-force commander Vice Admiral John S. "Slew" McCain. The I-14's new commander was also the father of future naval aviator, Arizona senator, and 2000 presidential candidate John S. McCain III.

The I-400 and I-401 were sailed to Pearl Harbor under U.S. Navy crews for further evaluation and were ultimately sunk in deep water in 1946. U.S. Navy personnel charged with getting the ships ready for transfer from Japan noted sizable numbers of rats and insects aboard the vessels. These were exterminated, but it is not known whether the vermin were tested for biological agents.

## Kamikaze Torpedoes

Like the German Kriegsmarine, the Imperial Japanese Navy built and deployed manned torpedoes as offensive weapons. Unlike the Kriegsmarine torpedoes, which were designed to be aimed and abandoned, the Japanese designed their torpedoes so that the crewmen knew they'd be making one-way trips.

The Kaiten "Special Attack" weapons preceded the kamikaze suicide aircraft conceptually, although kamikaze aircraft were actually used in action first. The initial Kaiten proposals were drafted in 1943 and approved early in 1944 with provisions for the survival of the crewman, but after June 1944, they were designed as suicide weapons.

Based on the Type 93 naval torpedo, the Kaiten I contained a 39-inch forward section, which housed the 3,400-pound warhead as well as fuel and oxygen tanks. The pilot's niche was grafted onto the torpedo's center section. The overall length was just over 48 feet. Speed could be varied from 12 knots, giving a range of some 85,000 yards. At 30 knots, the range was about 25,000 yards. Larger Kaiten II and Kaiten IV torpedoes were 7 feet longer, and boasted higher performance and a larger warhead. They differed in that the Kaiten II used a hydrogen-peroxide oxidizer. A similar Kaiten III was electrically powered. Reportedly there were 300 Kaiten Is, 50 Kaiten IVs, and a handful of the other models.

The first U.S. Navy vessel known to have been sunk by a Kaiten was the fleet oiler USS *Mississinewa,* which was hit on November 20, 1944, at Ulithi in the Caroline Islands. The destroyer escort USS *Underhill,* sunk in July 1945, was another victim of an Imperial Japanese Navy suicide torpedo.

# 16

## Jet Fighters

World War II saw the introduction of the first jet aircraft used in wartime. Jet aircraft revolutionized aerial combat for one simple reason. They were more than 100 mph faster than the fastest piston-engine fighter aircraft, and as much as twice as fast as most bombers. In aerial combat, speed is the most important factor in both offensive and defensive actions, so jets were a secret weapon that changed the equation in nearly every encounter.

It is axiomatic to say that the German aviation industry during World War II was far ahead of its counterparts in the rest of the world. All the major German aircraft manufacturers had advanced jet airplanes on the drawing boards by 1944 and several were already in squadron service.

The turbojet engine was invented by Frank Whittle in Britain in 1928, but the first aircraft to fly purely under jet power was the German Heinkel He.178, which first flew in August 1939, powered by an HeS3B engine designed by Hans-Joachim Pabst von Ohain. The Reichsluftfahrt Ministerium (RLM, German Air Ministry) took an early interest in jet propulsion and financed the development of the Heinkel He.280 and the Messerschmitt Me.262 twin jet fighters even before practical jet engines existed to power them. The He.280 flew in April 1941, powered by two of Ohain's experimental turbojets, which were later replaced by a pair of Junkers Jumo 004 turbojets. The Me.262 made its first flight in July 1942, powered by a pair of BMW 003 turbojets. The He.280 never proceeded past the experimental stage, but the Me.262 as to have an interesting service career.

Both would merely be the beginning.

These well-known German aerospace achievements were, however, only part of the story. There is a more enigmatic side that includes the dozens of even *more advanced* aircraft that were still on the drawing boards or in the wind tunnels when the war ended in May 1945.

These more obscure, unproduced types are known through both captured blueprints and captured prototypes. In the following pages, we discuss a selected number of the more interesting and important of the myriad advanced jet aircraft that were designed in Germany through 1945. The focus of this and the following chapter is on Germany because that nation was ahead of all others in every phase of jet development. The Luftwaffe had them operational before anyone else, and the unproduced aircraft on German drawing boards represented a level of technology that was roughly a decade ahead of the aircraft taking shape elsewhere.

## Allied Jet Fighters

Outside Germany, operational jet aircraft were farther from a reality. Only Britain's Gloster Meteor had moved beyond the test stage by the end of 1944, although the

American Lockheed P-80 Shooting Star was being delivered to operational USAAF units early in 1945. Most of the Allied jet fighters that did exist before 1945 were hardly more than advanced test aircraft that were being used to evaluate engine technology. They were classified projects, but hardly secret weapons that would have impressed the Germans.

Though some work had been done, neither Japan nor the Soviet Union was close to developing an operational combat jet during the war. Indeed, most of the Japanese secret jet projects were based on German prototypes. The same can also be said of the jets that took shape in the Soviet Union immediately after the war.

In the United States and the United Kingdom, jet fighters were flying routinely in 1945, but had not yet entered air-to-air combat. Britain's Gloster Meteor made its debut in May 1941, but it took three years to work the bugs out and get the aircraft into service. The Meteor's only aerial combat action during the war came in 1944 when Meteor Mk.Is were used against German V-1s over Britain itself. By January 1945, Meteor Mk.IIIs had started to reach operational squadrons, but the Royal Air Force was reluctant to fly them over enemy territory for fear that they'd be captured.

The first American jet fighter, the Bell XP-59A Airacomet, first flew in October 1942, but it had limited performance and was used only as a test aircraft. The Lockheed P-80 Shooting Star, destined to be America's first operational jet fighter, made its first flight in June 1944. As we said, production deliveries began in April 1945, but only a handful reached Europe in a demonstration capacity. VE day intervened before either a Gloster Meteor or a P-80 had a chance to meet a Luftwaffe Me.262 in aerial combat.

Both the Meteor and the Shooting Star remained as the star players within their respective air forces in the years immediately after the war, but by the 1950s, new aircraft that owed a debt to captured German technology had rendered them obsolete.

## Messerschmitt Me.262

Though it is well known, well documented, and hardly a *secret* weapon, it is difficult to begin any survey of Luftwaffe jet fighters without mentioning the world's first operational example. The Me.262 was sluggish on takeoff and had a very limited range, but in aerial combat, where speed matters more than anything else, there was no comparison. It was arguably the best operational fighter of any kind in World War II.

It was an aircraft whose full potential and effectiveness was never realized, not because of opposition from enemy aircraft, but because of opposition and indecisiveness on the part of Germany's own leadership. In the final weeks of the war, Adolf Hitler is recorded to have babbled incessantly amount imaginary secret weapons, but few who heard him realized that, two years earlier, he had squandered and even sabotaged a powerful secret weapon that might have altered Germany's fate.

The slow development of the Me.262 in the year after its first flight in July 1942 was due in part to developmental problems with the engines—an annoyance that dogged the Allies as well. However, the Me.262 program was also crippled by a general ambivalence on the part of the Reichsluftfahrt Ministerium (RLM, German Air Ministry) in Berlin. The bureaucrats there saw it as a program to develop new technology that was of lower priority than the production of established aircraft.

As testing proceeded though 1942 and 1943, the immense potential of the jet fighter was becoming apparent to everyone involved in the secret program who had any understanding of fighter aircraft operations. Fighter pilots—including General Adolf Galland, inspector general for fighters for the Luftwaffe—were delighted with the Me.262's speed and performance. They wanted it in production—and in combat—as soon as possible. They realized what the bureaucrats did not: that Allied fighters were steadily improving, and that instead of continuing to catch up or stay even, the Luftwaffe should—and could—leap ahead technologically.

Men such as Galland also knew that Allied bombing was a growing threat to Germany and that jet interceptors could be far more effective than piston-engine interceptors.

When Hitler was briefed on the promise of the Me.262, he came to the opposite conclusion of nearly everyone else. He was obsessed with offensive weapons and saw no reason to use such a wonderful secret weapon as an interceptor when it could be put on the attack!

Amazingly, Hitler insisted that the Me.262 be completed as a fighter-bomber rather than as an interceptor or air superiority fighter. This meant that when the first production Me.262As were finally ready in April 1944, they were further delayed by their need to retrofit them with bomb racks. Hitler's obsession with offensive operations would critically delay one of the best defensive weapons then in development.

In October 1944, Me.262s began service as fighter-bombers being used against the Allies' bridgeheads. They were quite effective at this task because they were too fast to be targeted by Allied fighters or conventional antiaircraft guns.

By now, however, the Allied bomber offensive had multiplied in its intensity and the pendulum was swinging

against Germany. Having lost half a year during which the
Me.262 might have been decisive, the Luftwaffe finally received permission to use its jets to their best advantage.

Kommando Nowotny, the first fully operational Me.262
unit, was set up in September 1944 under leading Luftwaffe ace Major Walter Nowotny. Cleared to attack enemy
aircraft as well as enemy bridges, the jets finally began to
prove their worth. Kommando Nowotny claimed 22 kills
by the end of September, but many Me.262s were also lost
because their pilots were unfamiliar with the new technology and had had limited training time to learn about takeoffs and landings and other handling characteristics
peculiar to jets.

In air-to-air combat, though, the Me.262s were truly superior. They could not turn as tightly as a piston-engine
fighter, but they could maintain speed in a turn much better.

A full-fledged jet-fighter wing, Jagdgeschwader 7, was
set up near Berlin in November, and this unit was to
achieve an impressive record of 427 victories, 75 percent
of them being Allied heavy bombers. Through the winter, a
number of additional jet fighter units were established, and
the toll they took on Allied airmen was equally devastating.

The Me.262A had a wingspan of 40 feet 11.5 inches
and a length of 34 feet 9.5 inches. It weighed 14,101
pounds fully loaded and fueled. It was powered by two
Junkers Jumo 004B turbojet engines, each delivering 1,980
pounds of thrust, giving it a top speed in excess of the rated
maximum of 540 mph. The highest speed achieved by the
Me.262 was 624 mph, recorded in July 1944—significantly faster than any piston-engine fighter. It had a service
ceiling of 37,565 feet and a range of 652 miles. Its armament consisted of four nose-mounted 30mm cannons, and
interceptor versions carried eight R4M missiles.

The Me.262B was a two-seat night-fighter variant

equipped with Neptun V radar and its distinctive nose-mounted "deer-antlers" antennae.

In March 1945, General Galland set up the ultimate jet-fighter unit, Jagdverband 44, staffing it with a group of Luftwaffe aces that included 10 pilots who'd earned the Knight's Cross. They were flying the Me-262A-1a/U1 variant, which was especially well armed with six cannons, including two 20mm MG151s, two 30mm MK103s, and two 30mm MK108s—in addition to the rockets. Though JV 44 scored 50 victories in a month of operations, it was far too late for the Luftwaffe. With their airfields captured or destroyed, JV 44 resorted to flying from sections of four-lane highway near Munich, and they kept going until U.S. ground forces took them into custody less than a week before Germany capitulated.

The Allies thoroughly analyzed the Me.262, and innovations designed into it by Willy Messerschmitt's designers found their way into postwar American jets. For example, Boeing and North American Aviation, among others, had jet projects on the drawing boards in 1945 that were changed from straight- to swept-wing configuration largely because of what they learned from the world's first operational jet fighter. Curiously, in the Soviet Union in the late 1940s, the Sukhoi design bureau produced a series of straight-wing copies of the Me.262 under the Su-9 and Su-11 series of designations.

## Messerschmitt Me.328 Family

In early 1943, as the Me.262 was inching toward its initial operational capability, the Messerschmitt engineers and designers at Augsburg were at work on several other jet-fighter projects. One was Projekt 1079, which was aimed at developing a small, lightweight, and inexpensive—yet fast—point-defense aircraft. Messerschmitt undertook this project in cooperation with the German Glider Research Institute (Deutsche Forschungsinsitut für Segelflug, DFS), which handled jet- and rocket-powered projects as well as gliders. The idea was to design a small aircraft that could be ground-launched from a rail or air-launched from a larger aircraft such as a Dornier Do.217 or Heinkel He.177.

The result was the Me.328, which was 22 feet 5 inches long and had a wingspan of 28 feet. Powered by a pair of Argus pulsejets, it weighed under 10,000 pounds fully loaded. Armament would consist of a pair of 20mm cannons in the nose.

Initial airdrop tests of the DFS-built wooden-wing prototypes began late in 1943, and were followed by tests of pulsejet-powered aircraft early in 1944. Though problems with the use of a pulsejet engine in a manned aircraft would eventually lead to the abandonment of the Me.328 project, numerous variants were discussed during 1944. These included a submarine-launched version and a fast-attack-bomber variant.

Even before the pulsejets proved impractical, Messerschmitt had been looking into developing a turbojet-powered version of the Me.328. This would become Messerschmitt Projekt 1095, which incorporated a pair of Junkers Jumo turbojets. The P.1095 had the straight wings of the Me.328 rather than the slightly swept wings of the Me.262, but one of two October 1943 P.1095 design variations borrowed the tail design of the Me.262. Also like the Me.262, the P.1095 was designed with a tricycle landing gear for conventional runway operations, rather than being designed to be rail-launched. It had a wingspan of just under 32 feet and was 31 feet 9 inches long. Takeoff weight would have been just under 8,000 pounds, and armament would have been nose-mounted 20mm or 30mm cannons.

The P.1095 program was terminated in 1944 when it became apparent that the aircraft's performance would be inferior to that of the Me.262. Messerschmitt could better utilize the time and talent of its engineering staff on aircraft that would become the next generation of jet fighters beyond the Me.262.

## Next-Generation Messerschmitt Fighters

The first aircraft of the next generation of jet fighters were taking shape on Messerschmitt drawing boards even as the Me.262 was in flight test. Among those working on these projects were Hans Hornung and Woldemar Voigt, with Willy Messerschmitt himself closely involved. One of their first aircraft was Projekt 1092, a multirole plane loosely based on the overall Me.262 design. The program was actually a series of designs that used the Me.262's wings and fuselage as a point of departure, although the resulting aircraft were about 15 to 20 percent smaller in their overall dimensions.

Whereas the Me.262 had a pair of wing-mounted engines, Projekt 1092 studied ways of incorporating the engine into the fuselage. American and Soviet jet-fighter designers would adopt this layout for their first postwar generation of jets. While most of the designs specified Junkers Jumo turbojet engines, the P.1092B interceptor variant studied the possibility of a Walter rocket engine such as that used in the Me.163 interceptor.

Like the Me.262, the various P.1092 aircraft also featured nose-mounted 30mm cannons and tricycle landing gear. They also boasted a cockpit with better visibility than earlier Messerschmitt aircraft such as the Bf.109. An exception to this would be the P.1092.3 variant, which moved the cockpit to the rear of the aircraft, just slightly ahead of the tail and above the engine exhaust, thus reducing rearward visibility. This aircraft was followed by the P.1192.4, in which the cockpit was moved forward, almost to the nose and well ahead of the wing.

The early P.1092s had a single large engine intake in the nose, but the P.1092.3, P.1092.4, and P.1092.5 would all have smaller split intakes located beneath the wing roots.

Another approach to next-generation jet fighters was seen in Messerschmitt's Projekt 1099 and Projekt 1100, which were unveiled early in 1944. Like the P.1092, they borrowed the wing and tail of the Me.262, but they also retained the wing mounting for their pairs of Junkers Jumo turbojet engines. While the P.1092 aircraft brought the engine or engines into the fuselage, the P.1099 and P.1100 kept them on the wing.

However, these new aircraft differed from most of the others by borrowing an idea from the P.1092.4, which placed the pilot far forward in the nose of the aircraft. This permitted a longer flight deck. Like the Me.262B night fighter, these aircraft could accommodate a crew of two or three.

Plans called for heavy armament, including a pair of 30mm cannons and multiple 20mm guns. This versatility led planners to consider the P.1100 for a variety of roles. In March 1944, variants were proposed as fast-attack bombers as well as night fighters. In the latter role, they would have been configured with Schrage Musik (Jazz Music) gunsights and two 30mm cannons that fired straight up into the belly of an enemy bomber.

In the postwar Soviet Union, the Lavochkin design bureau produced small numbers of many of the P.1092 variations. The P.1092.4 became the La-150, while the P.1092.2 and P.1092.3 influenced the La-152, La-154, La-160, and La-174.

## Messerschmitt Projekt 1101

Though it remained completely unknown to Allied intelligence until after the war, Messerschmitt's Projekt 1101 would later become one of the most famous second-generation jet fighters built in Germany during World War II.

In an era when swept-wing jet fighters were considered revolutionary technological innovations, the P.1011 went a step further. It was designed with a mechanism that the pilot could use to *change* the angle of the sweep while in flight. This remarkable and innovative feature would not be applied to operational aircraft until two decades after World War II. Although the P.1011 never flew during the war, it was roughly 80 percent complete when it was captured, and it cast a very distinct shadow across postwar military aircraft development.

The idea of a "variable geometry wing" originated with Professor Alexander Lippisch, who is best remembered for designing the Messerschmitt Me.163 rocket fighter. Although Lippisch patented the concept in 1942, it was Messerschmitt aerodynamicist Dr. Waldemar Voigt who first exploited it. Indeed, Projekt 1101 originated with Voigt, who conceived the aircraft in 1942 as a test bed for the variable geometry concept. By year's end, he had constructed a six-foot scale model and had run extensive wind tunnel tests.

As the urgent building of operational aircraft consumed Messerschmitt's resources, Voigt's P.1101 languished for two years, until the summer of 1944, when the Reichsluftfahrt Ministerium (RLM, German Air Ministry) issued a request for proposals to German aircraft manufacturers under its Emergency Fighter Competition. This program envisioned a single-engine jet fighter that was faster than the twin-engine Me.262 and capable of operating at above 45,000 feet. The Messerschmitt answer would be the P.1101.

At the secret Messerschmitt engineering design center near Oberammergau in the mountains of Bavaria, Voigt and engineer Hans Hornung headed a team that fashioned Voigt's preliminary work into a real airplane. The design was complete by mid November, and construction of the prototype began on December 4, 1944. Because of the sudden urgency of the project, Messerschmitt decided that the airframe would be built even as final design details were still being worked out.

The P.1011 would weigh 8,948 pounds fully loaded. It was originally designed to be powered by a Heinkel Hirth 011 turbojet delivering 2,866 pounds of thrust, but this engine was replaced by the Junkers Jumo 004 turbojet that was used in the Me.262. In the meantime, a Lorin ramjet engine was also considered.

The P.1101 prototype was 30 feet 1 inch long, with a maximum wingspan of just over 27 feet. The wings would sweep to a maximum of 45 degrees. This was greater than had been used for any aircraft yet built. The initial P.1101 aircraft was designed so that the sweep could be changed and locked on the ground only, although later aircraft were envisioned in which this could be done in flight.

The P.1101 pilot was seated in a pressurized cockpit equipped with an ejection seat beneath a high-visibility bubble canopy. Armament consisted of two 30mm or 55mm cannons, with space allowed for an additional two.

There was also room for 50mm upward-firing Jagdfaust (Fighter Fist) rocket launchers for attacking enemy bombers from beneath. Ruhrstall-Kramer X-4 air-to-air missiles were also planned as armament.

As the prototype P.1101 was taking shape, Messerschmitt was also working on an even more advanced variant under its Projekt 1106. The P.1106 aircraft would have been similar to the P.1101, but with its cockpit moved very nearly to the rear of the fuselage just ahead of a V-shaped "butterfly" tail. This idea never moved past the initial planning stage.

By the first of January 1945, the Luftwaffe decided to downgrade the priority of Projekt 1101 in order to concentrate on programs that were less revolutionary and, thus, closer to their initial operational capabilities. However, the Messerschmitt team at Oberammergau continued to work diligently on the P.1101.

While nearly every aircraft factory in Germany was aflame from Allied bombing raids, Oberammergau remained a quiet and tranquil place. The secret facility would remain a secret to the Allies until the end. It was never bombed.

Voigt and Hornung proceeded expeditiously and had even penciled in a first flight date for the P.1101 of June 1945. However, as the Allies began sweeping into southern Germany, it became clear that this schedule would never be met. Technical data was microfilmed and hidden, but no attempt was made to destroy the nearly complete P.1101 prototype. On April 29, the war came to an end for Oberammergau as U.S. Army forces stumbled across the secret facility.

A USAAF Combined Advanced Field Team was sent into Oberammergau to conduct a technical evaluation of the P.1101 and to interview the Messerschmitt engineering staff. Coincidentally, the American team was headed by Robert Woods of Bell Aircraft, who ultimately received the USAAF contract to continue Projekt 1101.

The ensuing intrigue was worthy of Hollywood. Woods arrived at Oberammergau on May 7, but by the time Voigt agreed to show him the hidden microfilm, it had already been discovered by a French team, who refused to share it with the Americans. Indeed, the USAAF would never get its hands on the technical data for the aircraft they had captured.

The P.1101 was crated and shipped to the Wright Field in the United States, where Waldemar Voigt agreed to work with Woods to continue Projekt 1101 under the auspices of the USAAF Engineering Division. However, the P.1101 was damaged in transit, so it was considered irreparable and unflyable. In the meantime, the USAAF had concluded that the P.1101 was too small to carry the necessary armament to make it an effective intercepter. Woods later convinced the USAAF and Bell Aircraft management that it would be valuable to continue the program if only to study the variable geometry concept. The P.1101 finally reached Bell Aircraft in Buffalo, New York, in August 1948.

Bell received an order from the USAAF (U.S. Air Force after 1947) to build two slightly modified P.1011s under the designation X-5. Powered by an Allison J35-A-17 turbojet, the first variable geometry X-5 made its debut flight on June 20, 1951.

The variable geometry concept eventually made its way into operational aircraft. In the United States, the General Dynamics F-111 first flew in December 1964 and entered service in 1967, while the Grumman F-14 Tomcat first flew in December 1970 and deployed to squadrons in 1974. In the Soviet Union, the Mikoyan Gurevich MiG-23 first flew in June 1967 and entered service in 1973. Clearly, the

Messerschmitt P.1101 was a secret weapon well ahead of its time.

## Messerschmitt Projekt 1110 and 1112

Even as Messerschmitt was working on the P.1101 variable geometry high-altitude jet fighter, the company was developing designs for other advanced aircraft with fixed-wing designs. Whereas previous fixed-wing types had borrowed from the slightly swept-wing design of the Me.262, the Project 1110 and 1112 jets explored newer technology. They were designed in 1944 for supersonic speeds, although no German jet fighter is known to have exceeded the speed of sound during World War II.

Variations of the Project 1110 and 1112 jets utilized the V-shaped "butterfly" tail that had been designed into such aircraft as the P.1106 and at least one variation of the earlier P.1092. However, one aircraft designed under Projekt 1110 had four wings and no horizontal tail surfaces. The forward wings were slightly shorter in a configuration known today by the French term *canard,* meaning "duck." The ducklike appearance was not lost on the Germans of the World War II era, who nicknamed this P.1110 variant *Ente,* meaning "duck."

The Projekt 1112 aircraft evolved directly from the P.1110 early in 1945. It was to have been powered by a single Heinkel Hirth 011 turbojet fed by a pair of side-mounted air intakes. As with the P.1101, there was a pressurized cockpit with an ejection seat for the pilot, and the armament would have consisted of four side-mounted 30mm cannons.

The P.1112 was seen by Messerschmitt as a step in P.1110 evolution that might have led to an operational jet fighter. Indeed Waldemar Voigt projected that such an aircraft would be ready for flight testing in the spring of 1946. Of course, World War II ended a year before this could become a reality.

Nevertheless, part of the P.1112 prototype had been built at the secret Messerschmitt engineering design center in Oberammergau in the mountains of Bavaria when the war ended. The United States confiscated the technical files related to Projekt 1112 and shared them with American planemakers. It is believed that the P.1112 wing design was adapted by Chance Vought for the 38-degree swept-wing of the F7U-1 Cutlass jet fighter, which first flew in September 1948 and which served with the U.S. Navy in the 1950s.

## Messerschmitt Wespe

One of the last Messerschmitt World War II projects was the sleek Wespe (Wasp) jet fighter. It had the "butterfly" tail of the P.1112, but it was a much trimmer and more graceful aircraft. It was designed to be 32 feet 9 inches long, with a wing spanning 28 feet 4 inches and having a shallower sweep than the P.1112.

## Focke-Wulf Ta.183

During World War II, the two leading makers of piston-engine fighter aircraft in Germany were Messerschmitt and Focke-Wulf. The Messerschmitt Bf.109 and the Focke-Wulf Fw.190 were two of the greatest piston-engine fighters ever made. While Messerschmitt produced an operational jet fighter in the legendary Me.262, Focke-Wulf never matched this accomplishment. However, if one were to create a "greatest jet fighter that *never* flew" category for World War II, the leading contender would certainly be the Focke-Wulf Ta.183 Huckebein (Raven).

Though the Ta.183 did not fly during the war, the design emerged soon after in the Soviet Union as the Mikoyan Gurevich MiG-15. This sleek, swept-wing fighter stunned the Americans during the Korean War and had a service life with dozens of air forces that spanned several decades. Clearly, this was a major accomplishment for a secret weapon of World War II.

As is implied by the "Ta" prefix (rather than "Fw"), the Ta.183 was the creation of the brilliant Focke-Wulf engineer Dr. Kurt Tank. The story of the Ta.183 parallels that of the Messerschmitt P.1101. Both evolved from initial engineering work that was done in 1942, but neither project really got off the ground until two years later, when the Reichsluftfahrt Ministerium (RLM, German Air Ministry) issued the request for proposals to German aircraft manufacturers under its Emergency Fighter Competition in the summer of 1944.

The initial work done in late 1942 by the engineering team led by Hans Multhopp formed the basis for Tank's proposal. The initial design called for an aircraft that was 30 feet 10.25 inches long, with a wingspan of 32 feet 9.75 inches. This was later to be trimmed to a length of 28 feet 8.5 inches and a span of 31 feet 2 inches. The wings were to have a sweep of 40 degrees, and the horizontal tail surfaces—neatly placed atop the vertical portion of the tail— were swept at 60 degrees. The gross weight rating was finalized at 9,150 pounds.

During the last days of February 1945, the RLM evaluated all the proposals. Although the P.1101 prototype was actually closer to completion, the Ta.183 was declared the winner. This is why it received a formal designation rather than a *P* for "Projekt" prefix like the Messerschmitt aircraft.

In March, the Luftwaffe formally ordered 16 prototype aircraft. The engine of choice would be the Heinkel-Hirth 011 turbojet, but since it was not expected to be available for several months, the Junkers Jumo 004 turbojet would be used in the first three prototypes. The projected top speed was to be just short of 600 mph, and the service ceiling topped 45,000 feet. Like the competing Messerschmitt aircraft, the Ta.183 would have a pressurized cockpit with "bubble" canopy and an ejection seat for the pilot. The armament would have consisted of two to four 30mm cannons mounted at the side of the intake in the nose.

The first test flights were planned for early summer of 1945, with initial operational deliveries intended for as early as October 1945. These plans came to an abrupt halt on April 8, however, as British troops seized the Focke-Wulf factories.

Of course, this turn of events was not the end of the Huckebein story. Less than a month after the British captured the Focke-Wulf facilities in northwestern Germany, Soviet troops took Berlin. Here, in the German capital, they rifled through the files of the RLM and found a full set of blueprints and engineering specs for the Ta.183 as well as for the larger Fw.250 jet fighter that was based on the earlier design. The Mikoyan Gurevich design bureau in the Soviet Union was given the task of picking up where Kurt Tank and his team left off. The result was the MiG-15, which first flew in July 1947 and made such a name for itself during the Korean War.

The British did not build a Ta.183 copy, but ironically, in a moment of ill-considered largesse, the Labour Party government allowed the export of the Rolls Royce Nene turbojet engine to the Soviet Union in 1946. Without this, the MiG-15 would have been delayed for several years and perhaps the air war in Korea would have gone differently.

As for Kurt Tank himself, he chose not to go to work for the victorious Allies as most of his colleagues had done. Instead, he found a new home in South America, where he, too, continued the Ta.183 project. Argentina had long had strong pro-German sympathies due in part to a large German ethnic minority. In 1943, the Argentine government of Ramón Castillo had been overthrown by a cadre of army officers who supported both Mussolini's Fascist government in Italy and Hitler's Nazis in Germany. One of the officers, Juan Perón, emerged as the Argentine strongman, and in 1946, he was elected president by a large majority. Among the nationalistic steps that Perón took to mold Argentina into a new world power was to invite men such as Kurt Tank and French engineer Émil Dewoitine to help create an indigenous Argentine jet-fighter industry.

Dewoitine's Pulqui (Arrow) first flew in 1947, and Tank's postwar version of the Ta.183, known as the Pulqui II, made its debut on June 27, 1950. Only six aircraft were built before the Pulqui II program was canceled in 1954. Argentina was never able to develop a successful indigenous jet-aircraft industry.

## Focke-Wulf Fw.250

The Focke-Wulf Fw.250 was strikingly similar to the Ta.183, and at first glance from certain angles, it could easily be mistaken for a MiG-15. It had the familiar tall tail and wings swept at 40 degrees. It differed from the Ta.183 in that it had two turbojets blended into its fuselage rather than one.

Kurt Tank introduced drawings for the Fw.250 in November 1944, proposing it as a multirole aircraft. Recalling how Adolf Hitler's insistence that the Me.262 be used as a bomber had held up that program, he designed the Fw.250 so that it could be used as a bomber capable of carrying 2,200 pounds of ordnance. The long-range-fighter variant would use this payload capacity for external fuel tanks.

Though Focke-Wulf never came close to cutting metal on the Fw.250 program, its design was further modified under Focke-Wulf Projekt 011, and together, this design work probably influenced that of the single-engine MiG-15.

## Focke-Wulf Ta.283

Though the designation implies a design relationship with the Ta.183, this dart-shaped aircraft had virtually no similarity with the prototype of the MiG-15. At 45 degrees, the wings were more acutely swept than virtually any swept-wing aircraft ever, certainly more than contemporary German jets. It would have been 38 feet 10.9 inches long, with a wingspan of 26 feet 3.2 inches.

Rather than conventional turbojets, Focke-Wulf design genius Kurt Tank proposed a pair of enormous Pabst ramjets mounted at the ends of the stubby tailplanes. This gave the Fw.283 the first-glance appearance of a swept-wing variation on the Republic A-10 Warthog of the 1980s. The ramjets would be boosted on takeoff by a Walter rocket engine. Had it flown, the Ta.283 would have probably been capable of supersonic speeds, but its range would have been limited.

A related, but apparently undesignated, project combined the unconventional tail-mounted Lorin ramjets with an airframe similar to that of the Ta.183. It would have been closer in size to the Ta.283, with a length of about 38 feet and a wingspan of about 25 feet.

## Focke-Wulf Projekt 011

Unveiled to the Reichsluftfahrt Ministerium (RLM, German Air Ministry) in March 1945, Projekt 011 obviously represents a very evolved level of technology, and it clearly shows how rapidly Focke-Wulf engineers were progressing in terms of the design of large jet aircraft. The program included a series of large night fighters, each powered by a pair of Heinkel Hirth 011 turbojets. They had wings swept to 30 degrees, and efforts were made to specify all-metal construction, although by 1945, materials shortages required at least some control surfaces to be made of wood.

Projekt 011 called for a crew of three, with the pilot and navigator side by side and the radio operator behind them facing aft. As with other German jet aircraft of 1944–1945, the plans also called for a pressurized cockpit. Also as with contemporary designs, armament would have included four forward-firing 30mm cannons, or two firing forward and two firing upward for attacking bellies of bombers.

Both variations on Projekt 011 were large aircraft, themselves the size of contemporary conventional medium bombers. The smaller one was designed to be 44 feet 4 inches long, with a wingspan of 46 feet 3 inches. The larger one was to have been 62 feet 8 inches long with a wingspan of 63 feet 8 inches. This would have made it about the size of a USAAF B-25 Mitchell, though it was nearly twice as fast.

The Projekt 011 files were scooped up by Soviet forces

in 1945. The smaller of the two designs was reportedly built by Mikoyan Gurevich, with a tail borrowed from the MiG-15, under the experimental designation Ye-320 (I-320). The first of three prototypes was first flown in April 1949. Though no production series followed, the design is said to have influenced that of the Yakovlev Yak-25 "Flashlight," a widely deployed Soviet interceptor of the 1950s.

## Blohm und Voss Jet Fighters

Toward the end of World War II, nearly every German planemaker had a jet fighter on the drawing boards, whether or not the company had a strong background in piston-engine fighters. Best known as a builder of U-boats and other marine systems, Blohm und Voss had an aircraft division that produced some of Germany's most important seaplanes. These included the widely used Bv.138 and the gargantuan Bv.222. The company also produced small numbers of several land-plane types, including the strange asymmetrical Bv.141, which is discussed in Chapter 22.

The initial Blohm und Voss entries in the Luftwaffe's top-secret quest for a single-seat jet fighter were Projekt 197 and Projekt 198. The former was a swept-wing, "T-tailed" aircraft that was to have been 29 feet 7 inches long with a wingspan of 36 feet 5 inches. It would have been powered by a pair of BMW 003 turbojets in the fuselage.

The P.198 was a straight-wing aircraft with a single BMW 018 turbojet. It would have been 42 feet long with a wingspan of 49 feet 3 inches. The large intake in the nose was capped by a tiny protrusion that made the P.198 look as though it had a huge yawning mouth. The Soviet Sukhoi design bureau copied this awkward-seeming intake configuration after the war for its Su-15 jet fighter.

Demonstrating the Blohm und Voss inclination toward unconventional airframe design—as evidenced by the Bv.141—the company also produced a series of designs for short, tailless, single-seat jet fighters. In general, each had a small, egg-shaped fuselage with swept wings that had a sinister batlike appearance when viewed from the front. Created by a team led by Blohm und Voss head engineer Dr. Richard Vogt, these designs began to emerge during the latter part of 1944. The jets were preceded by the Projekt 208, a tailless, piston-engine design.

The first Blohm und Voss tailless jet was the Projekt 209, which had a wingspan of 35 feet and was 24 feet long. It was to have been powered by a Heinkel Hirth 011. Next came the Projekt 210, a tailless craft that was to have been powered by a BMW 003 turbojet with elective rocket-assisted takeoff. The P.211 was an aircraft with a conventional fuselage and tail that utilized the P.210's wing. It was submitted to the RLM in September 1944 as part of the Volksjäger (People's Fighter) program.

The tailless P.212 was the Blohm und Voss entry in the Luftwaffe's Emergency Fighter Competition of late 1944—which was won by the Focke-Wulf Ta.183 (discussed above). It was similar to the P.210, but with a lengthened fuselage to accommodate larger fuel tanks. Wind-tunnel tests were conducted, and metal was cut. The first of three prototype aircraft was actually under construction when the war ended. Had the latter not obviated the development schedule, the first flight was to have come in August 1945.

The P.215 was a development of the P.212 that was proposed to the Luftwaffe as a night fighter. With a wingspan of 61 feet 8 inches and a length of 47 feet 3 inches, it was the largest of the Blohm und Voss tailless jet fighters. Intended to be powered by two Heinkel Hirth 011 turbojets, it was approved for further study in March 1945, but never came close to production.

## Heinkel Jet Fighters

As noted in the introductory remarks to this chapter, the firm of Ernst Heinkel built the first jet aircraft and the first to be designated as a fighter aircraft. Though officially a fighter, the He.280 never reached operational use. A straight-wing aircraft, it was clearly inferior to the Messerschmitt Me.262 in terms of performance. Nevertheless, eight prototype aircraft were built, and they were used for flight testing from April 1941 until early in 1945.

As the He.280 flight test program got under way, Heinkel also had a number of other secret jet fighters on the drawing board. These differing designs were grouped into Projekt 1078 and Projekt 1079. Both projects contained swept-wing aircraft similar to the Focke-Wulf Ta.183 as well as tailless jets similar to the Blohm und Voss P.212 and its relatives, which are discussed immediately above. The two types differed in that the Projekt 1078 craft were designed for the Luftwaffe Emergency Fighter Competition, which called for a fast, single-seat, second-generation jet fighter, while Projekt 1079 involved larger aircraft.

Projekt 1078 specified a single Heinkel Hirth 011 turbojet, while Projekt 1079 called for a pair of such engines in each aircraft. The P.1078s would have carried a crew of one, and the P.1079s were designed for more. Armament was to have been a pair of 30mm cannons for each, although placement varied from subtype to subtype.

The P.1078A was a swept-wing aircraft with an intake

configuration similar to that of the Blohm und Voss P.198. It was to be 31 feet long, with a wingspan of nearly 29 feet. The Heinkel P.1078B was a tailless aircraft with a fuselage less than 20 feet long and a wingspan of 31 feet. The cockpit was a separate module that was slightly offset from the centerline of the fuselage. The tailless P.1078C had a centered cockpit.

The twin engine, V-tailed P.1079A was designed as a night fighter and was similar to the Focke-Wulf Projekt 011 series. The crew consisted of a pilot and radar operator. It had a wingspan of 42 feet 8.2 inches and was nearly 47 feet long. The tailless P.1079B was similar in appearance to the Horten flying wings that are discussed later in Chapter 21.

## Skoda-Kauba Projekt 14

One of the more obscure aircraft designers who was active in the German Reich during World War II was an Austrian named Otto Kauba. His early proposals caught the eye of the Reichsluftfahrt Ministerium (RLM, German Air Ministry) in about 1942, and they set him up in a design office near Prague in occupied Czechoslovakia. His activities were apparently supported by the personnel and resources of the giant Skoda industrial firm, prewar Czechoslovakia's largest arms manufacturers. During World War II, Skoda would continue to be an important supplier of matériel for the German war effort.

Skoda-Kauba produced a series of small piston-engine aircraft designs that never entered production, including light trainers. As the story goes, the promising aircraft designs were sabotaged by Czechs who disliked the German occupation.

In early 1945, Kauba undertook Projekt 14, an aircraft

that has been described as "a ramjet with wings." Intended as an inexpensive interceptor, the P.14 was a barrel-shaped contraption in which the pilot would have lain prone atop the combustion chamber and fired at Allied bombers with a 30mm cannon. Like the Messerschmitt Me.163 Komet rocket interceptor, the P.14 would not have had internal landing gear. It would take off with a wheeled carriage that dropped away as the aircraft lifted into the air. For landing, the P.14 was equipped with a skid.

Because fuel was in short supply within the Reich by 1945, Kauba designed the aircraft to be fueled by a slurry of powdered coal and jet fuel. The first prototype had yet to be built when Soviet forces captured Prague in early May 1945.

## Luftwaffe Volksjäger Program

One of the most interesting footnotes to the story of jet fighters during World War II is that of the Volksjäger (People's Fighter) program. While most secret weapon stories captivate us with their advanced technology, the Volksjäger program is amazing for the audacity of its production scheme, and for the fact that this scheme *worked!*

Otto Saur, an influential deputy to Albert Speer at the Ministry of Armaments, came up the impossible notion of designing, building, and flying an all-new jet fighter and getting it into production in just *90 days.*

The idea of the Volksjäger was analogous to that of the Volkswagen (People's Automobile). The Volkswagen was conceived by Adolf Hitler and developed by Ferdinand Porsche before World War II as a simple, inexpensive automobile that could easily be mass-produced and made available to the maximum number of consumers in the minimum amount of time. The Volksjäger was conceived

in the summer of 1944 as a simple, inexpensive jet interceptor that could easily be mass-produced and made available to the Luftwaffe in the minimum amount of time.

Speer and Hitler loved the Volksjäger concept. However, the Luftwaffe high command and most of Germany's
aviation industry professionals saw it as an impossible task
that would soak up precious resources that could be devoted to the proven aircraft such as the Me.262. The Volksjäger was seen as an overly ambitious undertaking at a
time when Allied bombers were seriously damaging the
Reich's industrial infrastructure.

Nevertheless, the bureaucrats carried the day, and on
September 8, 1944, Arado, Blohm und Voss, Focke-Wulf,
Junkers, Heinkel, and Messerschmitt were each requested
to provide a Volksjäger design. They were given 12 days
(later cut in half) to come up with a design that could be
ready for production on January 1, 1945. The Volksjäger
was to have a gross weight of 4,410 pounds and to be capable of speeds in excess of 466 mph. The engine specified
was the BMW 003 turbojet.

The requirement also stated that the Volksjäger was to
be designed so that it could be constructed by semiskilled
laborers using inexpensive materials. The latter included a
generous use of plywood rather than aluminum.

Most of the firms submitted variations on work that was
then ongoing in their advanced project centers. For example, Focke-Wulf's Volksflugzeug (People's Airplane) was
similar to the early designs that were evolving toward the
Ta.183 aircraft. At Heinkel, head designer Karl Schwartz-
ler was already working on a light, inexpensive jet aircraft,
the Projekt 1073, also known as Spatz (Sparrow). At
Blohm und Voss, Richard Vogt had his Projekt 211 well on
its way.

None of the firms met the September 14 deadline; but
Heinkel submitted a preliminary design the following day.

This was rejected, and there was a flurry of submissions and evaluations over the ensuing week. At the Luftwaffe, the favorite was the Blohm und Voss P.211, but it was not considered simple enough to meet the mass-production requirement. Otto Saur favored the Heinkel entry, and on September 23, it emerged as the official winner.

The new Heinkel Volksjäger was originally designated as He.500, but this number was seen as so prominent as to stand out too much to Allied spies. It was changed to He.162 for the sake of secrecy.

The Volksjäger production program was code named Salamander, and inevitably, the He.162 itself came to be known by that name. Three widely separated factories—including the giant underground facility at Nordhausen—were earmarked for Salamander production, and these were fed by a group of furniture shops (making the wooden parts) and other subcontractors throughout Germany.

The He.162 was a straight-wing, twin-tailed aircraft with its BMW 003 turbojet mounted on top of the fuselage. It was 29 feet 8.3 inches long, with a wingspan of 23 feet 7.5 inches. It weighed 6,184 pounds fully loaded and fueled and had a top speed of 562 mph at 19,690 feet. Various armament—including R4M air-to-air missiles—was studied, but a pair of 30mm cannons was standard.

The first flight of the He.162 prototype came on December 6, 1944, less than three months after the Luftwaffe request for proposals. The first prototype crashed on December 10, but the second was flying just 12 days later, and more than a dozen were being flight-tested by the end of January 1945. A trickle of He.162 production aircraft followed soon after.

Even as production was beginning, later variants were being studied, including a swept-wing version and a twin-engine He.162B. The He.162C was equipped with the more powerful Heinkel Hirth 011 turbojet.

The first operational unit, I/Jagdgeschwader 1, began training with the He.162 in February 1945, but the transition to the new type was problematic against the chaotic backdrop of the war's final months. It also proved to be a difficult aircraft to learn to fly, so experienced pilots were required, and they were in short supply in 1945. By April, the He.162 was still not deemed officially ready, although a few aircraft were transferred to JV 44, General Adolf Galland's elite Me.262 unit.

Approximately 270 He.162s were completed by the time Germany was defeated. Of this, at least half had been delivered to operational units, although there are no confirmed reports of one actually going into combat against an Allied aircraft.

Though the Volksjäger had no practical impact on the war, the program had reached all of its milestones within a few days of the target dates set in the initial request for proposals. Early production-series aircraft really *were* under construction 90 days from the September 1944 date of the initial request.

Though the Luftwaffe made a concerted effort to destroy all the Volksjägers to keep them out of Allied hands, some were captured and at least seven still survived at the turn of the twenty-first century. Two of the once-secret He.162s are on display at the Canadian National Aviation Museum, and one each can be seen at the Royal Air Force Museum at Hendon, near London, at the Imperial War Museum in London, at the Musée de l'Air in Paris, at the National Air and Space Museum annex at Silver Hill in Maryland, and at the Planes of Fame Museum in Chino, California.

## 17

## Luftwaffe Rocket-Propelled Aircraft

Today, we know that jet propulsion is far more practical for routine powered flight than rocket propulsion. Rockets provide immense raw power and a great deal of speed; that's why they are used to put objects into outer space. On the other hand, jet engines are more easily throttled and controlled. They also provide longer range. During World War II, however, there was a clean slate on the subject of advanced propulsion systems. Nobody was really sure what potential might reveal itself as jet and rocket engine technology evolved.

While rocketry was born in the United States with Robert Goddard and widely studied elsewhere in the early years of the twentieth century—notably in the Soviet Union—it was in Germany that it was embraced most heartily.

The RLM and the Luftwaffe both encouraged both types of secret experimental programs to a greater extent than parallel agencies elsewhere in the world. Indeed, the Luftwaffe established a "Special Plenopentientiary for Jet and Rocket Aircraft" under Generalmajor Josef Kammhuber, who had previously served as inspector general for night fighters.

Not only did the German air arm take jets seriously, they naturally assumed that rocket propulsion had a similar potential.

## Messerschmitt Me.163 Komet

The world's first rocket-powered interceptor, the Messerschmitt Me.163 Komet was a shock to Allied airmen when it made the sudden transition from secret weapon to aerial scourge on July 28, 1944, over Merseburg, Germany.

The diminutive Komet was the creation of celebrated aerodynamicist Dr. Alexander Martin Lippisch, who had originally designed it under the designation DFS.194 as part of the super-secret Projekt X while he was working at the German Glider Research Institute (Deutsche Forschungsinstitut für Segelflug, DFS) in the late 1930s. Though the DFS did do work with gliders, it also handled secret rocket-powered projects. Indeed, the rocket-powered Komet was originally tested as an unpowered glider in order to evaluate its aerodynamic performance.

Gliders were a good cover for rocketry, but the level of secrecy at DFS was stifling. Late in 1938, Lippisch let it be known that he wanted a change of venue, and on January 2, 1939, the RLM transferred Projekt X from the DFS facility near Darmstadt to the Messerschmitt facility at Augsburg. Indeed, the RLM set the 45-year-old Lippisch up as head of his own aerodynamics "think tank" within the Messerschmitt organization. The designation of the rocket plane would eventually change from DFS.194 to Me.163.

The first German experimental rocket plane, the Heinkel He.176, made a powered test flight of less than a minute in June 1939, but by then, the RLM was clearly favoring the DFS.194, which was already "gliding through" unpowered test flights.

It was two years, however, before the first Me.163A entered its own glide-test phase. The first powered Me.163A flight came on October 2, 1941, and the operational Me.163B was introduced in April 1942. The Me.163B was just 19 feet 2 inches long, with swept wings spanning 30 feet 7 inches. It weighed 4,200 pounds empty and 9,500 pounds fully loaded and fueled. It was powered by a Walter HWK 509-series rocket motor fueled by T-Stoff (hydrogen peroxide plus a stabilizer) and Z-Stoff (a solution of calcium permanganate). Operational armament consisted of a pair of 20mm or 30mm cannons.

Because of its small size, the Komet was designed without internal landing gear. It took off with a wheeled carriage contraption that dropped away as the aircraft lifted into the air. For landing, the Komet was equipped with a skid, like the runner of a child's sled.

Capable of approaching an Allied bomber formation at nearly 600 mph, the Komet proved to be nearly unstoppable when it entered service in the summer of 1944 with Jagdgeschwader 400. However, the speed gave the pilot only a few useful seconds to fire his guns, and the rapid burn rate of the rocket fuel made it difficult for pilots to make a second pass.

As the Allied bomber groups learned of the Komet's limited endurance, they were able to play it to their advantage. More than 200 Me.163s were delivered to the Luftwaffe during 1944, but production fell in 1945 because of supply problems. This, coupled with fuel shortages, diminished the effectiveness of the Me.163B in combat.

The Japanese inspected the Komet in Germany in 1944 and saw its promise as a means of defending Japan. An Me.163B airframe and engine were purchased and sent to Japan, where a series of them was to have been manufactured by Mitsubishi under the designation J8M1. The first of these made its debut in a test flight on July 7, 1945. A month later, the war was over.

The Allies did not exploit the rocket technology of the Komet after the war, as they did with many other German jet fighters. The United States didn't even test a rocket-powered interceptor until well after the war, and it never achieved even the limited success of the Me.163. This aircraft, the Republic XF-91 Thunderceptor, was actually a jet/rocket hybrid. It first flew under jet power in May 1949, and the supplementary rocket engines were not used until late 1952.

Lippisch himself was captured by Americans forces and subsequently induced to relocate to the United States. As the RLM had set Lippisch up with his own think tank within Messerschmitt, so did the United States, and Lippisch settled briefly at Wright Field near Dayton, Ohio. After December 1946, he worked for the Naval Air Matériel Center in Philadelphia until 1950, when he was hired by the Collins Radio Company of Cedar Rapids, Iowa, as director of their aeronautical division. Among other craft, he created the Aerodyne, a wingless aircraft whose lift was supplied solely by engine thrust. He died in Cedar Rapids in 1976.

## Heinkel Projekt 1077 Julia

Even as the Messerschmitt Me.163 was entering combat with the Luftwaffe's Jagdgeschwader 400, the firm of Ernst Heinkel was at work on a rocket interceptor project of its own. With its stubby, straight wings, spanning just 15 feet, the P.1077 appeared crude in comparison with the swept-wing Me.163.

The pilot was originally to have lain on his stomach in

the tubular, 22-foot fuselage, but a later version put him in a seat. The original power plant was to have been a Walter HWK 509 rocket, similar to that of the Me.163. Like the Komet, armament was to have been a pair of cannons. The original full-scale mock-up was demolished in a bombing raid toward the end of 1944, but work inched forward. By April 1945, two prototype Julias were taking shape when Russian forces captured the Heinkel factory.

## Junkers Elli and Walli

The Junkers created a pair of experimental piloted inter-ceptor aircraft that were similar in size and appearance to the Fieseler Fi.103 Reichenberg, the crewed version of the V-1 (Vergeltungswaffe 1) cruise missile. Both received the "Ef" designation prefix for *Entwicklungsflugzeug*, which translates as "prototype" or "development" aircraft.

The Ef.126 Elli (also referred to as "Lilli") was pow-ered by an Argus pulsejet engine, while the Ef.127 Walli was powered by a Walter 509 liquid-fuel rocket engine and boosted by a pair of solid rockets. Though the Elli was similar in many ways to the piloted version of the Fi.103, it was to have been armed with a pair of cannons to attack enemy bombers rather than a warhead for hitting surface targets. When World War II ended, both Elli and Walli were under construction, although far from complete.

## Von Braun A6

As a corollary to the V-2/A4 intermediate-range-ballistic-missile program discussed in Chapter 5, Wernher von Braun proposed a manned version of this rocket to the Reichsluftfahrt Ministerium (RLM, German Air Ministry).

Designated as the A6, this vehicle was exactly like the A4b, except that it was equipped with aircraft-style landing gear for horizontal, rather than vertical, takeoffs and landings—and it had a cockpit in the nose. From some angles it looked like the North American X-15 rocket plane that set numerous speed and altitude records during the 1960s.

The A6 would have provided the Luftwaffe with an interceptor or reconnaissance platform capable of speeds exceeding twice that of sound. It would have been able to catch any Allied aircraft and fly with impunity through any Allied antiaircraft defenses. It was also based on existing technology, and its development and deployment was within grasp.

Of course, there was the limited range of the A4 rocket engine, which burned all its fuel in less than two minutes and would have to be recovered in a dead-stick landing. These characteristics were problematic but not insurmountable. Today, Space Shuttle Orbiters land without power—and many German World War II pilots had some glider experience. The range might have been extended somewhat with a more sophisticated throttle system.

Also on the downside was the fact that the issues of controlling and maneuvering such a vehicle were far from resolved. Finally, there were the problems related to training pilots for Mach-2 flight at a time when nobody had yet flown at Mach 1.

## 18

## Unorthodox and Unrecoverable
## Interceptor Aircraft

Deserving of separate discussion are a class of secret
weapons that are outstanding as much for the audacity of
their concept as for their technology. They are similar to
manned cruise missiles in that they were designed as ex-
pendable. These are the air-to-air equivalents of the unre-
coverable aircraft discussed in Chapter 18 that were
designed for use against surface targets.

Some of the German jet and rocket warplanes were the
result of many years of careful calculations, while others
were almost hysterical monsters brought to life by convul-
sions of sheer desperation. However, as we can see in the
XP-79, it was not only the Germans who indulged in such
strange notions as colliding with enemy aircraft to knock
them down.

**Bachem Ba.349 Natter**

Nicknamed Natter (Adder), the Ba.349 was designed as
target-defense interceptor to defend a single high-priority

target. It was the brainchild of Erich Bachem, the technical director at the Gerhard Fieseler firm, the same company that had produced the Fi.103 Reichenburg that became Hitler's first Vergeltungswaffe (Vengeance Weapon). During development of the Natter, Bachem had the technical support of Wernher von Braun and members of his team.

Briefly given the Fieseler designation Fi.166, the Ba.349 was a simple, yet very fast, aircraft that could be prepositioned near potential targets of Allied bombers and launched at a moment's notice. It was 18 feet 9 inches long, with straight, stubby wings measuring 11 feet 10 inches from tip to tip. Built primarily of wood and other noncrucial materials, the Ba.349 weighed 5,000 pounds fully fueled. It was designed to be launched vertically, thus eliminating the need for an airfield and permitting it to be stationed virtually anywhere.

In the operational scenario, Natters would be launched as the Allied bombers neared the target. A single Walter HWK 109 rocket motor, delivering up to 4,410 pounds of thrust, would kick the aircraft up to 29,000 feet in less than a minute. The aircraft would be under the control of ground-based radar operators until contact was made with the enemy, whereupon the pilot would assume control, jettison the nose cap, and begin attacking the bomber formation with two dozen 73mm Foehn (or 33 R4M 55mm) unguided rockets. Seven minutes after the plane reached altitude, the fuel would be expended and the pilot would save himself and the rocket motor by means of a primitive ejection system.

The remarkable thing about the Ba.349 was that it went from initial conception to first test flight in only six months. Conceived in August 1944, two months after the invasion of France, the first piloted Natter was hoisted into its launch tower on February 28, 1945. Before the day was out, that Ba.349 and its precious rocket motor were spread in pieces across the German countryside and test pilot Lothar Siebert was the program's first martyr.

Within two months, the Ba.349 had actually been successfully flown and a pilot recovered. Also by April 1945, a staffel of 10 had been put into position near Kirchheim. None of these was ever flown operationally, however. The entire site was later purposely destroyed to keep the aircraft from falling into American hands, although at least one was taken intact. In the end, hastily conceived and constructed Bachem death traps cost more Luftwaffe lives than those of Allied fliers.

## Messerschmitt Projekt 1103 and 1104

Among the designs that competed with the Bachem Natter for the favor of the Luftwaffe were two from Messerschmitt, which was already delivering operational examples of the much more sophisticated Me.163 comet rocket plane. The Projekt 1103 was born in the summer of 1944, a cheap wooden aircraft that was 15 feet 5 inches long with wings spanning 20 feet 4 inches. It was to have been towed by a larger aircraft, with its Schmidding 109-513 rocket engine ignited at higher altitude.

Conceived at about the same time as Projekt 1103, the Messerschmitt Projekt 1104 was the same size and differed in that the pilot sat in a seat rather than lying on his face. The P.1104 was to have been powered by a Walter HWK 509 engine similar to that used in the Me.163.

When the Luftwaffe decided to build the Natter, Messerschmitt abandoned its cheap rocket projects to focus on the Me.163 and other more sophisticated aircraft.

## Zeppelin Rammer

Proposed by Zeppelinwerke of Friedrichshafen, Germany, this aircraft was intended to ram Allied bombers not zeppelins. It was an unorthodox concept concocted in the desperate days of 1944 that called for destroying enemy aircraft by running into them at up to 600 mph!

The Rammer never received a designation from the Reichsluftfahrt Ministerium (RLM, German Air Ministry), implying that the agency probably never accepted it as a viable concept. Had it been accepted, built, and deployed, it would have been air-launched, probably after being towed aloft by another aircraft. The pilot would engage the Schmidding rocket engine and collide with the wing or tail of an Allied bomber at top speed. Alternately, or prior to the ramming attack, the pilot would have the option of firing a salvo of more than a dozen R4M air-to-air missiles. Maneuvering for such an activity would have been difficult, given that the solid-fuel engine could not be throttled or controlled.

The aircraft was to have been 16 feet 9 inches long, with stubby straight wings spanning 16 feet. It would have had to be heavily armored and heavily reinforced structurally in order to execute its attack, and the likelihood of any aircraft flying a second mission was remote.

Though it was equipped with a landing skid, the Rammer would almost certainly have been impossible to land. If the pilot survived an attack, he would probably have to bail out if he was going to survive. This is, of course, assuming that he was not knocked unconscious or otherwise injured in the collision.

## Zeppelin Fliegende Panzerfaust

Like the Zeppelin Rammer, the "Flying Tank Destroyer" or "Flying Fist" was a crude weapon conceived in 1944 by Zeppelinwerke of Friedrichshafen with little concern for the safety of its crew. It was a straight-wing aircraft that was 19 feet 8 inches long with straight wings spanning 14 feet 9 inches. Like the Rammer, it would have been towed aloft by a parent aircraft, whereupon the pilot would ignite six rockets engines clustered at the rear of the aircraft. Like the engine of the Rammer, these would be uncontrollable solid-fuel motors.

Though the term *Panzerfaust* is generally applied to antitank weaponry, the Fliegende version apparently was intended to be used as an interceptor. Operationally, the pilot would make one pass at enemy bombers and fire a brace of air-to-air missiles. The designers seem to have accepted the notion that the aircraft was impossible to land. The entire front section of the fuselage was a large escape capsule, which detached from the rest of the aircraft and descended by parachute—*theoretically* carrying the pilot to safety.

## Northrop XP-79

Deliberately colliding with an enemy aircraft is an act of what most of us would call desperation. To deliberately design an aircraft for such a purpose is far more so. When this was done in Germany with the Zeppelin Rammer, it was a response to the truly desperate air defense situation the Luftwaffe faced in late 1944. That the concept was also considered in the United States raises some eyebrows. That a prototype was actually designated and *built* (the Zeppelin Rammer was neither) makes for a curious tale of an extraordinary secret weapon.

John Knudsen "Jack" Northrop in regarded as the leading exponent of the flying wing in the history of American aviation. Though there were other creators of flying-wing aircraft, notably Walter and Reimer Horten in Germany, the largest and most successful of such aircraft ever built were Northrop products. Jack Northrop's flying-wing research in the 1930s led to some interesting and unusual prototypes. Probably the strangest of these was the Northrop XP-79.

Conceived in 1942 and developed under the secret MX-324 project designation, the XP-79 had more in common with the advanced German aircraft of 1944 than it did with anything else being done in the United States at the time. First of all, Northrop was alone among American planemakers to be a proponent of flying wings, an idea that gained favor in Germany in 1944–1945. Second, Northrop's XP-79 concept called for the pilot to be lying face-down rather than seated, something we usually associate with more radical German designs.

Of course, the notion of using deliberate collision as an offensive weapon was a 1942 tune straight out of the German desperation songbook of 1945. Finally, Northrop originally envisioned the XP-79 as a rocket-powered plane.

The Heinkel He.176 became the first rocket-powered aircraft in the world in 1939. The concept attracted the attention of several designers in Germany—notably Alexander Lippisch and Willy Messerschmitt—and Jack Northrop in the United States. Northrop's answer to the requirements of the MX-324 secret project called for a liquid-fuel Aerojet rocket main engine, delivering 2,000 pounds of thrust, which would be augmented by two solid rocket boosters for takeoff.

In March 1943, two months after the USAAF ordered three XP-79 prototypes, it was decided to complete one such aircraft with a pair of Westinghouse 19B turbojets instead of the rocket. It would be designated as XP-79B. Ultimately, the Aerojet engine was dropped entirely, and the other two aircraft were canceled. The first glide tests of the unpowered XP-79B began in July 1944. It was 14 feet long, with a wingspan of 38 feet. The wing had been constructed of heavy-gauge magnesium in order to facilitate the ramming mission and to allow adequate heat shielding for rocket fuel. Its twin vertical stabilizers stood seven feet six inches.

The jet engines were fitted during the summer of 1945, and the first flight occurred on September 12, less than two weeks after World War II officially ended. High over the USAAF test range at Muroc Army Air Field, the XP-79B became uncontrollable and test pilot Harry Crosby was killed attempting to bail out. The aircraft was destroyed in the crash, the project was canceled, and the concept was never revisited by the American military.

## 19

## Luftwaffe Very Long-Range Bombers

Prior to World War II, strategic airpower, the use of large numbers of very large bombers to strike an enemy's heartland, had been widely discussed as a theory. Britain and the United States, while not fully embracing the strategic doctrine, had taken steps toward developing large bombers.

In Germany, strategic airpower had largely been rejected in favor of tactical airpower, which is the use of smaller bombers in closer cooperation with ground forces. While the Reichsluftfahrt Ministerium (RLM, German Air Ministry) and the Luftwaffe embraced the notion of really huge flying boats, such as the Blohm und Voss Bv.222 and Bv.238, they were produced only in very small numbers.

When World War II began, large British aircraft such the Avro Lancaster and Handley Page Halifax were ready. In the United States, the Boeing B-17 Flying Fortress and Consolidated B-24 Liberator were in the early stages of their production career. In Germany, Luftwaffe planners envisioned a short war and intended to make do with medium-range bombers.

By 1943, as the above-mentioned British and American bombers were striking Germany's industrial heartland from bases in England, the Luftwaffe had no equivalent strategic bomber. There were, in fact, long-range aircraft in the Luftwaffe arsenal—such as the Focke-Wulf Fw.200 and the Heinkel He.177—but nothing was available in significant numbers and with a significant bomb load.

By the time that the RLM and the Luftwaffe woke up to the importance of bombers with the range of Lancasters and Fortresses, it was probably too late. Giving such a notion nary a thought, they went a step further. If the Allies were striking Germany from England, then Germany would respond by bombing *America* from Germany!

In the summer of 1944, the RLM issued its "Amerika Bomber" requirement for an aircraft with a range of nearly 7,000 miles, making it capable of taking off from occupied Europe, bombing New York or Boston, and returning to its base without refueling. Such an aircraft would, the RLM specified, be capable of carrying a bomb load of 4,000 kilograms (8,800 pounds). Many innovative designs were submitted, but nothing was deemed satisfactory in the first round.

Ironically, the aircraft that was ultimately chosen in 1945, the Horten XVIII intercontinental bomber, was one that came from the farthest afield, and one that would have probably been rejected out of hand in 1944 (see Chapter 20). Other secret long-range Luftwaffe bomber programs are discussed below.

Coincidently, a bomber capable of an unrefueled round-trip across the Atlantic had been taking shape in the United States since 1941. Deemed unnecessary for World War II, it would finally emerge from the cocoon of secret weapons after the war, in 1946, as the Consolidated B-36 Peacemaker.

## Messerschmitt Me.264

Before the Amerika Bomber of 1944, there had been the Amerika Bomber of 1941.

Though the Luftwaffe and the Reichsluftfahrt Ministerium treated it as a novelty prior to the summer of 1944, the notion of an intercontinental bomber had been on their agenda since at least 1940. In the late 1930s, Messerschmitt had reconnaissance aircraft with ranges up to about 12,000 miles on its drawing boards, and at the end of 1940, the RLM had asked for proposals for a transatlantic aircraft. For this, Messerschmitt submitted a proposal that was accepted.

Despite the fact that the RLM had earmarked Messerschmitt as a producer of fighters, not bombers, six examples of the proposed Messerschmitt bomber were ordered early in 1941 under the designation Me.264. Internally, Messerschmitt referred to the Me.264 as the "Amerika Bomber." Thus it was that Messerschmitt anticipated the 1944 project by nearly three years. It should also be pointed out that, while the United States would not enter the war until December 1941, this eventuality was considered inevitable on both sides of the Atlantic.

Competing demands of Messerschmitt resources delayed the Me.264 project, and ironically, it would not make its first flight until after the one-year anniversary of the United States' entry into the war. Throughout this nearly two years of development, the RLM apparently treated the Me.264 with no sense of urgency.

Curiously, the RLM seems to have lost interest in the idea of transatlantic missions at about the same time as the United States actually entered the war. The Me.264 was reclassified as a maritime patrol plane rather than a strategic bomber. This fact clearly illustrated how the RLM and the

Luftwaffe perceived the overall doctrine of strategic air-power.

The long-anticipated first flight of the Messerschmitt Me.264 finally came on December 23, 1942, at Augsburg, with veteran test pilot Karl Baur at the controls. The aircraft was larger than any Allied strategic bomber then in service—68.5 feet long, with a wingspan of 127 feet 7.5 inches. The latter was subsequently increased to 141 feet 1 inch in the second and third prototypes.

The Me.264 flew initially with Junkers Jumo 211 radial piston engines, but the operational aircraft were scheduled to be equipped with more powerful BMW 801 radials. With the latter engines, the Me.264 had an estimated gross weight of over 100,000 pounds and an estimated maximum bomb load of 4,400 pounds. The estimated maximum range was over 9,300 miles.

Comparisons are occasionally made with the Boeing B-29 Superfortress, the American "super-bomber" of World War II. Though both very-long-range-bomber programs were "super-secret," certain of their similarities are uncanny. The unusual "all-glass" nose and flight deck was nearly identical in the two aircraft, and the Me.264's wingspan was revised in early 1943 to be within *two inches* of that of the B-29. Apparently a German spy in Seattle had gotten hold of the specifications.

The B-29 was ordered in September 1940 and made its first flight on September 21, 1942, three months before the Me.264, which had a lower priority at the Luftwaffe than the B-29 had within the USAAF. Indeed, this difference in perception would sidetrack the Me.264 program at the same time as the B-29 was being fast-tracked. Before the end of 1945, the B-29 demonstrated a range of nearly 8,000 miles and routinely flew operational missions in excess of 3,000 miles.

As the Me.264 flight test program proceeded in early

1943, Messerschmitt again brought up the Amerika Bomber concept, but it fell on deaf ears at the Luftwaffe.

The second prototype was completed, but destroyed in a late 1943 air raid before its first flight. The third prototype was never finished. The last flight of the first Me.264 came in June 1944; a radio message intercepted a month later suggested that it was to have been used to evacuate Adolf Hitler to Japan if the July 20 coup attempt had been a success. It was reportedly through the incident that the Allies learned of the existence of the secret Me.264.

Despite renewed interest by the RLM and the Luftwaffe in the Amerika Bomber concept, the Me.264 program was officially canceled in October 1944. However, Messerschmitt continued to work on the project at company expense. Among the scenarios it studied was the idea of equipping the big bomber with turbojet engines.

## Focke-Wulf Fw.238

The most commonly used long-range four-engine land plane in Luftwaffe service during World War II was the Focke-Wulf Fw.200 Condor. Introduced in the late 1930s as an airliner, it established a reputation for range with a number of spectacular long-distance flights. These included one from Berlin to New York City, during which the plane covered 4,075 miles and stayed aloft for over 24 hours.

When the war started, its great range made the Condor ideal as a maritime patrol aircraft. However, attacking ships at sea was different from wading through interceptors to bomb cities, and the fragile Fw.200 was not a serious contender as a strategic bomber.

Because of the RLM's reluctance to encourage manufacturers to develop strategic bombers, the Fw.200 never evolved into one, and subsequent long-range Focke-Wulf projects were conceived primarily as maritime reconnaissance aircraft.

Among the first of the secret strategic bomber projects undertaken by Focke-Wulf was the Fw.238. Design work on the program began in 1941, with the goal of designing an aircraft with a range of 8,000 miles and a payload capacity of 11,000 pounds. The Fw.238 was to have been 115 feet long with a wingspan of nearly 171 feet. Four BMW 803 piston engines were specified. Defensive armament would have consisted of four remotely controlled turrets, each containing a single 20mm cannon.

When the prototype was not ready for testing by February 1943, the project was canceled and many details were lost in the mists of time.

### Focke-Wulf Ta.400

In 1943, at about the same time that the Focke-Wulf Fw.238 was canceled, Focke-Wulf's legendary designer, Kurt Tank, was starting work on his large Ta.400 project. An ambitious secret project, it was to have contained two pressurized crew compartments for its 9-man crew in a 96-foot fuselage. The wingspan of 137 feet 10 inches made it one of the largest aircraft conceived by a German planemaker during World War II. It was intended to have a range of around 3,000 miles, less than the Fw.238, but still exceptional when compared with most Luftwaffe bombers.

The Ta.400 would have been a piston-turbojet hybrid, with six BMW 801 radial engines augmented by a pair of Junkers Jumo 004 turbojets mounted beneath the wings.

The payload capacity was immense, and sufficient for 11 tons of ordnance. This would have included conventional bombs as well as Fx.1400 Fritz X smart bombs and

Henschel Hs.293 and Hs.294 guided missiles. Defensive armament would have included three remotely controlled turrets—each with a pair of 20mm cannons—two atop the fuselage and one beneath. A tail turret would have held four 20mm guns.

Though it could not have reached the United States from Europe, the Ta.400 might have made an extraordinary strategic bomber for missions against targets in the United Kingdom. With such defensive and offensive firepower, it would have been clearly superior to any Allied strategic bomber of the war except the Boeing B-29 Superfortress.

## 20

Jet Bombers

When World War II began, jets were a novelty, and building a jet bomber was among the most remote ideas for serious military planners. As the war was coming to a close, German designers were frantically working on numerous such projects. In the United States and the United Kingdom, the pace was more leisurely, but a number of projects were taking shape. Only in Germany, however, would jet bombers actually reach operational units.

## Arado Ar.234 Blitz

Like the Messerschmitt Me.262, the Arado Ar.234 Blitz (Lightning) is a well-known milestone in the history of aviation technology, but familiarity does not detract from its immense significance. Like the Me.262, it was an extremely important secret weapon in the arsenal of the Luftwaffe. Just as the Me.262 was the world's first widely used jet fighter, the Blitz was the world's first jet bomber.

It was late in 1940 when Arado undertook the study of

a large, fast turbojet-powered aircraft. At the time, the Reichsluftfahrt Ministerium (RLM, German Air Ministry) was urging such a project with an eye toward using the plane for reconnaissance. The speed and altitude promised by turbojet power would make the weapon practically invincible to interception by Spitfires over the United Kingdom.

As with other German jets of its era, development of the Ar.234 lagged because of the lack of availability of engines. Bugs were finally worked out of the first-generation Junkers Jumo 004s by the spring of 1943, and a first flight of the Ar.234 occurred on June 15. By this time, the Luftwaffe had adopted the notion of arming the aircraft with bombs so that they could be used in either the reconnaissance or the strike role.

Originally, Arado planned for the Ar.234A production variant to be landed on a skid, but flight testing showed that this scenario left a great deal to be desired, and the skid was replaced with conventional tricycle landing gear. This led to the revised Ar.234B aircraft, now known officially as Blitz, which made its debut on March 10, 1944.

The Ar.234B was 41 feet 5.5 inches long, with a wingspan of 46 feet 3.5 inches. Powered by a pair of Junkers Jumo 004 turbojets, it had a gross weight of 21,715 pounds, including an offensive bomb load of up to 3,300 pounds. It had a range of over 1,000 miles when stripped down for reconnaissance work, or just under 700 miles with a full bomb load. Defensive armament included a pair of 20mm cannons in the tail. Unlike most medium bombers, the Blitz could be operated by a single crewmember.

Though a prototype aircraft actually ventured into action in the skies over Normandy on June 6, 1944, routine Ar.234B operations did not get under way until later in the summer. As planned, the aircraft were able to conduct reconnaissance missions over the United Kingdom without being intercepted. Initially, they were based in northern France and tasked with keeping an eye on British Channel ports to provide intelligence on Allied shipping.

The Luftwaffe began using the Blitz as a bomber in October, and it saw a great deal of service during the December 1944 offensive in the Ardennes that resulted in the Battle of the Bulge. Operationally, the Ar.234B was used to hit high-priority and heavily defended targets because it was fast and, therefore, hard to shoot down. Though only about 200 Ar.234Bs were built, they were used widely—from the Western Front to northern Italy.

Arado experimented with various four-engine Ar.234, and several such prototypes were built and flight tested. By early 1945, plans were under way for a four-engine Ar.234C, with four Jumos paired into two nacelles. A few had been built when the war ended. Other theoretical plans included an Ar.234P night fighter and the idea of using the Blitz as an airborne launch platform for Fieseler Fi.103 (V-1) cruise missiles.

As the Allies, especially the Soviets, closed in on German territory, the Luftwaffe made a concerted effort to destroy existing Blitz aircraft to keep them out of enemy hands. By the time World War II finally came to a close, however, the straight-wing Blitz, a revolutionary concept just a few years earlier, was already becoming obsoleste.

## Arado E.560

Among the high-speed secret aircraft projects that made the Ar.234 obsolete was Arado's own E.560. The *E* stood for *Entwurf,* meaning "design" or "rough draft." In general terms, it was like an enlarged Ar.234 with a crew of two in a pressurized flight deck.

Little is known of the E.560 because most of the project documentation was destroyed at the end of the war. However, it is known that Arado completed a number of rough drafts under the general 560 heading. These included a version with four BMW 003 turbojets that would have been 73 feet 2 inches long with a wingspan of 78 feet 9 inches. A smaller version that was 59 feet 1 inch long, with a wingspan of 76 feet 1 inch, would have had *six* BMW 003 turbojets. Bomb loads for the E.560 projects ranged up to 8,000 pounds, and a turboprop variant promised a range of over 2,000 miles.

## Blohm und Voss P.188

The Hamburg shipbuilding firm of Blohm und Voss was best known in the aviation world during World War II for its large flying boats and a passion for strangely asymmetrical aircraft. The firm also entered the world of jet bombers with a series of designs undertaken as Projekt 188. This work culminated in a large bomber with a pressurized, two-person flight deck and four Junkers Jumo 004 turbojets. The aircraft would have been 57 feet 8 inches long, with a wingspan of 88 feet 8 inches, making it significantly larger than operational German jets of the 1944–1945 era. What made this aircraft unusual was the Blohm und Voss trademark of unorthodox configuration.

While other manufacturers were incorporating swept wings—and even *forward* swept wings—Blohm und Voss used both forward- and back-swept wings in the same wing! From the top, the wings looked like a pair of letter *V*s attached to the fuselage. The inner segment was swept back 20 degrees, and the outer part was swept forward at the same angle.

It seems that this would have focused a great deal of aerodynamic drag at the center of the wing. Had the aircraft flown, its unusual appearance would certainly have evoked unknowing witnesses's notion of an archetypal secret weapon.

## Daimler Benz Airborne Aircraft Carriers

The idea of a larger aircraft carrying a smaller one as a "parasite" was not new in World War II. The U.S. Navy had done extensive testing of fighters carried by dirigibles during the 1930s. During World War II, the Japanese Yokosuka MXY7 Ohka was a piloted aircraft that was air-launched operationally. After the war, the U.S. Air Force conducted tests in which F-84 and F-85 fighters were launched and recovered aboard B-29 and B-36 bombers.

During the war, the most ambitious such project was actually a series of projects undertaken by Daimler Benz. The company, whose products include the ever-popular Mercedes-Benz automobiles, was best known at the time as a producer of internal combustion engines. These ranged from power plants for trucks and tanks to the famous DB 605 that powered the Messerschmitt Bf.109G fighter. However, the giant industrial firm also designed enormous aerial aircraft carriers.

The first of these was an enormous aircraft that would have been larger than any that had ever flown. Lifted by six engines, it would have had a wingspan of more than 308 feet. The engines were to be Heinkel Hirth 021s, the turboprop engines based on the Heinkel Hirth 011 turbojets.

This "mother" of all "mother ships" would have had a fixed landing gear widely spaced to accommodate a high-speed jet bomber hanging beneath it.

The plan called for the latter aircraft also to be quite large—with a wingspan of more than 85 feet. This bomber held a crew of four in a pressurized flight deck and would have been powered by BMW 018 turbojets mounted under the wings. Because it would not have to expend fuel taking off by itself, this aircraft could carry a very large bomb load. It has been reported that engineers calculated a barely imaginable payload capacity in excess of 30 tons.

The scaled-down second version was still enormous and still promised a 30-ton bomb load. It called for a mother ship that was 117 feet long with a wingspan of slightly over 117 feet. The jet bomber would have been huge—101 feet long (about the same as a B-29 Super-fortress) with a wingspan of 72 feet. For this aircraft, Daimler Benz planned to use its own DB S06 turbojet engine, which delivered over 28,000 pounds of thrust.

In 1945, a variation on the project replaced the single jet bomber with as many six smaller ones that were actually manned cruise missiles. These aircraft are discussed in Chapter 8.

## BMW Strahlbomber I

The BMW (Bavarian Motor Works or Bayerische Motoren Werke) company is best known today—as it was before World War II—as a leading manufacturer of automobiles and motorcycles. During World War II, the company was a prominent producer of military motorcycles as well as very large numbers of piston engines for surface vehicles and aircraft. BMW was also an important pioneer in the development of turbojet engines.

Like Daimler Benz (another World War II engine maker that is now best known as a carmaker), BMW dabbled secretly in the world of jet aviation in 1944–1945. Among their projects were their straight-wing Strahljäger (jet-fighter) designs as well as their swept-wing Strahlbomber (jet bomber).

The first Strahlbomber was a very large aircraft—60 feet 9 inches long, with a wingspan of 87 feet. It was to have been powered by six of the company's own BMW 003 turbojets, two of them mounted side by side in the nose. This made the aircraft look like it had a large screaming mouth. The other engines were located in the wings. There was a vertical stabilizer, but no horizontal surfaces aft of the wing.

The second BMW Strahlbomber design was the same length as the first, but its wingspan of 113 feet 3 inches was significantly greater. Engineers promised an increase in bomb capacity from 8,000 pounds to 11,000.

As with Daimler Benz, BMW built many thousands of aircraft engines during World War II but no aircraft. After the war, the company returned to manufacturing motorcycles as well as the tiny Isetta two-person automobile. BMW turned to full-size cars in the 1960s and later to luxury automobiles. In 1990, BMW was back to aircraft engines through a joint venture with British Aerospace aimed at the business jet market.

## Focke-Wulf "1000x1000x1000" Program

As the Reichsluftfahrt Ministerium gradually awoke to the potential of jet bombers in 1944, they issued the secret "1000x1000x1000" bomber requirement. What they had in mind was an aircraft that could carry a bomb load of 1,000 kilograms (2,200 pounds) for 1,000 kilometers (621 miles) at a speed of 1,000 kph (621 mph). The payload and range were within the capabilities of existing bombers, but the third part of the triad, the speed criterion, called for a jet aircraft.

Focke-Wulf created three distinct designs in an effort to meet the needs of the 1000x1000x1000 specifications. The first aircraft, Projekt A, was a sleek, swept-wing bomber with a "fighter-style" cockpit that looked at first glance like the postwar Boeing B-47 Stratojet. It was to have been 46 feet 6 inches long with a wingspan of 41 feet 6 inches. A pair of Heinkel Hirth 011 turbojets would have been mounted under the swept wings in a manner nearly identical to the outboard engines of the later Stratojet.

The Projekt B variant of the Focke-Wulf 1000x1000x1000 bomber also utilized a pair of Heinkel Hirth 011 turbojets, but it was there that the similarity ended. The airframe was a boomerang-shaped flying wing spanning 46 feet. It was aerodynamically clean except for an egg-shaped pressurized flight deck attached to the center leading edge of the wing, and two "winglets" attached at the wingtips.

Projekt C was generally a variation on Projekt A in which the engine nacelles were canted slightly outward. The idea is reported to have been that such an arrangement would provide asymmetrical thrust from one engine to compensate for the loss of thrust from the other.

The 1000x1000x1000 aircraft remained on the drawing board when World War II ended. No evidence has been found to suggest that Boeing engineers specifically studied the Projekt A bomber when creating the Stratojet (Boeing Model 450). Boeing's famed aerodynamicist George Schairer did, however, revise the project as a swept-wing rather than straight-wing aircraft after reviewing captured German data.

## Douglas B-43 Jetmaster

The first American jet bomber was ordered in 1944 but did not make its first flight until after the war. The Douglas Aircraft Company's Jetmaster was actually a follow-up to another secret project, which was also an intriguing aircraft in terms of its propulsion system.

Originally ordered in 1943 as the XA-42, the Douglas XB-42 was designed as a faster, cheaper aircraft that could match the range of a Boeing B-29 Superfortress, if not its bomb load. Aerodynamic drag was reduced by burying two Allison V-1710 engines inside the fuselage and using them to drive a pair of contra-rotating "pusher" propellers in the tail. Because of its appearance, the aircraft was given the name "Mixmaster," inspired by the Sunbeam kitchen appliance that was introduced in the 1930s. The first of two Douglas Mixmaster aircraft had its maiden flight on May 6, 1944.

Though there was no production contract, America's first jet bomber borrowed the clean lines of the Mixmaster. The wing and fuselage of the new aircraft was similar to those of the XB-42, and both had a crew of three. Ordered in March 1944, the Douglas XB-43 Jetmaster made its historic first flight on May 17, 1946, powered by a pair of General Electric J35-GE-3 turbojets that were buried in the fuselage. It was 53 feet 10 inches long, with a wingspan of 70 feet 7 inches and a gross weight of 39,000 pounds.

With the war over, and because of its limited range—no more than 4,000 miles—the Jetmaster did not go into production, but Douglas built a YB-43 for further flight testing.

# 21

## Stealthy Flying Wings

The first flight of one of the ultimate secret weapons of the
Cold War occurred on July 17, 1989, at Edwards AFB in
California, after much publicity by the U.S. Air Force. Bil-
lions had been spent in absolute secrecy over a decade to
create what was rightly seen as a remarkable technical
achievement. The debut of the Northrop B-2 "stealth
bomber" made aviation history.

It was a huge aircraft that was *all wing*. The engines and
crew compartment were blended into the wing itself. There
was no fuselage and no vertical surfaces of any kind. For
many reasons, including its surface coating, and especially
its shape, the B-2 was "stealthy," meaning it had virtually
no visible radar signature.

However, as extraordinary as the B-2 was, it was not the
original of its kind.

## Horten IX (Gotha Go.229)

On February 2, 1945, at Oranienburg in Germany, a handful of engineers and Luftwaffe personnel celebrated the first flight of what might have been one of the ultimate secret weapons of World War II. The debut of the Horten IX (officially designated as Gotha Go.229) was an historical event.

It was a large aircraft that was *all wing*. The engines and crew compartment were blended into the wing itself. There was no fuselage and no vertical surfaces of any kind. The principles of "stealth" had yet to be discovered, but the Horten IX was certainly 44 years ahead of its time.

The Horten IX was the brainchild of Walter and Reimer Horten, a pair of brothers who were, by 1945, Luftwaffe officers. Like John Knudsen "Jack" Northrop, whose company later produced the B-2, the Horten brothers had experimented with flying wings during the 1930s. The idea they shared was that eliminating the fuselage would eliminate a great deal of aerodynamic drag and make an airplane faster and more fuel efficient.

The first Horten flying wing was a glider, but in 1935, the brothers tested their Horten II with a small piston engine. Their subsequent experiments included both gliders and powered aircraft. By 1938, their work had attracted the attention and encouragement of the Reichsluftfahrt Ministerium (RLM, German Air Ministry). Though this interest began to wane by 1943, the brothers decided to continue their work.

Without official sanction, however, they could not really do so. Just as it seemed to be the end of the road for the Hortens, they were discovered by Reichsmarschall Hermann Göring, head of the Luftwaffe. He was very interested in their work and ordered that their latest project, the

Horten XI, be given the necessary support to get it off the ground.

The first glide tests of an unpowered Horten IX occurred in February 1944 at Göppingen, and work proceeded on a second prototype that would be equipped with a pair of BMW 003 turbojets.

It was decided that the Horten IX would be manufactured by Gotha (Gothaer Waggonfabrik) at Friedrichsroda under the designation Go.229. Seven prototypes and 20 preproduction Go.229As were ordered in the summer of 1944.

By the end of 1944, two powered prototypes were taking shape. They would be 24 feet 6 inches long, with a wingspan a quarter inch less than 55 feet. They would weigh 10,450 pounds empty and 19,840 fully loaded and fueled. Armament in operational aircraft was to have included four 30mm cannons as well as two 2,205-pound bombs.

As noted, the first flight came on February 2, 1945, at Oranienburg, with test pilot Erwin Ziller reporting good flying characteristics. The potential for extremely high speed was observed but not explored. Some have suggested that the Horten IX/Go229 had the potential to exceed the speed of sound, but such a test never happened. A second flight two weeks after the first turned tragic when an engine cut out and the aircraft went out of control. The prototype crashed and Ziller was killed.

Despite this setback, Göring remained enthusiastic and the program continued, with several additional Go.229s nearing completion. A second powered prototype was completed and nearly ready to go when U.S. Army troops captured Friedrichsroda on April 12.

After having amazed the GIs who first saw it, this sleek secret weapon was taken back to the United States for evaluation. However, it was never flown and apparently had little influence on postwar aircraft development. Today this aircraft sits in a hanger—its wings removed, but stored nearby—at the Smithsonian Institution's Paul Garber facility in Silver Spring, Maryland.

## Simultaneous Gotha Projects

As noted above, the Reichsluftfahrt Ministerium (RLM, German Air Ministry) intended for the Horten IX to be manufactured by Gotha (Gothaer Waggonfabrik) at Friedrichsroda under the designation Go.229. This firm, which had built large bombers for the Kaiser's air force during World War I, was dormant from 1919 to 1933. After reopening, the company built gliders and light-powered aircraft. Receiving the nod to build the Luftwaffe's most advanced jet fighter was clearly an anomaly.

During the time that Gotha was preparing for production of the Go.229, its own designers went to work on a parallel series of similar aircraft under the umbrella of a secret undertaking called Projekt 60. It remained secret from Allied intelligence until after the war, but it is not clear whether Projekt 60 was also secret from Walter and Reimar Horten *during* the war.

The Projekt 60-series designs were swept-wing, tailless fighter aircraft that were similar to the Horten IX. However, the Horten IX—like the Northrop B-2 of four decades later—was truly all wing, with crew compartment, landing gear, and engines all molded into the wing structure. Each of the Projekt 60 aircraft had a fuselage. These were was a very aerodynamically clean fuselages, but they were distinctly not part of the wing. While the Horten IX—like the B-2—had no vertical tail surfaces whatsoever, the Projekt 60 designs had vertical rudder structures at the wingtips.

Another important feature of the Projekt 60 aircraft was that the engines were attached to the fuselage rather than blended into the structure of the craft. One engine was attached to the top of the fuselage, with a second below the fuselage. The engine choice was initially the BMW 003 turbojet, although the Heinkel Hirth 011 turbojet was mentioned as an alternate for the P.60B and P.60C.

As with most Luftwaffe jet-fighter designs of the 1944–1945 period, the armament specified was four 30mm cannons.

In an effort to reduce the fuselage cross-section as much as possible, the initial Projekt 60 design, designated P.60A, had both crewmembers lying prone. This feature, which was common to some of the more desperate German jet fighter designs of the era, was eliminated in the P.60B, which called for the crew to be seated.

The P.60A was to have been 31 feet 2 inches long, with a wingspan of 40 feet 9 inches. The P.60B, which was substantially different and not simply scaled up, was 32.5 feet long and had a wingspan of 44 feet 9 inches. The former was abandoned in late 1944 in favor of the P.60B. The RLM gave Gotha the go-ahead in early 1945 to begin cutting metal for a prototype of this aircraft.

Gotha engineers were apparently on a roll, for the P.60B was quickly superseded by a design for the P.60C. This was the largest of the three, and the one whose fuselage appears to be the least radical and the least "Horten-like." The P.60C would have been 35 feet 10 inches long, with a wingspan of 44 feet 4 inches.

## Subsequent Horten Projects

While the Horten IX was moving toward flight testing, its creators were working on additional "flying wing" projects.

As noted earlier, in the summer of 1944, Otto Saur of Albert Speer's Ministry of Armaments came up the idea of an inexpensive and easy-to-build jet fighter that could be manufactured quickly in very large numbers. This was the Volksjäger (People's Fighter) program. Though they clearly had more important fish to fry, the Horten brothers did as other designers across Germany did. They designed a Volksjäger. It seems to have been the patriotic thing to do in the summer of 1944.

The Horten X Volksjäger was naturally a flying wing, but it was simpler than the more advanced IX, and it had a single engine. It was smaller than the Horten IX—23 feet 7 inches long with a wingspan of 46 feet. The Horten X did not win the competition for the Volksjäger program, and the brothers moved on to other things.

These included the dart-shaped Horten XIIIB, which was designed to operate at supersonic speeds in excess of 1,000 mph. Based on the Horten XIIIA glider, it had wings that were radically swept back to 60 degrees. As such, the wingspan dimension of 39 feet 5 inches was the same as that of the fuselage length.

### Horten XVIII Intercontinental Bomber

Probably the most ambitious project the brothers undertook was the Horten XVIII intercontinental bomber. It was to have been a massive all-wing aircraft with its massive wing spanning 131 feet. This compares with 141 feet 3 inches for the Boeing B-29 Superfortress, the largest operational, land-based bomber of World War II. (Today's all-wing Northrop B-2 has a wingspan of 172 feet.)

The Horten XVIII was created in response to the 1944 RLM request for proposals for an "Amerika Bomber." As discussed in Chapter 19, such an aircraft would have had a range of nearly 7,000 miles, sufficient to drop 4,000 kilograms of bombs on New York City and return to Europe without stopping. The first round of requests went only to manufacturers with bomber experience, which excluded the Hortens. However, when they heard in December 1944 that no other designer could meet the range requirements, the brothers went to the drawing board. They realized that the curtailment of aerodynamic drag inherent in a flying-wing design was an easy prescription for long range.

The result was the Horten XVIII, which theoretically met the range and payload capacity by using six Junkers Jumo 004 turbojets, which were blended into the wing.

Like the Northrop B-2 of the 1980s, the structure was primarily nonmetal. While the B-2 is made up of carbon-fiber composites, the Horten XVIII was to be made of glue-impregnated wood. This idea was similar to the Duramold process that Howard Hughes used for the H-4 "Spruce Goose," which was taking shape in Culver City, California, at the same time as the Horten brothers were designing their aircraft.

The Luftwaffe approved the Horten XVIII project in February 1945. The flying-wing concept was itself a convincing argument for range capabilities. However, the Horten brothers had two things going against their ambitious project. First and most obvious was that time was running out for the Third Reich, and anyone with any sense of current events knew that the end was near. Second, the Hortens were "prototypers," with a small shop and no mass-production capability. Just as they had to go to Gotha for the Horten IX, they would have to find some other industrial partner to join them in the bomber project. In this case, it would be the Junkers firm.

It is axiomatic that any machine designed or modified by a committee automatically loses any sparkle of innovation and falls behind schedule. To make a long story short,

Junkers engineers, who'd had more than a decade of experience with large aircraft built in very large numbers, asserted themselves in the Horten XVIII program. They insisted on adding vertical tail surfaces and moving the engines to external locations. This, of course, increased aerodynamic drag on an aircraft that was remarkably clean aerodynamically. Of course, it also added many weeks to the development schedule.

The Horten response was a further refinement and simplification of the original design, which was designated as Horten XVIIIB. In March 1945, the RLM apparently agreed to permit the Hortens to go ahead with construction of a prototype that would be ready for flight tests by about October 1945. As we have seen so often in these pages, by that time, the Third Reich was just a bitter and fading memory.

In the United States, however, Jack Northrop was moving forward with his own flying-wing designs. His first such aircraft were already a reality, and June 26, 1946, would mark the first flight of his large XB-35 flying-wing bomber. It was a piston-engine aircraft, but it would be re-engined as the all-jet YB-49, which first flew on October 21, 1947. The wingspan was 172 feet, identical to that of the much later Northrop B-2.

Jack Northrop died in 1981 when the B-2 was still a very secret project and far from its first flight. The Horten brothers, on the other hand, lived to see the big flying wing become a reality. Reimar died in 1994, and Walter in 1998.

## Lippisch Flying Wings

Of course, not all the flying wings were Horten products. Several memorable designs were created by Dr. Alexander Lippisch, the legendary aerodynamicist who had conceived the Me.163 rocket fighter. Indeed, Lippisch had been halfway to the flying-wing concept from the very beginning. Dating back to his early glider projects, he minimized the importance of the fuselage and maximized the wings in order to maximize lift. His Me.163 and the various hypothetical aircraft from which it evolved were mostly wing, with only a vertical stabilizer in the tail.

In 1943, after four years at Messerschmitt, Lippisch became director of the Luftfahrtforshungsandstalt Wien (LFW), an aeronautical research institute in Vienna. It was here that many of his advanced flying-wing designs evolved. The most advanced was his Projekt 11 of 1944.

Unlike the boomerang-shaped Horten and Northrop flying wings, the Lippisch P.11 was essentially a large triangle that measured 23 feet from front to back with a wingspan of 35 feet 5 inches. The wingtips were slightly clipped, and there was a slightly protruded nose where the cockpit was located. The intakes were located adjacent to the cockpit, and the two Junkers Jumo engines were completely buried within the wing. There were two vertical stabilizers, but aside from that it was a very aerodynamically clean aircraft.

In a series of meetings held in late November of 1944, the RLM made tentative plans to acquire this aircraft, along with the Go.229. However, no official designation seems to have been assigned to the Lippisch P.11. At least one model, though probably not a wind-tunnel one, is known to have been built before events overtook the development of this Lippisch flying wing.

Designed in late 1944, the Lippisch Projekt 12 and Projekt 13 were ramjet flying wings loosely based on the Lippisch DM-1 glider of the late 1930s. Essentially, they were composed of two triangles at right angles from each other like a child's paper airplane. Take the Projekt 13 aircraft, for example. The wing was a triangle 22 feet long and 19 feet 5 inches at the base. Aligned perpendicular with the centerline of this triangle was the vertical stabilizer, which was a second triangle that was just as long but half as wide. The cockpit was squeezed into the stabilizer and the ramjet engine was rammed though the center of the contraption where the two triangles intersected.

Unlike the Horten projects, none of the Lippisch flying wings ever took to the air.


## Arado E.555

Best known for the Ar.234, the world's first jet bomber, Arado also produced a series of ambitious designs for large flying wing bombers. These were all developed under the general secret project designation of E.555, with the prefix representing *Entwurf*, which, as we have said before, means "design" or "rough draft."

The Arado E.555 program was initiated late in 1943 while, elsewhere in the company, the Ar.234 was working through its flight test program. The idea was to present the Reichsluftfahrt Ministerium with a bomber with a range of better than 3,000 miles that was capable of carrying 8,800 pounds of bombs. Most important, it would have to be fast enough—better than 500 mph—to outrun Allied fighters.

Over the course of a year, about a dozen distinct E.555 designs came off the Arado drawing boards. Of these, the first was the most visually impressive, which probably led to its being chosen a half-century later to become a Revell model kit. The E.555.1 was mostly a huge wing, spanning nearly 70 feet, with a small, stubby flight deck with a glazed nose. It accommodated a crew of three, including a rearward-facing bombardier-navigator.

Defensive armament included two remote-control turrets—one atop the fight deck and one aft—each of which carried a pair of 30mm cannons. Additional such weapons were fixed to fire forward from the leading edges of the wings. Six BMW 003 turbojets were arrayed above the rear fuselage and between two vertical stabilizers.

The E.555.2, the E.555.3, and the E.555.4 were similar to their predecessor, but with different turbojet engine scenarios—four Heinkel Hirth 011s, two BMW 018s, and three BMW 018s respectively. The E.555.6 used the latter engine layout, but it was scaled up to a wingspan of more than 93 feet, with a range of more than 4,600 miles.

The E.555 designs from late in 1944 abandoned the pure flying-wing configuration by pushing the vertical stabilizers well aft of the wing on long booms. The E.555.10 had a wingspan of 77 feet 8 inches, with the stabilizers pushed back to 63 feet from the nose. As with most later variations, three BMW 018 turbojets were specified for the E.555.10.

Probably the program's final design, the E.555.11 had a conventional fuselage that was 82 feet 4 inches long. It used the same wing as the E.555.10, and had a conventional tail with both horizontal and vertical surfaces. Four BMW 018 turbojets were mounted in pairs atop the wing. The trade-off in the reversion to a conventional configuration seems to have been the bomb capacity, which increased to over 13,000 pounds.

In December 1944, a year after the program was born, the E.555 project was quietly and formally terminated. The secret program had run its course without seeing any of the aircraft built or seriously considered for prototyping. However, five decades later, a German named Josef Poisinger, with the help of his friends Alwin Müller and Hans Rupp, constructed and flew a large flying model of the E.555 flying wing. They used a small piston and propeller engine rather than a turbojet.

# 22

## Strange Aircraft Configurations

Before and during World War II, Germany produced many aircraft with configurations that defied notions of "what airplanes should look like." While these secret programs would probably not have resulted in weapons that tipped the scales dramatically, they are worth mentioning because they are historically important efforts to shape warplane technology. Indeed, they fall into that category of aircraft that explored technologies that were well ahead of their time. In some cases, we are *still* waiting for that time.

### Forward-Swept Wings

By the late 1940s, the notion of high-performance jet aircraft having their wings swept *back* was been accepted and even expected. However, even today, the idea of such aircraft with their wings swept *forward* seems entirely unorthodox. Nevertheless, even before World War II, it had been suggested that such a configuration could improve an aircraft's maneuverability and high-speed performance.

Air moving over the forward-swept wings flows in toward the root of the wing instead of out toward the wingtip. This results in maximum lift focused at the wing root, which is where the fuselage needs to be lifted. Theoretically, this reverse airflow would not allow the wingtips and their ailerons to stall or to lose lift when the aircraft is in a steep dive or steep climb. In other words, forward-swept wings allow an aircraft to remain more maneuverable in extreme situations.

Several gliders with forward-swept wings were tested before World War II, and in the United States, the Langley Memorial Aeronautical Laboratory of the National Advisory Committee on Aeronautics (NACA, later NASA) did some wind-tunnel work on the concept in 1931. No powered aircraft would test the potential of the concept for a decade.

During World War II, a number of secret projects involving forward-swept wings were committed to paper. One such jet aircraft was secretly built and flight-tested. Exactly four decades would pass before the evolution of aviation technology allowed for a second such flight-test program!

In Germany in 1942, Focke-Wulf considered and abandoned a jet-fighter concept with wings swept forward at 30 degrees. A year later, Dr. Hans Wocke, an engineer at Junkers, was exploring unorthodox methods in an effort to create a large bomber that could outrun Allied interceptors. Given a great deal of latitude, Wocke and his team dusted off the forward-swept concept, which had been studied in Germany as well as in the United States.

Wind-tunnel tests confirmed the theoretical data, and Wocke received a green light to proceed as quickly as possible. In order to get the first test aircraft flying quickly, the wings—swept forward at 25 degrees—were attached to an existing fuselage from a Heinkel He.177. The tail surfaces were pulled from an "off-the-shelf" Junkers Ju.388. The forward landing gear was from a captured American B-24. The resulting hybrid was designated as Ju.287. It was 60 feet long, with a wingspan of just under 66 feet. The gross weight was 44,000 pounds. Operational bombers might have carried more than 4,000 pounds of bombs.

The prototype was completed at the Junkers facility at Dessau early in 1944 and trucked to an airfield at Brandis, near Leipzig. Four Junkers Jumo 004 turbojet engines were fitted, two under the wings and two bolted to the sides of the forward fuselage. For the tests, an extra boost came from a Walter 501 rocket that was attached beneath each jet engine. These gave a total of 10,000 pounds of extra thrust for takeoff and then were jettisoned.

The first flight of the radical concept occurred secretly on August 16, 1944. Through the 16 outings that followed, the big aircraft was deemed easy to handle despite the unorthodox wing. Though it was intended as a low-speed prototype, the Ju.287 was successfully tested in dives exceeding 400 mph. A second prototype and a preproduction aircraft (Ju.287.V3) were under construction when the Ju.287 program was abruptly canceled in July 1944. That might have been the end of the story, but in January 1945, the RLM suddenly revived the Ju.287 and ordered it into production!

The second two Ju.287s were scheduled to be retrofitted with BMW 003 engines, and the Ju.287.V3 preproduction aircraft was to be equipped with a tail cannon. However, this work was not completed because the Junkers facility was captured by Soviet troops in April. The Soviets rounded up the engineering and flight-test personnel and shipped them east along with the Ju.287.V3.

Work resumed on the project under Soviet auspices and under intense secrecy. The Ju.287.V3 made its first flight near Moscow in May 1947 with German test pilot Paul Julge at the controls. A reverse-engineered fourth aircraft was built under the designation Ef-140 (or I-40) and reportedly first flown in March (some sources say October) 1949 at Podberze near Moscow.

Little was learned in the West for half a century about the Soviet tests. However, captured German data that was evaluated in the United States after World War II indicated that the forward-swept wings were not entirely successful because the technology and materials did not then exist to construct a wing that was rigid enough to overcome bending and twisting forces without making the aircraft too heavy.

Three decades later, the introduction of composite materials opened a new field of aircraft construction, making it possible to design lightweight airframes and structures that were stronger than those made of conventional materials, and, thus, able to withstand immense aerodynamic forces.

In 1977, the United States Defense Advanced Research Projects Agency (DARPA) and the U.S. Air Force Flight Dynamics Laboratory (now the Wright Laboratory) issued proposals for a research aircraft designed to explore the forward-swept-wing concept. Grumman Aircraft Corporation was chosen in December 1981 to receive a contract to build two such aircraft under the designation X-29. The first of these made its debut on December 14, 1984, just over 40 years after the Ju.287. The two X-29s would make a total of 436 flights through 1992.

In 1997, half a century after the Ju-287.V3 was first flown in the Soviet Union, the Russian design bureau Sukhoi unveiled and first flew its Su-37 Berkut (Royal Eagle), a high-performance jet fighter with forward-swept wings. At 74 feet, it was longer than the Ju.287 bomber, although its wingspan of 54 feet 9.5 inches was less.

## Blohm und Voss Asymmetrical Aircraft

Although the firm is best known to the aviation world for building Germany's World War II flying boats, Blohm und Voss is most notorious for its profoundly eccentric asymmetrical aircraft, notably the Bv.141 (see the section on the P.188 in Chapter 20). It was precisely this eccentricity that doomed an otherwise operable and reportedly reliable airplane.

The story of the "deformed" Bv.141 began in the late 1930s when the Luftwaffe was shopping for a light ground-attack aircraft to supplement the Junkers Ju.87 Stuka, which was already in production. Focke-Wulf proposed its Fw.189, while at Blohm und Voss, designer Dr. Richard Vogt came up with what is certainly the most unconventional design to be built during the war.

The Bv.141 was also probably the most asymmetrical airplane ever flown. The right wing was *longer* than the left wing, and the crew compartment was *not* in the fuselage. It was located in a pod mounted on the right wing. The center of gravity was between this compartment and the fuselage.

It would be intriguing to know what Vogt had in mind when he conceived such a design, as it would be interesting to know what charisma he must have brought into play in order to convince his employers to take it to the RLM. In any case, the RLM was predictably appalled by this strange contrivance and refused to appropriate a single pfennig for its production. There were scowls and snickering and suggestions that Blohm und Voss stick to flying boats. Focke-Wulf's Fw.189 won the production contract.

Blohm und Voss, however, was sufficiently impressed with the Bv.141 that they actually undertook to build it at their own expense. The airplane that emerged from Vogt's drawings was remarkably aerodynamic, which he'd already known. It was 39 feet 10 inches long, with a wingspan of 50 feet 8 inches and a weight of 8,600 pounds, putting it in almost exactly the same size and weight class as the familiar Messerschmitt Bf.110. Powered by a BMW 132 radial engine, the Bv.141 had a respectable top speed of 248 mph and a ceiling of 29,530 feet, while its 700-mile range was almost *twice* that of the Fw.189.

Its first flight, on February 25, 1938, proved the Bv.141 to be more airworthy than its detractors wanted to believe. Several prototypes and 10 Bv.141A production aircraft were followed in 1941 by 5 Bv.141Bs with larger BMW 801 engines, but the poor bird never shook the stigma of its disfigured appearance.

Blohm und Voss continued to explore the asymmetrical concept throughout the war. The two-seat Bv.141 was succeeded by a smaller, faster, single-seat Bv.237, which was 35 feet 3 inches long, with a wingspan of 47 feet 5 inches. Powered by a BMW 801, it had essentially the same asymmetrical configuration as the Bv.141.

The Bv.237 was never built, but design studies continued with Blohm und Voss Projekt 194, which evolved in 1944 as a high-speed fighter closely based on the size and shape of the Bv.141. It would have augmented the piston engine in the nose of the fuselage with a single BMW or Junkers Jumo turbojet in the pilot's module. This would have combined an asymmetrical airframe with asymmetrical thrust that would probably have made the P.194 a difficult aircraft to control.

Blohm und Voss also studied the concept of an asymmetrical flying boat. Dr. Vogt's Projekt 111 was essentially a variation on Blohm und Voss's familiar Bv.138 flying boat. The Bv.138 had three engines; one in the main fuselage and one in each of the two parallel side booms that supported the tail. Under Projekt 111, the main fuselage of the Bv.138 remained largely unchanged, but it was moved to the right. The left boom remained the same, but the right boom was removed. The engine in the left boom remained, and the two engines were relocated to the wing on either side of the fuselage.

## 23

## Strange Vertical Takeoff Aircraft

The idea of a vertical-takeoff-and-landing (VTOL) fighter aircraft has appealed to operational air force commanders since the beginning of military aviation.

Though helicopters existed before World War II and were used in small numbers during it, they were a very slow and delicate craft compared with the robustness of a combat aircraft. Yet combat aircraft needed runways. Military planners yearned for an aerial vehicle that could take off and land like a helicopter, yet fly and fight like an airplane. Such a secret weapon would clearly provide an important advantage to the side that possessed it.

Numerous technologies were studied and tested throughout the 1950s, but success was finally achieved in the 1960s by Hawker Siddeley (later part of British Aerospace, BAe) through the use of a vectored-thrust jet engine. This would lead to the legendary Harrier "Jump Jet," which became operational in the 1970s.

Meanwhile, the first—and arguably the most radically innovative—VTOL designs originated in Germany during

World War II. Allied bombers were destroying German airfields, and the Luftwaffe was interested in VTOL aircraft. The Bachem Natter may be considered as such an aircraft, but it was really designed for vertical takeoff alone. Landing was not considered to be a necessary part of the scenario.

## Focke-Wulf Triebflügel

While the Natter was being developed, work was proceeding on a VTOL interceptor that would be recoverable and reusable. In September 1944, Heinz von Halem at the Focke-Wulf firm proposed an aircraft that he called the *Triebflügel,* which roughly translates as "floating wing." In fact, the aircraft would have *no* wings.

The Triebflügel was a wingless airplane that stood on its tail like a rocket, with a huge three-bladed propeller around its waist. This propeller had a diameter of 37 feet 9 inches, which was greater than the 30-foot length of the fuselage. The propeller was powered by a vectorable Pabst ramjet engine at the tip of each blade. Von Halem designed his Triebflügel to be capable of speeds up to 621 mph.

Armament would have consisted of two 30mm and two 20mm cannons mounted in the nose adjacent to the cockpit.

The Triebflügel would need no runway. It could take off from any patch of level ground. Had there been enough time left in the war for the Triebflügel to actually go into production, it might have been the ideal air defense fighter because the Luftwaffe could have based it almost anywhere.

After World War II, the U.S. Navy became interested in the same idea. It would be to their advantage to have a fighter aircraft to provide air defense for operations that took place when and where an aircraft carrier was not available. In March 1951, less than a year after the start of the Korean War, the U.S. Navy ordered prototype VTOL fighters from both Lockheed and Convair under the designations XFV-1 and XFY-1. Both were to be designed around the huge Allison 6,825 hp XT40-A-16 double-turboprop engine, and whichever design proved itself superior would be ordered into production. The pair of contra-rotating propellers, while huge, were smaller than the one imagined for the Triebflügel.

The first Lockheed XFV-1 was completed in 1953. It stood 36 feet 10 inches in its vertical stance and had straight wings that spanned 30 feet 11 inches. However, the XT40-A-16 wasn't ready, so the XFV-1 was fitted with the less powerful 5,332 hp XT40-A-14. Because of this, it was decided not to attempt any vertical takeoffs, and the aircraft was fitted with a crude auxiliary landing gear for horizontal takeoffs. Taxi tests began in December 1953, and test pilot Herman "Fish" Salmon made the first horizontal takeoff on June 16, 1954. In the course of 32 test flights, Salmon never made a vertical takeoff, but while in flight, he made the transition from horizontal to vertical mode many times.

Convair's delta-wing XFY-1 stood 32 feet 3 inches tall and had a wingspan of 27 feet 8 inches. It was first flown on August 1, 1954, six weeks after the XFV-1. Because the XFY-1 had a gross weight of 14,250 pounds, a ton lighter than the XFV-1, Convair decided to attempt a vertical takeoff. This proved successful, but both Convair and Lockheed soon discovered that it wasn't the takeoffs that were the inherent design flaw in the concept, it was the landings.

As a test pilot of the Focke-Wulf Triebflügel would certainly have discovered in 1945, the pilot literally had to look over his shoulder and *back* the aircraft down. Thus, landings were considered impractical and even dangerous!

Kelly Johnson, the great aircraft designer who was responsible for many of Lockheed's greatest aircraft, said of the XFV-1, "We practiced landing on clouds, and we practiced looking over our shoulders. We couldn't tell how fast we were coming down, or when we would hit. We wrote the Navy: 'We think it is inadvisable to *land* the airplane.'"

Both the XFV-1 and XFY-1 programs were canceled in 1955 at the request of the contractors.


## Heinkel Wespe

At the same time that Focke-Wulf was working on the Triebflügel, the Vienna office of the Ernst Heinkel firm was developing a similar project. Known as the Wespe (Wasp), it was similar to the Triebflügel in that it stood on its tail, with the pilot sitting at the top near the nose. It stood 20 feet 4 inches tall, roughly two-thirds the height of the Focke-Wulf aircraft.

While the Triebflügel was powered by ramjets at the tips of the massive propeller blades, the Wespe—like the postwar XFV-1 and XFY-1—was powered by an internal turbine engine that drove a smaller propeller. However, unlike the postwar aircraft, the Wespe's engine and propeller were in the waist, not the nose. This six-bladed propeller measured 16 feet 5 inches in diameter and was powered by a Heinkel Hirth 021, the turboprop engine based on the Heinkel Hirth 011 turbojet. The latter was widely specified for German experimental aircraft in 1944–1945. As with the Focke-Wulf VTOL design, armament for the Wespe would have included nose-mounted cannons.

The Wespe was never produced and was succeeded as a design concept by the Heinkel Lerche, which was also created at the Vienna facility.

## Heinkel Lerche

By late February 1945, Heinkel went back to the drawing board to come up with a larger and improved version of the Wespe VTOL aircraft. Unveiled on March 8, after two weeks of intensive engineering, the Lerche (Lark) was like the Wespe in terms of its overall configuration and its armament. At 30 feet 10.4 inches, it was half again taller than the Wespe and would have been roughly the same height as the Focke-Wulf Triebflügel.

Instead of a single engine and a single propeller, as specified for the Wespe, the Lerche was powered by a pair of Daimler Benz DB.605 engines driving two contra-rotating propellers with diameters of just over 13 feet.

Vienna fell to the Soviets less than two months after the Lerche design was finalized, and the prototype was never completed.

# 24

## Poison Gas

On August 13, 1918, near Ypres, Belgium, a young German corporal was caught in a poison gas attack and temporarily blinded. Three months later, while recovering in a military hospital, he heard of the abdication of Kaiser Wilhelm II and felt so betrayed that he decided to become a political activist.

The corporal's decision helped change the course of twentieth-century world history. His injury helped ensure that the most horrible weapon of World War I would not be used on European battlefield during World War II.

It is hard to know whether Germany might have used poison gas in World War II if Corporal Adolf Hitler had *not* been gassed at Ypres, but his stated horror of the experience is often cited as the reason it wasn't.

In World War II, the use of chemical weapons was shunned by all combatants except Japan, who used gas extensively against Chinese forces in Manchuria. Japan considered using it against U.S. forces, but realized that the American capability to retaliate with gas exceeded their ability to attack with it.

Though it was to be eclipsed in degree of horror by the nuclear era after 1945, poison gas was the most feared weapon in any arsenal for the four decades leading up to 1945.

The poison gas era of modern warfare began in 1915. Artillery shells containing gas were used on the Eastern Front in January, but the first full-scale German gas attack occurred on April 22, 1915, against French troops at the village of Langemarck near Ypres. For the next three years, the British and French used poison gas often as did the Germans. It is estimated to have resulted in 100,000 deaths, not to mention a million veterans who suffered permanent disabilities.

The first gas to be used was chlorine, known as a suffocating gas because it slowly fills the lungs of the victims with fluid, asphyxiating them. Other deadly asphyxiants were phosgene (carbonyl chloride), introduced in 1915, and diphosgene (trichloromethylchloroformate), introduced in 1916.

As terrible as they were, these gases pale when compared with the so-called blister gases, which include mustard gas (dichlorethylsulphide). The most awful of World War I gases, mustard attacks the skin, especially the eyes, creating large burnlike blisters. If inhaled, it does the same to the lungs, where the blisters cannot be treated. The result is usually an agonizing death. Mustard would later be a favorite of Iraqi leader Saddam Hussein, who readily used it against Iranian troops—as well as Iraqi civilians—during the 1980s.

Poison gases were particularly effective in trench warfare because they are heavier than air. The huge, billowing clouds of gas would be released upwind from containers and settle in the trenches, which were, by definition, below ground level. Soldiers hiding from enemy fire would choke to death. Those who leaped out of the trenches to catch their breath were also likely to catch the fire of an enemy sniper.

Gas masks were developed to prevent the gas from reaching the eyes or lungs of intended victims, but less lethal gas, such as tear gas, would be used to trick the enemy into exhausting the protective capability of their masks. The Germans also used vomiting gases such as diphenylchloroarsine, which forced victims to remove their gas masks.

Hydrogen cyanide gas, which is instantly lethal, was not widely used because it is lighter than chlorine or mustard, and there was always a risk of it drifting over friendly territory or dissipating before it could be effective. The British and French, who had the prevailing winds in their favor, used it more often than the Germans.

In 1925, the "Geneva Protocol for the Prohibition of the Use in War of Asphyxiating, Poisonous or Other Gases, and of Bacteriological Methods of Warfare" was adopted. It prohibited only the *use* of poison gas and germs in warfare. Between 1932 and 1937, unsuccessful attempts were made to work out an agreement that also prohibited the production and stockpiling of biological and chemical weapons.

Despite the Geneva Protocol, poison gas was used occasionally in the interwar period, notably by the Italians in Ethiopia in 1935, where they killed approximately 15,000 people with mustard gas.

When World War II began, all the major combatant nations had stockpiles of various types of poison gases that were loaded in shells or canisters and ready for use. It is commonly assumed that chemicals were not used because of the threat of retaliation in kind. While this may have been a factor, available documents also show that military staffs on both sides were skeptical about the utility of chemical weapons and did not recommend their use. Of course, each side knew that the other had generally good antichemical protection.

## German Nerve Gases

Though Hitler refused to attack his battlefield enemies with poison gas, the defenseless inmates at the concentration camps were not so fortunate. As with the Japanese attacks on the Chinese, the Germans used gas only on people they considered to be "racially inferior."

The Führer's skittishness about battlefield gas also did not hamper German research and development into newer and more terrible gases. Several important new weapons were created to augment the large stockpiles of mustard and other agents. These new gases were nerve gases, which attack the central nervous system rather than the respiratory system, as the first-generation military gases did.

Tabun (ethyl-dimethyl-amidophosphorocyanidate) was first isolated in 1936 as a by-product of weed-killer research being done by a scientist named Gebhardt Schraeder. It was soon discovered that tabun provided a tenfold increase in lethality over phosgene. The asphyxiant gases could kill in hours; tabun was deadly within minutes of exposure. Zyklon-B, the gas used in the death-camp gas chambers, is related to tabun and was originally invented as an insecticide.

In 1942, a tabun factory was established at Dyhernfurth in Silesia, and it manufactured an estimated 500,000 tabun artillery shells and 100,000 tabun bombs before Soviet forces captured it in 1945. Those munitions found by American and British forces were reported to have been subsequently destroyed, but Soviet forces retained the German stockpiles that they discovered.

Another nerve gas, sarin (isopropyl-methyl-phosphoroflouridate) was discovered in 1938. As with tabun, attempts were made to undertake a manufacturing program. However, sarin is an anticholinesterase organophosphate compound, and the complexity of its manufacture prevented scientists from producing and stockpiling large numbers of munitions.

On March 20, 1995, a half-century after the end of World War II, terrorists belonging to Chizuo Matsumoto's Aum Shinrikyo religious cult released sarin at several points in the Tokyo subway system, killing 11 and injuring more than 5,500 people.

The last of the German World War II nerve gases was soman (pinacolyl-methyl-phosphoroflouridate). It was not discovered until 1944, and no attempt was made at mass production.

## The Long Dark Shadow of Japanese Chemical Weapons

Ironically, it was in 1995, about the same time as the Aum Shinrikyo terrorists poison-gassed the Tokyo subway, that the secrets of Japan's own history as a *user* of poison gas began to emerge.

Though it was not widely discussed in the West until the mid-1990s, Japan used poison gas, especially mustard gas, extensively in China between 1937 and 1945.

The involvement of the Japanese Empire in World War II was a direct outgrowth of a prewar foreign policy that called for its political and economic domination of the Far East. Japan's aggressiveness had been a half-century in the making when it launched an all-out war on China in 1937. In 1931, Japan had incorporated the Chinese territory of Manchuria into its empire, renaming it Manchukuo and setting up a puppet emperor. In 1937, Emperor Hirohito's forces moved on China itself. Shanghai, Beijing (then known as Peiping), and Nanking were battered into submission and occupied. Japan reportedly used poison gas in the fighting around Wusung and Shanghai in August 1937, and on more than a thousand occasions thereafter.

According to a 1995 Reuters news report, Keiichi Tsuneishi, a professor at Kanagawa University, obtained copies of Imperial Japanese Army memoranda concerning the use of chemical weapons in China. These documents state that the army produced as many as 5 million poison-gas shells between 1931 and 1945 at facilities on Okuno Island in Hiroshima Prefecture. Further production is said to have occurred in Manchuria.

World War II ended with the Japanese still in possession of a sizable portion of China. Before withdrawing, the Imperial Japanese Army realized the need to conceal the "smoking gun" evidence of its chemical weapons. The huge stocks were buried at sites throughout China or dumped in waterways. These dumps remained largely undiscovered for the next four decades, but by the late 1980s, so many had been accidentally unearthed that a diplomatic crisis in relations between China and modern Japan was provoked.

Beginning in 1989, the two sides began negotiations at governmental level aimed at locating and disposing of the weapons. Over the ensuing years, the Japanese conducted 15 field inspections of its leftover chemical weapons. On July 30, 1999, the two governments signed the "Memorandum on the Destruction of Japanese Discarded Chemical Weapons in China Between the governments of the People's Republic of China and Japan."

According to Japan's official Ministry of Foreign Affairs documents, there were approximately 700,000 abandoned chemical weapons still in China as of December 1999. This estimate was based on an official Japanese interpretation of the results of joint Japanese-Chinese on-site investigations. Meanwhile, the Chinese estimate was *2 million* weapons.

The Japanese Foreign Ministry has admitted that the Imperial Japanese Army also disposed of chemical weapons by dumping them in Lake Kussharo on the northern Japanese island of Hokkaidō. These were reported to have been recovered in June 1999.

The government of Japan also acknowledged that the Chemical Weapons Convention, which came into effect in April 1997, had obliged it to deal with the destruction of these weapons. The Japanese government has stated that it intends to carry out its duty "sincerely in cooperation with the related ministries and government agencies."

The actual destruction of Imperial Japanese Army poison-gas stockpiles is under the direction of the high-profile Office for Abandoned Chemical Weapons, which was established within the prime minister's office on April 1, 1999. Since then, it has proceeded with such activities as a study of destruction technology and a destruction plan.

According to an official statement issued in 2000 by the Ministry of Foreign Affairs of the People's Republic of China, "The discarding of the chemical weapons in China was one of the serious crimes the Japanese militarists committed during the War of Aggression against China. . . . The Japanese discarded chemical weapons have so far been found in more than 30 places in over 10 cities and provinces in China. Eroded by wind and rain for over half a century, some of those chemical weapons are corroding by rust, and some others are leaking, which is greatly endangering the safety of the Chinese people and the ecological environment as well."

The buried caches continue to be dug up. According to a December 2001 article in the *Los Angeles Times,* a Chinese road crew stumbled across a stash of about 20,000 chemical weapons canisters near Nanjing in February of that year.

## Britain Grows Desperate

On at least one occasion during World War II, Britain flirted with the notion of using poison gas from its arsenal against the Germans. This was in response to the notorious Vergeltungswaffen (Vengeance Weapons). In 1944, Prime Minister Winston Churchill instructed his Joint Planning Staff to examine whether chemical weapons might be useful against the German V-1 and V-2 sites in France that were launching missiles against England. The report sent back to Churchill concluded: "Gas attacks are unlikely to be any more effective than bombing with high explosives."

## The United States Prepares for Chemical Warfare

Like Britain, the official policy in the United States during World War II was to avoid the use of poison gas. However, the Americans were not immune from a moment of temptation.

President Franklin D. Roosevelt, in a statement warning the Axis powers against the use of chemical weapons, had expounded: "Use of such weapons has been outlawed by the general opinion of civilized mankind. This country has not used them, and I hope we never will be compelled to use them. I state categorically that we shall under no circumstances resort to the use of such weapons unless they are first used by our enemies."

The United States initially showed little interest in developing or using chemical weapons in World War II, but as casualties mounted in the Pacific Theater, the notion was revisited. The invasion of Japan was scheduled to begin in November 1945 with Operation Olympic, landings on the southernmost Japanese home island of Kyushu. This would be followed in March 1946 by Operation Coronet, an invasion of the main Japanese home island of Honshu. Based on experiences with the Japanese defense of Iwo Jima and Okinawa early in 1945, officials expected a million U.S. casualties. The use of poison gas was evaluated as a means of last resort to break the Japanese will to resist. Planners highlighted approximately 50 urban and industrial areas that were seen as being suitable for gas attacks. These secret studies were almost certainly conducted without knowledge of the extremely secret Manhattan Project nuclear weapons program.

By 1945, the U.S. Army had stockpiled nearly 5 million chemical artillery shells, more than a million chemical bombs, over 100,000 aircraft spray tanks, and 43,000 mustard-gas land mines made from 1-gallon rectangular tin cans. These were available in the Pacific for use by April 1945. The nuclear strikes four months later rendered this arsenal unnecessary. Half a century later, most of the stockpile was finally destroyed.

# 25

## Biological Warfare

Few weapons have been so universally condemned as inhumane and contrary to civilized behavior, yet the deliberate use of biological weapons in warfare has long been discussed and theorized about.

Known as germ warfare during most of the twentieth century, biological warfare actually predates human knowledge of the existence of germs. Centuries ago, it might have involved such tactics as dumping livestock carcasses in enemy drinking water. It is understood that the smallpox virus was responsible for decimating a sizable proportion of the native population of North America during the eighteenth and early nineteenth centuries. There is an ongoing controversy over whether the U.S. government deliberately used the smallpox virus to eradicate certain tribes, but there was probably too little technical understanding of smallpox at the time to make this likely.

The systematic isolation of microorganisms for offensive purposes is a twentieth-century invention. Considerable evidence suggests that the Germans had such a program during World War I that involved covert contamination of cavalry animals and livestock feed with such things as anthrax. Such agents were used, for example, on French mules in the Middle East, and on Romanian sheep set for export to Russia.

After World War I, biological warfare was the prohibited in the same 1925 "Geneva Protocol for the Prohibition of the Use in War of Asphyxiating, Poisonous or Other Gases, and of Bacteriological Methods of Warfare." However, as with poison gas, the treaty condemned only the *use* of germ warfare, not the production or possession of such weapons. Though many nations maintained stockpiles of such agents, Japan was the only nation to cross the line during World War II and actually use biological weapons on a widespread basis.

## Japan's Secret Unit 731

It has been suggested that Japan initially developed its biological warfare program as a means of deterring the Soviet Union from using biological warfare against it in any future conflict. However, it was China that would bear the brunt of Japanese germ warfare.

In 1932, Dr. Shiro Ishii of the Imperial Japanese Army began a biological weapons research program that evolved into the secret Unit 731 organization in 1936. Established under Ishii's direction, Unit 731 was headquartered at Pingfan in occupied Manchuria, where it was composed of a sprawling campus of more than 150 buildings, staffed by more than 3,000 scientists and technical personnel. Satellite facilities were also located at Mukden, Changchun, and Nanking.

The purpose of the Unit 731 complex was to create offensive weapons and to conduct experiments on human subjects. The latter appears to have been undertaken with particular enthusiasm, as an estimated 10,000 persons were killed with biological agents through 1945. Among these were a number of captured American civilians and military personnel.

The specific toxins Unit 731 tested are named in a 1997 article in *The Journal of the American Medical Association*. It was authored by Lieutenant Colonel George W. Christopher, a doctor with the U.S. Air Force Medical Corps, along with Lieutenant Colonel Theodore J. Cieslak, Major Julie A. Pavlin, and Colonel Edward M. Eitzen Jr., all doctors on the staff of the U.S. Army Medical Corps. Among the Unit 731 pathogens were anthrax (*Bacillus anthracis*), meningitis (*Neisseria meningitidis*), and cholera (*Vibrio cholerae*).

Imperial Japanese Army field trials of the products of the Unit 731 laboratories had begun by 1940. These included contaminating Chinese food and water supplies with anthrax, cholera, and salmonella by aerial spraying or through direct application by ground troops. It has also been asserted that Unit 731 cultivated bubonic plague and that millions of infected fleas were airdropped over Chinese cities. At least 11 Chinese cities are thought to have been attacked with Unit 731 biological agents.

In 1942, Kitano Misaji replaced Shiro Ishii as head of Unit 731, and later that year the Imperial Japanese Army stopped using biological warfare on the battlefield because of the high numbers of friendly casualties that were suffered. In a 1941 attack against Changde (then called Changteh) in northern Hunan Province, an estimated 1,700 Imperial Japanese Army troops were reported to have died as a result of a Unit 731 field trial.

These trials were described in great detail during war

crimes prosecution of participants in the Unit 731 program who had been captured by the Soviet Union during and after World War II.

As the war neared its end, however, and Japan became encircled, it was prepared to use biological warfare against the continental United States as a weapon of last resort.

In 1944, Tokyo's military planners considered sending biological agents into the United States by means of balloon bombs (see Chapter 2) to create epidemics of plague or anthrax. In 1945, Unit 731 embarked on an operation called "Cherry Blossoms at Night," which would have used submarine-launched kamikaze aircraft to infest the San Diego, California, area with the plague (see Chapter 15). It was a close call. The huge Japanese I-400–class submarines were on their way. The target date was to have been September 22, 1945, but by that time, the war was over.

## The German Biological Weapons Arsenal

As was the case with poison gas, the Germans did not use biological weapons on the battlefield during World War II, but they did use them on the inmates of their concentration camps, and they did maintain a contingency battlefield arsenal. There is, however, a case of the Germans deliberately dumping sewage into a reservoir in Czechoslovakia.

It is well known that concentration camps were used as a grisly test bed for brutal "medical experiments." Among these were deliberate infection of humans as part of studies of potential vaccines. The pathogens injected into people are recorded to have included both rickets (*Rickettsia prowazekii* and *Rickettsia mooseri*) and the hepatitis A virus.

While gas was used for the wholesale slaughter of inmates, biological weapons were apparently not. This was probably to avoid secondary infection and to prevent epidemics that might spread to the general population.

## The American Arsenal

As with Germany, the United States created and maintained a biological weapons research program during World War II, but did not use such weapons on the battlefield. A civilian agency, the War Reserve Service, directed the American program, but its primary research and development facility was at the U.S. Army's Camp Detrick (later Fort Detrick) in Maryland. The size of the U.S. biological weapons arsenal was minimal compared with that of the Japanese, with only 5,000 bombs containing anthrax (*Bacillus anthracis*) produced.

After the war, the United States took the threat of biological weapons so seriously that it undertook extensive secret debriefings of Japanese Unit 731 participants. In a controversial step that was not widely known for decades, the United States granted immunity from war crimes prosecution to Japanese scientists—including Kitano Misaji and Shiro Ishii—in exchange for their disclosing Unit 731 research data.

In 1969 and 1970, President Richard Nixon issued executive orders officially terminating the United States' offensive biological weapons program. The United States adopted a policy never to use such weapons, including toxins, under any circumstances whatsoever. National Security Decisions 35 and 44 mandated the cessation of offensive biological research and production and the destruction of the biological arsenal. Research efforts were directed exclusively to the development of defensive measures such as diagnostic tests, vaccines, and therapies for potential biological weapons threats.

Stocks of pathogens and the entire biological arsenal were destroyed between May 1971 and February 1973 under the auspices of the U.S. Department of Agriculture, the U.S. Department of Health, Education and Welfare, as well as state agencies in Arkansas, Colorado, and Maryland, where stockpiles existed. Small quantities of pathogens were retained at Fort Detrick for testing of antigens.

## 26

## Rumors of Very Strange Weapons

At the distant fringes of the lore of the secret weapons of World War II, the line between documented fact and science fiction becomes blurred. This chapter deals with some of the most far-fetched and unconfirmed rumors of wartime secret weapons without offering an opinion as to their veracity. Almost never are such rumors precisely true, but often they are based on some small kernel of reality. On the other hand, such rumors are frequently planted as deliberate efforts at misinformation. Either or neither explanation may be operable here.

The obvious question to ask is: Why are these things still unconfirmed?

Certainly, after more than half a century, some concrete evidence must have leaked out, or someone must have come forward. Many World War II secrets remained so for 20 or 30 years. The British code-breaking Ultra program (see Chapter 4) was secret until the 1970s, and even the Navajo Code Talkers could not discuss their code until the 1960s. By the 1970s, though, the U.S. government was going to great lengths to declassify American and captured enemy material from World War II, but not everything was declassified.

There are numerous possible reasons why the items listed below are still unconfirmed. These begin, of course, with the view that they are pure fantasy. On the other hand, a conspiracy theorist would answer that the projects were considered to be so secret or so sensitive that the "powers that be" went to great lengths—even including the killing of witnesses—to keep things secret.

Another explanation is that things were so secret and so sensitive for so long that they were forgotten. They were simply filed away in an "X-File" and lost, just as we tend to lose things that we tuck away in the back of a closet for safekeeping. People who were involved retire and pass away, and new generations who were not on the need-to-know list come and go.

Whatever the reasons, these strange secret weapons still intrigue us. You be the judge.

## Invisibility and Time Travel

People have been interested in defeating the laws of physics since well before H. G. Wells wrote *The Time Machine* (1895) and *The Invisible Man* (1898). While the sorts of invisibility and time travel imagined by Wells and countless science-fiction writers of the twentieth century are still, of course, considered impossible, recent studies in theoretical physics have indicated that forward time travel may be possible by using wormholes that are known to exist in deep space—although reaching the wormholes remains impossible. Nevertheless, conspiracy theorists, people who take science fiction way too seriously, and people with too much time on their hands still insist not only that invisibility and/or time travel are possible, but that agencies of the U.S. government have made secret use of them.

It has long been rumored that such experiments took place during World War II, but there has never been any hard evidence or official confirmation. It is not known whether this is because the rumors are just pure fantasy, or that the secret projects became the objects of deep and long lasting cover-ups.

In the summer or autumn of 1943 (depending on which telling of the story one hears), the U.S. Navy destroyer escort USS *Eldridge* (DE-173) was allegedly made invisible, moved forward and backward in time, and teleported from the Philadelphia Naval Yard to Norfolk, Virginia. The incident is known as the "Philadelphia Experiment."

The USS *Eldridge*'s deck log and war diary indicate that the actual ship was in neither place during this period. Repeated searches of records in the Operational Archives Branch of the Naval Historical Center have located no documents that confirm either the event or any interest by the Navy in teleporting its vessels.

The history of the USS *Eldridge* is well documented. She was launched on July 25, 1943, by the Federal Shipbuilding and Dry Dock Company of Newark, New Jersey, and commissioned on August 27, 1943, with Lieutenant C. R. Hamilton, USNR, in command. Between January 4, 1944, and May 9, 1945, the *Eldridge* operated in the North Atlantic, escorting convoys carrying men and matériel to support Allied operations in North Africa and Southern Europe. She made nine voyages to shepherd convoys to Casablanca, Bizerte, and Oran.

On May 28, 1945, the *Eldridge* departed New York for service in the Pacific. En route to Saipan in July, she made contact with an underwater object and immediately attacked, but no results were observed. She arrived at Okinawa on August 7 for patrol duty, and the war ended a week later. She continued to serve as an escort on the Saipan–Ulithi–Okinawa routes until November. The ship was decommissioned and placed into reserve in June 1946. In January 1951, she was transferred to Greece under the Mutual Defense Assistance Program and recommissioned as the *Leon* (D-54). In 1991, she was decommissioned, but she continued to serve as a permanently berthed training facility.

According to the Philadelphia Experiment story now in circulation, the project grew out of a super-secret "Project Rainbow," not to be confused with the Project Rainbow that was a series of war plans drafted between 1939 and 1941. While the Project Rainbow in the Philadelphia Experiment story was said to be aimed at making large objects invisible, this may simply be someone's interpretation of a project that was, in reality, aimed at *reducing* visibility of large objects to *radar*—clearly a different matter altogether.

It has been theorized that a magnetic field surrounding an object would distort light waves or radar waves sufficiently to make it seem to disappear. The first of at least two experiments is said to have occurred at the Philadelphia Naval Yard on July 22, 1943. When large generators were turned on, a fog reportedly enveloped the ship, and when it cleared, the ship had apparently vanished. When the generators were turned off, the fog, and then the ship, reappeared.

Three months later, on October 28, the ship faded from view, disappeared in flash of light, and rematerialized at Norfolk. After a few moments, it vanished from Norfolk and reappeared in Philadelphia. The crewmembers were reportedly sick and disoriented. The Philadelphia Experiment was supposedly continued after World War II under the so-called Montauk Project, named for the U.S. Air Force facility at the eastern end of Long Island.

Not counting the crew, there would probably have been dozens, if not hundreds, of witnesses to the Philadelphia Experiment. Incredibly, no eyewitnesses and no member of the crew have ever come forward to comment on allegations of the experiment.

The story of the Philadelphia Experiment apparently originated with Carlos Allende, a.k.a. Carl Allen, who claimed to have been a seaman in the Port of Philadelphia area while the alleged events were occurring and to have had knowledge of them. Interest in the rumor grew so much that books were published and two motion pictures, *The Philadelphia Experiment* (1984) and *The Philadelphia Experiment II* (1993) were released.

The Navy did, in fact, conduct secret research in Philadelphia to find methods for ships to evade detection by enemy forces. Allende/Allen apparently mistook research on evasion as research on invisibility. He may have gotten the idea in part from an article that has occasionally been reprinted in the Philadelphia papers about a ship (not USS *Eldridge*) and crew that suffered damage from a storm at sea.

## Adolf Hitler and the Concave Earth Cult

There are people who still believe that the earth is either flat or hollow. The strangest of all theories concerning the planet's physical configuration was the one reportedly held by Adolf Hitler and many members of Nazi Germany's ruling elite. It was suggested after World War II that Hitler had believed that the world was neither spherical, flat, nor hollow—but concave!

Hitler is said to have been convinced by the hollow earth theorists that the surface of the earth was actually the concave *inside* surface of a spherical bubble surrounded by an infinite mass of solid rock. This theory holds that the sky is actually a cloud of blue gas in the center of a sphere that is illuminated by the sun, which is much smaller than mainstream astronomers have postulated.

This strange conviction is discussed in such books as *In the Name of Science* (1946) by Gerard S. Kuiper; *Pseudo-Sciences Under the Nazi Regime* (1947) by Willy Ley; and *The Morning of the Magicians* (1968) by Louis Pawels and Jacques Bergier.

As the story goes, Hitler sent Dr. Heinz Fisher, one of Germany's leading experts in radar and infrared radiation, to the Baltic Sea island of Rügen in April 1942. Fisher was told to undertake a long-distance search for the British fleet. Because the world was concave, he had only to direct his radar straight *up* in order to detect China. Thus, using a 45-degree angle, he ought to have been able to "see" the British fleet in the North Atlantic. A great deal of rare, high-technology equipment was allegedly devoted to the project. Needless to say, Fisher's attempt to locate Hitler's adversary proved futile. In spite of such "technological set-backs," some members of the Oberkommando Wehrmacht, the German High Command, are said to have continued to believe in the theory of a concave earth.

After the war, Dr. Fisher came to the United States to work on advanced weapons projects. As late as 1957, he was reported to have been working on the American hydrogen bomb program.

## Flying Saucers

At 2 P.M. on the afternoon of Tuesday, June 24, 1947, a private pilot named Kenneth Arnold took off from the airport at Chehalis, Washington, en route to Yakima. The 32-year-old Boise, Idaho, businessman had no idea that he was about to fly into the opening scene of one of the major controversies of the twentieth century.

The founder and chief salesman for Great Western Fire Control Supply, Arnold traveled the airways of the rural Northwest in his three-place Callair selling and installing automatic and manual firefighting equipment, and he had just completed a service call at Central Air Service in Chehalis.

The air was smooth and visibility excellent, so Arnold decided to take time out to look at the wreckage of a U.S. Marine Corps/Curtiss R5C-1 Commando transport plane that had crashed sometime before near Ashford, Washington, on the southwest slope of Mount Rainier. Arnold approached the extinct volcano at 9,500 feet and then took the Callair lower to investigate some of the deep canyons on Rainier's south side. He turned at Mineral, Washington, and climbed back to 9,200 feet, noting a commercial Douglas DC-4 airliner behind and to his left, about 15 miles distant at 14,000 feet altitude.

At 2:59 P.M., shortly after making his turn, Arnold was startled by a bright flash that looked like the sun reflecting off a shiny object. Thinking he might be too close to another aircraft, he quickly glanced around to locate the source of the reflection. He then observed a "chain" formation of nine aircraft to his left at roughly 9,500 feet and a heading of 170 degrees, rapidly approaching Mount Rainier from the vicinity of Mount Baker to the north.

Arnold noted in particular the ability of the nine aircraft to maintain a close formation at high speed as they passed very near to the slopes of Mount Rainier. As they passed between him and the snow-covered peak, he observed from their silhouettes that they were disk-shaped aircraft that lacked tails. By timing their flight between Mount Rainier and Mount Adams (about 40 miles distant), Arnold calculated their speed at 1,350 mph.

The nine disk-shaped aircraft were in view for less than three minutes, but they set the stage for a controversy that would sweep the nation and the world for the next 40 years. Upon landing, Arnold compared the flight pattern of the nine disks to "saucers" being "skipped across water."

The news media seized upon his choice of words and the "flying saucer" phenomenon was born. The phrase quickly entered the lexicon and became the buzzword for thousands of movies, books, and other forms of entertainment. Soon, the U.S. Air Force acronym *UFO* for such unidentified flying objects also became part of popular folklore. Before long, and for no explicable reason, the theory of flying saucers and UFOs being of extraterrestrial origin was proposed, and it has become the default explanation for what he Arnold saw that afternoon over Washington.

What neither Arnold nor the news media realized at the time was that less than three years earlier, disk-shaped aircraft of a much more earthly kind may have been flying in the skies over Europe.

An often repeated, but never confirmed legend holds that a disk-shaped, gyroscopically stabilized German aircraft exceeded the sound barrier in a test flight near Prague in February 1945. Dates for the test flight vary depending on which account one reads, but most fall within the first three weeks of that month. The February 1989 issue of the German periodical *Flugzeug* contains what is alleged to be an eyewitness account of a person who saw disk-shaped aircraft at Praha-Kbely airport (Prag-Gbell in German) near Prague.

There seem to be two ways of looking at evidence of such aircraft. On one hand, there is the notion that they were aircraft constructed with highly advanced technology that had yet to be publicly reported by any official source. On the other hand, references to them has in recent years, become intertwined with the belief in the extraterrestrial origin of UFOs. Certain people have theorized that the German disk-shaped aircraft were built with the assistance of extraterrestrial beings living inside the earth and/or humanoid aliens from the vicinity of the star Aldebaran. There are also a number of accounts that link the German engineers working on advanced propulsion systems to various occult secret societies, such as Thule and Vril.

Although the extraterrestrial notion is so improbable that it can safely be dismissed, the story of German disk-shaped aircraft has some basis in fact. It is simply hard to know where to draw the line between fact and fantasy.

As noted previously, German aeronautical research created the most technologically advanced aircraft of World War II. In the course of their work, German engineers created myriad advanced concepts and unconventional configurations. When the war ended, Allied aeronautical engineers evaluating captured German data were amazed by what they discovered.

Among the most unusual aircraft designs they found among the German blueprints were several disk-shaped aircraft developed by aeronautical engineering groups working within the Luftwaffe or other government-funded programs.

The basis in fact begins with numerous accounts of specific scientists working on such projects and numerous German technical drawings from the era that have been circulated since the 1950s. Of course, these drawings could easily be clever forgeries and part of an elaborate hoax, but the sheer volume of the reports indicates that something is there.

The cast of characters begins with Viktor Schauberger, an Austrian inventor who seems to have begun working on such projects with official sanction in 1938. He was in his early fifties at the time and had apparently been working for many years on a form of fluid oscillation that could produce high energy and a form of levitation.

Next are a group of four scientists who are widely discussed as having worked on disk-shaped aircraft both as a team and independently. They include Rudolf Schreiver, who is often identified as heading the team, as well as Dr. Walter Miethe, Klaus Habermohl, and an Italian engineer named Giuseppe Bellonzo (sometimes called "Belluzzo"). The project name "Diskus" or "Flugdiskus" is occasionally associated with the work of this team. Another project name that is mentioned is "Haunebu."

The Diskus team is often recognized as having completed a prototype or subscale model of a disk-shaped aircraft as early as the spring of 1941, with a prototype being tested in June 1942. The team and its members are often associated with the February 1945 supersonic flight, but in some accounts Schauberger's name is linked to this event.

Little seems to be known about any of the members of this group, although there is believed to be some evidence linking Miethe to Wernher von Braun in the early 1930s.

The Discus effort is thought to have been centered at a BMW plant near Prague. It was here that a Miethe-designed disk with a central cockpit and a diameter of 138 feet was reportedly completed and tested in the famous February 1945 flight. It is claimed that the disk climbed to nearly 40,000 feet in three minutes, achieving a speed of more than 1,200 mph in level flight. This reported speed is very close to that of the disk-shaped aircraft Kenneth Arnold observed two years later over the Cascade Mountains.

The location of a secret facility near Prague has a plausible explanation. By 1944, many important aspects of the German aircraft industry had been moved from Germany's traditional industrial centers, such as the Ruhr River Valley, to Czechoslovakia and Austria. The idea was to get them as far away as possible from the Anglo-American combined strategic bombing offensive, which was beginning to exact a costly toll from German heavy industry. Messerschmitt, for example, established a major piston-engine-fighter manufacturing facility at Wiener Neustadt near Vienna, and another facility in Czechoslovakia to build the Me.262 jet fighters. (After the war, the Czech firm Avia took over the plant and built Me.262s for the Czech air force.)

Schreiver is reported to have completed his own somewhat smaller prototype at Breslau simultaneous with the completion of the Prague disk. By this time, however, the Soviet army was closing in on both Breslau and Prague.

After the war, Schauberger, Miethe, and Schreiver are all rumored to have been brought to the United States to continue their secret work. Habermohl is believed to have been captured by the Soviets and to have been involved in building advanced aircraft for them during the postwar years.

Some accounts suggest that the Diskus program remained a secret German program after the war, and that it was shifted to a secret underground facility in, of all places, Antarctica. Those who suggest such a theory point out an interest in Antarctica by high level Nazis. This is evidenced by their effort to claim portions of the frozen continent for Germany in 1938—and by German commando operations against Norwegian whaling activities in the Antarctic that are known to have happened in 1941.

According to certain conspiracy theorists, the well-documented U.S. Navy expedition to Antarctica under the command of Admiral Richard Byrd in 1947 was a "cover" for a mission against the secret Nazi "flying saucer base." Byrd returned to the United States in March 1947, and the Arnold sighting occurred three months later.

That the Miethe disk—*if* it existed—could have been

captured near Prague, and could have found its way to the United States, is also plausible. The U.S. Third Army, under General George S. Patton, actually captured large portions of western Czechoslovakia at the end of the war. As German defenses collapsed during the latter part of April 1945, disagreement arose among Allied leaders over *which* areas of the fallen Reich would be captured by *which* Allied armies. General Dwight Eisenhower, the supreme Allied commander, favored allowing the Red Army to capture Berlin, while other Allied leaders—British prime minister Winston Churchill included—sought to have Anglo-American armies vigorously attempt to reach the German capital. Churchill saw no reason why Patton shouldn't attempt to capture Prague, to the south, while Eisenhower leaned toward the idea of American forces securing the vast German state of Bavaria but halting their advance at the Czech border.

As history was actually played out, Eisenhower had his way—almost. In northern Germany, Eisenhower halted Field Marshall Bernard Montgomery's 21st Allied Army Group at the Elbe River on April 25, while the Red Army took Berlin on May 2.

To the south, however, it was a somewhat different story. The Soviet armies here were not advancing nearly so fast as expected. In fact, the forces earmarked to capture Prague were still short of Dresden on April 20. General Patton's immediate superior, 12th Allied Army Group commander General Omar Bradley, echoing Eisenhower's sentiments, had, on April 11, ordered him to halt at the Czech border. However, on May 4, two days after the fall of Berlin, Bradley for some reason changed the order and gave Patton and the Third Army the green light to move into Czechoslovakia.

Patton, who had himself long advocated such a strategy, was immediately ready to roll, and within two days he had seized a sizable slice of western Czechoslovakia, including the major cities of Pilsen and Ceske Budejovice (Budweis).

Some days before, meanwhile, American agents of the Office of Strategic Services (the forerunner of today's Central Intelligence Agency) had reached Prague and determined that the Third Army could take the Czech capital with minimal resistance. When Eisenhower suggested that the Third Army meet the Red Army in Prague, Soviet Chief of Staff General Alexei Antonov strongly objected. Eisenhower relented and on May 6 directed Bradley to order Patton not to move past Pilsen, which was about 50 miles to the west of the Czech capital. The Red Army finally entered Prague on May 9.

Given the confusion of western Czechoslovakia's final week of Nazi occupation, it is not presently known what became of Miethe's project, its associated papers, and the disk aircraft prototype, if it still then existed. The Germans associated with the secret weapons projects destroyed much of the material relating to them to prevent such evidence from falling into Allied hands. However, a large number of less-shortsighted German scientists and engineers realized that the Reich was doomed and that it would be worth their while to surrender to the Allies with their files intact.

Leaving the extraterrestrial hypothesis for Hollywood, one is left to ponder whether or not aeronautics might ever be able to exploit a scientific principle according to which a circular electromagnetic device creates lift. For half a century, the answer was a firm "probably not." Then, in July 2002, the BBC reported that the controversial Russian scientist Yevgeny Podkletnov was trying to "create a device that will defy gravity."

Such a news item would hardly have been worth repeating had BBC not also said that Podkletnov's work was being taken seriously by the world's largest aircraft maker, Boeing. BBC went on to say that George Muellner, the head of Phantom Works, the advanced R&D unit for Boeing, had told the security analysis journal *Jane's Defence Weekly* that the science appeared to be valid and plausible. The BBC reported erroneously that "the hypothesis is being tested [by Boeing] in a programme code named Project Grasp."

In a response to the BBC news item, Boeing issued a press release that stated that Phantom Works was always monitoring potentially breakthrough ideas and technologies and were aware of Podkletnov's work on "anti-gravity" devices. However, the release went on to say that Boeing was not funding any activities in this area at the time. It was also pointed out that GRASP was not a code name for a current project, but rather an acronym for a presentation titled "Gravity Research for Advanced Space Propulsion," in which a Boeing engineer discussed Podkletnov's theory and proposes.

Podkletnov claimed to have countered the effects of gravity in an experiment at the Tampere University of Technology in Finland in 1992. He explained that he found that objects above a super-conducting ceramic disk rotating over powerful electromagnets lost weight. However, the BBC reported that NASA had attempted to reproduce Podkletnov's experiment, but that a preliminary report indicated that tests "gave a null result."

Nevertheless, it is true that the characteristics attributed to the Schreiver and Meithe disks of World War II were still the subject of serious scientific inquiry nearly six decades after the original projects.

## Foo Fighters

During the winter of 1944–1945, Allied pilots in the skies over Europe started reporting strange glowing balls flying around their aircraft at night. The objects seemed to maneuver with great speed, and the Allies began to worry that the Germans had developed a new weapon with startling capabilities.

These were given various nicknames, including "Kraut Balls" and "Foo Fighters." The latter name, adopted by a late-twentieth-century rock band, was actually based on the popular *Smoky Stover* comic strip, which used the phrase *Where there's* foo *there's fire*. Certainly the Allied fliers were seeing something that looked like fire.

After the war, it was learned that German pilots had seen the same things, and German military authorities had correspondingly feared an Allied secret weapon. The phenomenon has been explained as an unusual electrical or optical effect such as ball lightning or St. Elmo's fire.

On the other hand, UFO aficionados often explain Foo Fighters as mysterious spacecraft. Despite having a completely different physical description, they are also frequently linked to stories of Schreiver or Miethe disks or other such aircraft.

## From Focke-Wulf to Avrocar

No discussion of disk-shaped aircraft is complete without mention of the legendary VZ-9-AV Avrocar. Although these craft were built more than a decade after World War II, they have long been described as having their roots in secret German designs from that era.

The VZ-9-AV Avrocar was the very embodiment of the Hollywood image of a flying saucer. It was a silvery metal disk 18 feet in diameter with two bubble canopies for the crewmembers. Unlike the Hollywood saucers of the 1950s, the Avrocar was real. Not only that, it was nurtured with the research and development funding of at least two national governments.

It originated with Avro-Canada in 1952 as the secret program known as Project Y. In the early 1950s, the Canadian government was anxious to encourage a world-class aviation industry in their country, and such advanced projects as Project Y were part of it. It was to be a disk-shaped supersonic aircraft that could be used as a high-altitude fighter or an attack aircraft. Project Y was to possess vertical-takeoff-and-landing (VTOL) capability through the use of a powerful engine in the center of the disk, which directed its thrust straight down.

Coincidentally, a similar design had emerged from the drafting tables at Focke-Wulf during World War II. The Avro-Canada engineers almost certainly had access to this information by way of the British intelligence services. Whereas the Project Y Avrocar was destined to be perfectly circular, the Focke-Wulf aircraft was slightly elliptical in order to accommodate a vertical stabilizer at the rear. The Avro vehicle had no vertical surfaces of any kind.

In theory, the propulsion concept was the same in both aircraft. In the center of the Focke-Wulf, there were two huge contra-rotating propellers that turned parallel to the ground. The propeller blades were, thus, the lifting surface, like the rotors of a helicopter. Because the props turned in opposite directions, their torque would be balanced and the aircraft would be quite stable. The Project Y vehicle would be jet-propelled, with jet exhaust radiated to the edges of the machine and redirected downward by means of a series of valves.

Within two years, the Canadian government abandoned Project Y, but it was picked up by the United States, where it would be developed under the designation VZ-9-AV. The *VZ* stood for "VTOL Research," while the *AV* stood for the manufacturer. The fact that it was the ninth in the series of

VTOL Research vehicles indicated how serious the Americans took the quest for vertical flight.

Two prototypes were completed in 1959, although flight testing did not take place until 1961. The U.S. Air Force primarily and the U.S. Army secondarily would have an interest in the vehicle. When it was discovered that the VZ-9-AV could barely get off the ground and would not be able to operate at high altitude, the Army evaluated it as a hovercraft to carry troops across swamps. It was here that the nickname "Avrocar" was appropriate.

The Avrocar achieved top speeds of under 40 mph, less than the average speed of an army truck. Helicopters were more practical for flying troops over swamps. The project was canceled in 1961, but amazingly, both prototypes still survive. One is at the U.S. Army Transportation Museum at Fort Eustis, Virginia, and the other is at the Smithsonian's Paul Garber facility at Silver Hill in Maryland.

Conspiracy theorists still maintain that the Avrocar was a "cover" for other German-derived disks that actually did achieve high-altitude supersonic flight.

## 27

## Offensive Spacecraft

While the existence of disk-shaped aircraft in Germany during World War II is a matter of conjecture, an even more ambitious project is, amazingly, not only confirmed but very well documented. The Germans had a spacecraft in the design phase during World War II!

This vehicle was actually more sophisticated than the first generation of spacecraft that took humans into space two decades later. The Mercury, Gemini, Vostok, and Vokshod spacecraft the United States and the Soviet Union used in the 1960s were all ballistic return capsules. They were, to use the crude but apt vernacular of the times, "man-in-a-can" spacecraft. They were little more than slightly maneuverable containers in which people—all but one were men—were blasted into space. They returned to Earth dangling from parachutes. The capsules, or "cans," could be used only once.

The German spacecraft of World War II had wings that would have permitted it to land on Earth like an airplane. It was also designed to be reused. Such a winged spacecraft, the American Space Shuttle Orbiter, would not actually be

flown into space and back to Earth until 1981—four decades after the German spaceplane was originally designed. The Russian space program, meanwhile, continues
to rely on capsules in the twenty-first century.

## Sänger-Bredt Raketenbomber (Rocket Bomber)

It is well known and well documented that Austrian-born
aerodynamicist Dr. Eugen Sänger was already under contract with the Reichsluftfahrt Ministerium (RLM, German
Air Ministry) to build the world's first winged spacecraft
when World War II began. His project envisioned a craft
faster than any imaginable Allied interceptor. It would be
able to bomb the United States from a base in Europe and
then orbit the earth to return to Germany. In the 1930s,
such a thing was simply the stuff of science fiction, but
Sänger had worked out the necessary calculations to show
that it was possible.

It was in Vienna in 1933 that the 30-year-old Sänger
published a book titled *The Technique of Rocket Flight*. He
introduced the idea of a rocket-powered aircraft that could
fly *50 times* faster than the the 305 mph that was the
world's record speed for an airplane at the time. This was
to have been accomplished by Sänger's revolutionary
"boost-glide" trajectory, which accelerated the aircraft out
of the earth's atmosphere at supersonic speeds, whereupon
it would glide across the top of the upper atmosphere like a
stone skipping across a lake, covering vast distances at extremely high speeds.

While the exploits of the daring pilots setting the subsonic airspeed records of the 1930s easily captured the
world's attention, Eugen Sänger's promising, but unusual,
notions attracted little notice outside the rarefied academic

atmosphere of the Technische Hochschule (Technical University) in Vienna. Around the *Konditorei* (coffee shops) frequented by the engineering students of the Austrian capital, however, Sänger had become something of an eccentric folk hero with an ever-growing following.

Having obtained his doctorate in 1929, the scientist remained at the university as a research assistant, pursuing his rocket projects on the side. Between 1930 and 1935 he conducted a great many tests with a model of his Silbervogel (Silverbird), an aerospace vehicle powered by a liquid-fuel rocket engine. He subsequently published his findings in the June 1935 and February 1936 issues of the magazine *Flug* (*Flight*).

Meanwhile, across the border, Germany was in the process of a massive rearmament and the RLM and the Luftwaffe had their eyes out for the best aviation engineers in the German-speaking world. Though its institutional creativity would atrophy in the 1940s, the RLM was still quick to spot farsighted ideas that could be transformed into a qualitative superiority in weapons system technology.

It was exactly this line of thinking that gave the Germans operational jet fighters and medium-range ballistic missiles well ahead of the rest of the world. It was also this line of thinking that led the Luftwaffe's Hermann Göring Luftfahrt für Schungsanstalt (Aviation Research Institute), Germany's leading development center for advanced aeronautical research, to offer Eugen Sänger a job in the autumn of 1936. Two years later, Sänger's native Austria was absorbed into the German Reich.

Sänger settled in at a special laboratory in Trauen with the 10-year mandate to create a practical design for a rocket-powered "spaceplane" with an intercontinental range and the speeds suggested in his book and magazine articles. Joined by a small staff that included the brilliant mathematician Dr. Irene Bredt (who became Frau Sänger in 1951), the Viennese visionary soon created a remarkable design. Not only did it meet the German goverment's specifications, it was probably the world's first realistic design for a manned spacecraft!

Designed to utilize his boost-glide principal, Sänger's 110-ton aircraft was remarkably similar in many ways to the Space Shuttle. It had low, swept wings that turned up into the same sort of wingtip vertical stabilizers that would eventually be utilized in the American craft. Also like the Space Shuttle, Sänger's conception was configured with a tail-mounted rocket motor.

While the design of the vehicle presaged that of familiar reusable manned spacecraft of the future, the means by which it was to have been launched remained untried through the end of the twentieth century—although it was still considered a viable option. Sänger imagined a two-mile horizontal track on which a rocket sled accelerated the craft to Mach 1.5. This would provide the momentum for it to climb at an angle of 30 degrees before firing its own engines at an altitude of 5,500 feet. Thereupon the craft would continue to an altitude of 175 miles, climbing at a relatively shallow angle.

Initially, the Sänger-Bredt rocket spaceplane was conceived as a research aircraft, but with the start of World War II in September 1939, the specs were inevitably adapted to make this promising hypersonic intercontinental craft into a bomber.

Sänger then drafted a flight plan by which a Silbervogel bomber would be launched into space from Germany to reenter the atmosphere in time to bomb New York. The reentry would be required to avoid the rather comical notion of the bombs remaining weightless in space after their release, floating harmlessly high above the unsuspecting target below. Of course, when their orbit finally decayed and they did enter the atmosphere over a populated area, it would be no laughing matter.

Having dropped its ordnance, the craft would continue to glide through the upper atmosphere to a landing on a Japanese-owned Pacific island, or even perhaps a landing in Germany after achieving a full orbit of the earth.

By June 1941, Sänger's team had built and tested an engine that delivered 2,200 pounds of static thrust (1 percent of the thrust of that intended for the operational craft) for over three minutes, and it appeared that the project was well on the way to completion.

By December, Sänger was able to go to the RLM with a completed plan for the global rocket bomber he had nicknamed "Rabo" for Raketenbomber. The skeptical bureaucrats insisted that the untried technology must be ready within 18 months, which Sänger could not promise. The Rabo program was officially terminated, and Sänger— along with Irene Bredt—relocated to the German Glider Research Institute (Deutsche Forschungsinstitut für Segelflug) facility in Ainring, Bavaria. The erstwhile glider center was now engaged in studies for high-speed ramjet engines.

Though he was almost killed when a malfunction occurred in an experiment with a ramjet engine mounted atop a Dornier Do.217 bomber, Sänger made a great deal of technical progress. By the time the war ended in 1945, he was getting close to developing a ramjet capable of propelling an aircraft through the sound barrier.

In the meantime, his Rabo report, finally published at Ainring in 1944, made its way to Peenemünde on the Baltic coast, where Wernher von Braun and his rocket scientists had successfully developed the A4 intermediate-range ballistic missile. At Peenemünde, the Rabo report was not only well understood by engineers in the same field, but elements of it were incorporated into von Braun's A-10 intercontinental ballistic missile.

After World War II, as von Braun and his team went to work for the United States, Sänger and Bredt were commandeered by the French Air Ministry and resettled in Paris. It was here that a team of Soviet secret agents (reportedly including Josef Stalin's son) attempted unsuccessfully to kidnap them.

It would not be until the 1980s that the French National Center for Space Studies (Centre National d'Études Spatiales, CNES) announced the development of the French winged spaceplane called Hermes. Like the American Space Shuttle, the Hermes owed a technological debt to the Silbervogel and Rabo. Like the Silbervogel and Rabo, however, Hermes would be quietly canceled before reaching flight status.

Also during the 1980s, the German government decided to resume development of a spaceplane. Not only would this project be based on Sänger's original concept, it would be named for him. The German Ministry for Research and Technology (Deutsche Ministerium für Forschung und Technologie, DMFT) and the German Aerospace Research Agency (Deutsche Forschungsanstalt für Luft und Raumfahrt, DLR) sponsored the program, with participation by other members of the European Space Agency (ESA) as well. Unveiled in August 1986, the Sänger vehicle was described by the Germans as an important element in ESA developing an indigenous manned-space-flight capability that was independent of reliance on the American Space Shuttle.

As exhibited at the Paris Air Show in June 1989, the Sänger was a horizontally launched, completely reusable craft consisting of two stages, each of which was to be an aerodynamic spaceplane. The larger of these, the first stage, was to be 275 feet long, with a gross weight of

700,000 pounds, making it the same size as the largest jet-liners. The second stage was to consist of either the manned Hypersonic Orbital Upper Stage (HORUS) or the unmanned Cargo Upper Stage (CARGUS). The huge SCRAMJET (Supersonic Combustion Ramjet) powered first stage was to carry the second stage to Mach 6.8 and an altitude of 19 miles, where it was to be released to fly into space under its own rocket propulsion. Both HORUS and CARGUS were to be over 100 feet long and, as such, in the same size and weight class as the American Space Shuttle.

The Sänger spaceplane would have been a fitting tribute to the man who conceived winged, horizontal takeoff spacecraft, but little work was done toward realizing the project during the 1990s. At the beginning of the twenty-first century, it remained an unfulfilled dream. The twenti-eth century had ended with only one winged spacecraft type having achieved flight status, and with no offensive weapon having been delivered in anger from outer space.

# Index